Curriculum Politics, Policy, Practice

SUNY series, Innovations in Curriculum
Kerry Freedman, Editor

Curriculum Politics, Policy, Practice

CASES IN COMPARATIVE CONTEXT

Catherine Cornbleth, Editor

State University of New York Press

Published by
State University of New York Press, Albany

© 2000 State University of New York

For information, address State University of New York Press,
State University Plaza, Albany, N.Y. 12246

Production by Diane Ganeles
Marketing by Dana Yanulavich

Library of Congress Cataloging-in-Publication Data

Curriculum politics, policy, practice : cases in comparative context / Catherine Cornbleth, editor.
      p. cm. — (SUNY series, innovations in curriculum)
   Includes bibliographical references (p.) and index.
   ISBN 0-7914-4567-4 (alk. paper) — ISBN 0-7914-4568-2 (pbk. : alk. paper)
      1. Education—Curricula—Political aspects—Cross-cultural studies. 2. Curriculum change—Cross-cultural studies. I. Cornbleth, Catherine. II. Series.

LC71.3 .C87 2000
379.1'55—dc21
                                                                                    99-043440

10   9   8   7   6   5   4   3   2   1

Contents

1

Viewpoints

Catherine Cornbleth

Imagine stopping by the busy suburban mall where you shop occasionally. It is April, prior to Easter and to hotly contested school board elections in your district. Someone dressed as "the Easter bunny" is distributing slingers and hands you one. It warns, in bold print, that if so-and-so is elected to the school board, "our children" no longer will be able to acknowledge the "traditional" Easter and Christmas holidays in district schools with classroom and hall decorations or with holiday assemblies, concerts, and parties. "Our way of life" and "values" are threatened, the bunny and his slinger claim, by those who support the recently enacted district religion policy directing the study and prohibiting the celebration or furtherance, of religion generally or particular denominations.

The religion policy emerged from acrimonious debate following protests from Jewish, Muslim, and other parents and community members against the schools' promotion of Christmas and other Christian observances. In this case, the religious right mobilized noisy opposition to the change but was unsuccessful in doing much more than intensifying existing tensions and dividing an affluent suburban school district. The religion policy became the centerpiece of the district's multicultural policy and practice, in effect minimizing attention to racial/ethnic diversity. It left many teachers uncertain about what was acceptable classroom practice and generated grumbling backlash about how things just weren't like (or as good as) they used to be.

This brief, anonymous but actual scenario illustrates key aspects of the curriculum politics-policy-practice nexus that are further explored in this volume. Of particular interest here are questions of knowledge control and the distribution of benefits. By knowledge control I refer to means by which power is exercised to influence the selection, organization, and treatment of curriculum knowledge—the knowledge, broadly defined, that is made available to students, including opportunities to critique and construct or reconstruct knowledge as well as to acquire knowledge offered by teachers, texts, and other sources. Once decisions are made (for the time being since they rarely remain uncontested), who benefits or is disadvantaged, individually or collectively, by a particular selection, organization, and treatment of curriculum knowledge? What does it matter, for example, which or whose history and literature and religion are included in school curricula? Once included, what does it matter how those topics and issues are treated? Controlling curriculum knowledge has long been a means of exercising power beyond school walls by shaping how we understand ourselves, others, the nation, and the world. Curriculum knowledge affects individual and collective identity, capacity, attitude, and action. These questions are particularly important at times such as the present when the culture is in flux.

Of course "it's political!" Instead of claims to neutrality, now it is more common to hear that this or that aspect of education is political—as if that explains it. Saying that education in general or curriculum in particular is political isn't saying much unless one describes what political means, how the politics operate, and why politics matters. The political, for me, refers to the means by which power is exercised to shape if not direct others' actions, in this case curriculum policymaking processes, the policies made, and classroom curriculum practice. What, for example, did conservative religious groups actually do to influence state-level curriculum policy in New York? Or in California or Kentucky or elsewhere? Relatively few contemporary observers or analysts have explicated education politics beyond abstractions that are not very helpful to people outside the academy who are enmeshed in or otherwise affected by particular cases.

Politics and policymaking—including the discourse that surrounds and is prompted by specific political and policy actions and events—are a key aspect of curriculum context. By context, I mean the setting in which curriculum plays out in practice and that shapes how it plays out. Closing the classroom door does not close out the outside world. The outside world not only seeps in through the cracks, but closing the door *shuts in* the various, supposedly external, influences on teaching and learning. Ignoring them hardly renders them powerless. My interest is less in curriculum politics and policy *per se* than in their influence on curriculum practice or curriculum-in-use, that is, what students actually have opportunities to learn in school classrooms.

This volume—or one much like it—has existed in my head for almost a decade. *Curriculum Politics, Policy, Practice: Cases in Comparative Context* can be seen as an extension of my own prior work on curriculum context (e.g., *Curriculum in Context*, 1990) and the recursive connections within and between cultural politics and curriculum policymaking illustrated in the New York and California case studies in *The Great Speckled Bird* (Cornbleth and Waugh, 1995) as well as the work of others in curriculum studies.

In this volume, our intent is to go beyond the state-level, politics-policy cases and sketches of practice in *The Great Speckled Bird* and various publications spawned by the Consortium for Policy Research in Education (e.g., Massell, 1994) to offer a range of contextualized cases of the intersections of curriculum politics, policy, and/or practice—instead of the more common abstractions unencumbered by specific instances or evidence. Although only a few authors in this volume explicitly use the language of curriculum politics, policy, practice, and their interrelationships, the phenomena—both macro- as, for example, in the case from South Africa, and micro- as, for example, in the case of a U.S. special education placement—are highlighted. While my own illustrations are U.S.-based with a focus on cultural identities, the cases span school levels, subject areas, and national boundaries, thus enriching possibilities for cross-case analysis, interpretation, and insight. While some of that analysis and commentary is offered here, most remains to our readers who will, no doubt, expand the curriculum conversation in drawing on their own experiences and perspectives.

Thus *Curriculum Politics, Policy, Practice* is both more focussed and broader than typical curriculum readers. Its focus on the too often overlooked relations among politics, policy, and practice offers clear implications for other aspects of curriculum such as design and evaluation that are not addressed directly here. It is broader insofar as chapters draw on a range of curriculum contexts within and beyond the United States. Its difference, in sum, lies in its interweaving of curriculum politics, policy, and/or practice in a range of particular, contextualized cases that reveal the experiences and perspectives of participants as well as the authors' interpretations. Instances of curriculum politics, policy, and/or practice are both brought to life and situated in their contemporary and historical contexts with particular attention to questions of knowledge control and distribution of benefits.

In the remainder of this introductory chapter, I present the theoretical framework motivating and underlying this volume and its implications here, followed by commentary about the public schools as sites for curriculum politics and social policy contests, the key role of discourse as part of the context shaping curriculum practice, and cross-case interpretation. Finally, I offer an overview of the eight cases. The critical pragmatist theoretical frame is my own and that of the volume as a whole, not necessarily that of individual authors.

A Political Perspective: Critical Pragmatism

The hybrid perspective, critical pragmatism (Cornbleth and Waugh, 1995, ch. 2), is a response to the insufficiencies of both conventional critical theory and pragmatism.

> Bringing together critical and pragmatic traditions . . . links the contextual emphasis and equity goal of critical theory with the self-questioning and pluralism of pragmatic philosophy. The critical perspective gives depth and direction to pragmatic inquiry and dialogue. Pragmatism, in turn, reminds us that cultural critique encompasses us all; none of us or our cherished beliefs, individually or collectively as a member of one or another group, is above or beyond question. Emergent and oriented toward action, this critical pragmatism eschews materialist and theological determinisms on one side and postmodernist quicksands on the other. Critical pragmatism employs standards or principles of judgment, and it subjects them to ongoing scrutiny and possible modification. (Cornbleth and Waugh, 1995, p. 33)

Since all views are partial and necessarily distorting, approaching knowledge (or truth) and justice

> requires the interaction (not merely the availability or pres-
> ence or pasting together) of multiple perspectives. For crit-
> ical pragmatists, this interaction is governed by criteria or
> principles agreed upon by participants—principles of access
> and participation as well as of justification—principles
> which are subject to scrutiny and renegotiation as are the
> substantive points in question. (p. 34)

Critical pragmatism's assumption of cultural critique makes it
especially appropriate as a framework for examination of curriculum politics, policy, and practice. Its location between authoritari-
anism and anarchy would be uncomfortable both for those who
claim acceptance for their views, without reference to substantive
guiding principles, simply because they exist and perhaps have
been excluded or marginalized in the past, as well as for those who
claim unquestioning acceptance for their preferred principles and
conclusions. "Whereas the former emphasize principles of access
and participation (theirs), the latter emphasize principles of justification (theirs). Critical pragmatism encompasses both [sets of prin-
ciples] and works toward 'ours'" (p. 34), where "ours" is a more
encompassing community. One of the clearest implications of this
stance is its "opposition to efforts to limit or close off debate, either
by putting topics or issues out of bounds or by *a priori* rejecting particular viewpoints or the participation of particular individuals or
groups" (p. 34).

Thus critical pragmatism is consonant with political democracy and with democratic dialogue more than competitive debate.
Acknowledging the politics of pragmatism, Gunn (1992) notes that,
without advocating a particular politics, pragmatism possesses a
politics

> distinguished by the democratic preference for rendering
> differences conversable so that the conflicts they produce,
> instead of being destructive of human community, can
> become potentially creative of it; can broaden and thicken
> public culture rather than depleting it. (p. 37)

The case studies in this volume, in contrast, reveal less concern
with "rendering differences conversable" than with avoiding conflict in the schools. For example, in "They Don't Want to Hear it,"
Suzanne Miller and Gina DeBlase Tryzna document apology for
and subsequent silencing of non-mainstream views of US race rela-

tions—and the future avoidance of explicitly racial topics in the perceived interests of classroom and schoolwide peace and seeming harmony. In this case, an African American student's expression of a "different" view in the context of studying Claude Brown's *Man-child in the Promised Land* was seen as destructive of community, not creative of it.

Further implications of a critical pragmatist perspective for study and understanding of curriculum politics, policy, and/or practice are several. One is the interweaving or overlapping of theory and practice. Theory is seen to emerge from practice and to act back on it; theory has practical consequences. How we "see" the world or a part of it—our theoretical perspective, assumptions, conceptions, explanations, and so forth—influence how we think about and act within or on it. In "Science for All Americans?" for example, Margery Osborne and Angela Calabrese-Barton invite readers to witness science education practice informed by critical feminist conceptions of science, curriculum, and pedagogy. Instead of the more common assimilationist "science for all," they illustrate a liberatory science for all students that is inclusive of and responsive to differences among their students.

Not only are theory and practice intertwined in a critical pragmatist perspective, but there is no practice apart from theory, although operative theory may remain tacit knowledge. It may be that often-encountered practitioner hostility to theory "usually means an opposition to other peoples' theories and an oblivion to one's own" (Eagleton, 1983, p. vii). The connections and clashes among theories and practices in high tech business and public education are vividly revealed in "A Tale of Two Cultures and a Technology" by Vivian Forssman and John Willinsky who are attempting to construct business-education partnerships that will reconstruct technology education in Canadian secondary schools from computer programming to service learning projects that enable students to support their schools' and communities' technology needs in ways consistent with the emerging work world.

Akin to my emphasis on curriculum practice—shaped by but not synonymous with curriculum policies, guides, and good intentions—is critical pragmatism's emphasis on decision and action in particular, specific circumstances. Pragmatic inquiry is not only situated and contingent, but cognizant of its contingency. Interpretations and conclusions are judged in part by their consequences in action. The attention to practice, action, context, and consequence are inextricably theoretical and practical.

Perhaps the clearest implications of critical pragmatism for curriculum politics, policy, and practice concern opposition to efforts to limit or close off dialogue, either by putting topics or issues out of bounds or by *a priori* rejecting particular viewpoints or the participation of particular individuals or groups. Research from a critical pragmatist perspective would, for example, examine how the dialogue is framed and who is allowed or invited to participate. Multiple perspectives and questioning of received views are present in all of the chapters and prominent in several.

For example, in "Curriculum as a Site of Memory," Nadine Dolby provides an account of privileged white female students' responses to their history teacher's apartheid unit in an integrated, academically advanced history class in Durban, South Africa during the period of Truth and Reconciliation Commission hearings in 1996. Most white students were experiencing at least two "new" perspectives—the widely broadcast, publicized, and talked about Commission hearings and their teacher's "restoring" of South African history 1948–60—and they were trying to make sense of the recent past and their own places in it. Dolby's case illustrates the difficulties of sustaining a dialogue consistent with critical pragmatist tenets in what she calls a "struggle for history." There are parallels here with Miller and DeBlase Tryzna's case insofar as many students just "don't want to hear it" even though the teacher in Dolby's case introduces rather than silences some of the more disturbing topics and issues.

In addition to highlighting a case of limiting curriculum practice to a narrow range of acceptable dialogue, Miller and DeBlase Tryzna provide illustrations of more multivocal curriculum practice in literature classrooms. More inclusive curriculum knowledge and practice also are illustrated in Osborne and Calabrese-Barton's "Science for All Americans?" and my "National Standards and Curriculum as Cultural Containment?" where some school districts and teachers are found to ignore and/or move beyond limiting social studies curriculum policies and history textbooks. And multiple perspectives and wide participation are not only racially/ethnically/culturally-based as the other chapters in this volume aptly show. Jason Tan's "Politics of Religious Knowledge in Singapore," for example, highlights the contradictions in the government's positions with respect to diversity and to morality vs. utilitarianism.

Similarly, questions of equity and social justice are raised in all of the chapters and prominent in several. Gaby Weiner deals directly with questions of equity and social justice in "Understanding Shifts in British Educational Discourses of Social Justice" where she compares the politics, policies, and related discourses of the 1940s and 1990s. Despite political rhetoric and promises to extend social justice in both periods, the new Labour governments' education policies were "profoundly conservative." Weiner broadens the conversation about equity and social justice not only by providing historical perspective but also by employing Iris Young's conception of justice and "five faces of injustice" in her analysis—a conception that likely will break new ground for many readers. Moving from macro- to micro-politics and policy, Diana Lawrence-Brown addresses equity questions in the context of special education placement and curriculum practice. She too provides significant historical perspective but then takes us from broader movements to "The Segregation of Stephen" and a face-to-face case of practice and effects.

Curriculum Politics and Policy: Schools as Arenas

Given the purposes for which national systems of mass public schooling have been established over the past two centuries, it is not surprising that school curriculum frequently becomes the arena for public discussion and debate of national social, political, and even economic issues. Public schooling was established for nation-building and maintenance purposes: to prepare citizens and obtain their loyalty; to provide knowledge that will enable students to participate productively in the economy; and to confer credentials and allocate young people to different positions in society (see, e.g., Cornbleth, 1990, chs. 2 and 6).

In the United States a primary purpose of the so-called common school of the nineteenth century was to transmit an emerging American identity to an increasingly non-Anglo population. In this century the public schools have been charged with major responsibilities for the Americanization or assimilation of the children of immigrants. Rarely, until recently, has even the possibility of multiple, coexisting visions of America been considered seriously. Insofar as school curriculum is seen as a major vehicle of cultural definition and transmission, battles for control of curriculum knowledge are fierce. Schooling has been the site of numerous contests over community and societal values and priorities. Curricular inclusion serves to legitimate and sustain one's views or position by having the schools endorse and transmit them via curriculum policy and practice.

As I have observed elsewhere (Cornbleth and Waugh, 1995),

> How or on what basis curriculum knowledge is selected has been obscured by the so-called classic curriculum question, 'What knowledge is of most worth?' which dates to an 1859 essay and subsequent book, *Education: Intellectual, Moral, and Physical*, by Herbert Spencer. 'Worth,' for Spencer, meant anything that contributed to the self-preservation of a people and its civilization. Although subject to varying definition, 'worth' has been widely accepted or at least proferred as the primary criterion for selecting curriculum knowledge. (p.50)

Framing the question of the selection of curriculum knowledge in this way gives the appearance of beneficence in the public interest while deflecting questions of what, or who, or which, peoples are left out "in the public interest" (see, e.g., Appleby, 1992.) The case studies that follow illustrate quite clearly the clash of interests that shape the knowledge that actually is sanctioned by curriculum policy and incorporated in curriculum practice.

Within and across school subject areas, selection of curriculum knowledge has been shown to be less than coherent and more a result of tradition and politics than any public determination of worth (see, e.g., Cornbleth and Waugh, 1995; Goodson and Ball, 1984; Kliebard, 1995; Popkewitz, 1987; Reid, 1990). And the decisions that are made are continually contested so that both victories and defeats are rarely if ever complete or long-lasting. Curriculum policy is continually being made, remade, and unmade in hundreds of thousands of schools and classrooms. Multiple political and policy influences, sometimes at odds with one another, work themselves out in myriad ways in classroom practice across the nation, or within a single school in the United States. Despite the historical record of conflicting values, interests, and traditions in curriculum policymaking, the "most worth" claim holds continuing appeal. It gives the appearance of wisdom and good intentions as well as conveying the assumption of common interests and universality across time, place, and person. And it well supports calls for common culture.

Curriculum Practice and Context: Discourse Matters

Curriculum practice results from the ongoing interaction of students, teachers, knowledge, and the context in which that interaction occurs—both the immediate classroom, school, and community setting and the broader milieu of education system and society. Changing curriculum practice, for example, to make it more inclusive, multicultural, or otherwise equitable, requires not only designing or planning the desired practice but also bringing about the necessary supporting conditions or context. This is a recursive process that I envisage as a double helix, moving back and forth between design and context (see Cornbleth, 1990, ch. 7). Ignoring contextual considerations is like planting seeds in dry clay—or bringing in rich soil but no water. Thus, conventional curriculum policy, planning, and product development are not sufficient to reform classroom curriculum practice.

The political and policy aspects of context on which we focus in this volume have both direct and indirect effects on curriculum practice. Indirect effects include the mediation or interpretation of state policies by local school districts and building administrators. I recall, for example, one veteran high school teacher and department chair in whose classroom I spent considerable time as an observer telling me that he doesn't pay much attention to what comes out of Albany (meaning the state capital and education department). He does consider what the district subject area coordinator and his principal say, and he takes the required state exams very seriously.

Substantial indirect influence appears in the form of "expert" and public discourses that surround curriculum politics and policymaking. Discourse does matter, in some cases perhaps more than the policies made. That is, curriculum practice may be influenced less by official state policies than by continuing and widely accessible dialogues or debates about what should be taught, to whom, and how. How the discourse is shaped and plays out affects the perceptions and practices of policymakers, teachers, and other school personnel whether or not they are active participants (see, e.g., Cornbleth and Waugh, 1995, and my chapter in this volume). By discourse I refer to the prevailing language (including symbols and images) and manner of argument or rules of engagement, both tacit and explicit.

More than fifty years ago, Walter Lippmann observed that "he [or she] who captures the symbols by which the public feeling is for the moment contained, controls by that much the approaches of public policy" (cited in Alterman, 1992, p. 19). Lippmann's observation about the power of symbols (e.g., family values, common culture, cultural literacy, multiculturalism), and the power to shape policy by capturing or controlling public symbols, presaged Foucault's (1970) analysis of power, knowledge, and discourse.

Power, Foucault pointed out, resides not only in individuals and groups but also and perhaps more importantly in social organizations, institutions, and systems—in their familiar, formal or authoritative roles and relationships (such as government bureaucrat, high school teacher, and principal) and in their less obvious, historically shaped and socially shared conceptions and symbols (such as literacy, equality, student). In modern societies, power increasingly operates through the definition of these conceptions and symbols as well as through the definition of appropriate patterns of communication, including rules of reason and rationality, what Foucault called "regimes of truth." A residue of past practice and conventional ways of thinking can exert a powerful hold on everyday life and discourse.

Knowledge about prevailing conceptions, symbols, patterns, and roles—and with that knowledge the opportunity to instigate change—is enhanced by further understanding of the nature of prevailing discourse or discursive practices (see Cornbleth and Waugh, 1995, pp. 43–49). The discourse of common culture and of history as cultural literacy, for example, seems to have become a code for Eurocentric or western-dominated, upper class history. As code or symbol, cultural literacy can be seen as an attempt to control curriculum knowledge not only by means of official curriculum policy but also by dominating the public and professional discourse that (re)defines legitimate or appropriate curriculum knowledge and teaching.

Of importance here is not only opportunity to participate in the discourse—to be heard—but also to shape it. For example, the adversarial discourse—the culture wars or "America debate"— since the mid-1980s in the U.S. has been cast in dichotomous terms by defenders of the status quo as a choice between pluralism or unity. Various groups' objections to marginalization, exclusion, and misrepresentation were recast as threats to national unity (e.g., Schlesinger, 1991). Tyack and James (1985), in their historical analysis of the efforts of various "moral majorities" to "legalize virtue" (p. 513) by obtaining the passage of laws that prescribed inclusion of their preferred knowledge and values in school curricula, conclude:

> Not until the recent generation would excluded groups
> develop the power legally to challenge the precedents set by

this earlier legalization of values in order to broaden the scope of schooling and legitimize their values as well as those of dominant WASPs. Then, ironically, the results of their efforts to secure equality of dignity in public education would be labeled legislative meddling and litigiousness, partly because the pressure came from people who had traditionally lacked power. (p. 533)

In addition to polarization, the America debate in New York State during the early 1990s period of social studies curriculum review and reform efforts was characterized by a "discourse of derision" directed at both multiculturalism and the state commissioner of education who supported it until his 1994 change of direction. Borrowing from Ball's (1990) account of neo-conservative education politics in Britain, "discourse of derision" refers to efforts to undermine a position, person, or argument by first caricaturing and then ridiculing and dismissing it. In New York, multiculturalism in social studies education was linked to an extreme ethnocentric version of Afrocentrism and then both were scornfully dismissed (Cornbleth and Waugh, 1995, pp. 131–132) as "self-esteem pablum" (by the *New York Post*), "ethnic cheerleading" (by Diane Ravitch who served as Assistant Secretary of Education during this period), and leading to "the Tower of Babel" (by historian Arthur Schlesinger, Jr.). By advocating their preferred version of U.S. history and demeaning a strawperson, that is, "by setting reason against madness" (Ball, 1990, p. 44), critics of more multicultural curricula were able to dominate the discursive terrain and thereby shape curriculum policy and perhaps practice. For example, Schlesinger's admonition against "too much multiculturalism" was repeated more than once by more than one member of the 1992–95 New York State social studies committee on which I served until March 1994 when I resigned (Cornbleth and Waugh, 1995, ch. 5).

I mention these examples to illustrate symbols or images that have entered into both public and professional discourse and become part of how policymakers and educators talk about and act on matters of curriculum knowledge. The discourse about history, social studies, and multicultural education in New York, California, and elsewhere redirected attention to the selection of knowledge to be included in curriculum, particularly to the purposes that different selections might be expected to serve and to the criteria for knowledge selection. Such attention might well have prompted school districts, schools, and individual teachers to reexamine their social studies programs and modify curricula in multicultural directions even if official state policies did not change very much—as I illustrate in "National Standards and Curriculum as Cultural Containment?"

All of the cases in this volume illustrate context and discourse dynamics in one way or another. For example, Weiner interrogates the "social justice" discourse in 1940s and 1990s Britain. Tan examines apparent contradictions in the official discourse about morality and religion in a secular state, diversity and appropriate behavior, and the efficacy of knowledge, facts, and values in fostering appropriate behavior—in relation to the short-lived religious knowledge policy in Singapore. And Dolby shows how the discourse of "truth and reconciliation" enables white South Africans to avoid confronting systemic violence and inequity.

Cross-Case Interpretation

Here I suggest that particular chapters in this volume and/or different national contexts can inform each other and curriculum understanding more generally. It may seem that the suggestion of cross-case analysis and interpretation is at odds with my theoretical and practical emphases on context and contingency. This would be the case only if one assumes a technical analysis whose results are to be generalized, used instrumentally as guidelines if not prescriptions for practice, or simply applied to or implemented in other situations.

The kind of cross-case analysis I have in mind, however, is conceptual and interpretive. It is characterized by trying out conceptual frameworks, by wondering and questioning, by raising questions to be tested against available data or pursued in future inquiries. It actively involves readers interacting with the text, drawing on their experiences and perspectives to enrich the interpretive possibilities and decide what they will take from the encounter. These notions of conceptual and interpretive analysis and use date at least to the work of Dewey (1929) and Waller (1932) who argued that education research should help educators gain social insight, "insight into the social realities of school life" that can enhance their observation and interpretation of events in their own situations (see Cornbleth, 1982, pp. 9–10).

For me, such cross-case analysis and interpretation highlights the widespread importance (and local variability) of diversity—of class and gender differences as well as racial/ethnic/cultural ones—not surprising given my long-standing interests and recent work. Others no doubt would focus elsewhere.

Diversity is no longer unseen, unheard, or automatically glossed over in curriculum and school classrooms. Difference is no longer something to be controlled statistically or otherwise in the interests of generalizability or social equilibrium. It may not always be welcome (for example, in the cases of Derek's outspokenness or Stephen's school placement), but it is there to be reckoned with, no longer hidden away or simply segregated. As I read the chapters for this volume, I wondered how the students and teacher in Dolby's history classroom in South Africa would deal with a black student's statement of feelings akin to Derek's in the urban U.S., or how Osborne and Calabrese-Barton might encourage and support diversity in both of those classes. Even in a seemingly highly centralized education system and regulated society such as Tan describes in Singapore, diversity makes itself felt. And I wonder whether the education reform rhetoric and policies in Britain described by Weiner aren't as much an effort to contain diversity as to promote equity.

A second aspect of diversity that I "see" in these cases is diversity's non-categorical quality. Gender, for example, is not simply a category for statistical analysis. It represents a configuration of historically and socially contextualized expectations and relations both intra- and interpersonal. Gender matters but not to the same extent or in the same way for every (fe)male in every circumstance. The meanings of ability/disability and of ethnic and cultural group categories are similarly relational and contingent. What it means to be Italian-American, for example, has been constructed and modified *in relation to* the identities of and interactions with other groups both mainstream and subordinate (e.g, Conzen et al., 1990).

I have come to view race and ethnicity in similarly non-categorical or nonessentialist terms. What does it mean to be black? in South Africa today? in northeastern U.S. urban areas? in Great Britain? for an individual African-American young man in an urban high school where he is a star player on the championship basketball team? or that same young man in an affluent suburban high school where basketball is not a major sport? I am not arguing for an individualism that eschews all group characterizations and affiliations to celebrate some ideal-type, supposedly autonomous or unique individual. The individual is, after all, formed in social circumstances. This is to argue for treating group categorizations and characterizations as partial, multiple, situation-specific, and fluid (e.g., McCarthy, 1995).

The relational, fluid nature of identity and diversity also serve to remind that the world does not stand still, that further movement in one or more directions might be expected in all of the schools and settings presented here. The cultures of high-tech business and of public education, for example, while seemingly different realms, are neither mutually exclusive nor immutably fixed. So, we invite readers to talk with the text and its authors as well as each other. To facilitate that curriculum conversation, we include our email addresses along with our brief bios at the end of this volume.

Overview of the Cases

Eight contextualized cases are offered readers. They might have been grouped in a number of ways. As editor, I decided not to group them because to do so might unnecessarily limit readers' insights into various connections among them. Placing Forssman and Willinsky's unusually-told case of business-school partnership efforts at the beginning is intended to set the stage for thinking differently. Ending with my own case of policy in seeming conflict or opposition to social change is not merely an editorial courtesy to contributing authors; it seems to encompass several themes developed in the other case studies.

In "A Tale of Two Cultures and a Technology," Vivian Forssman and John Willinsky explore cultural politics, practice, and conflict in describing their forging of a business-educational partnership dedicated to creating a new curriculum for high schools that (a) is project-based and directed at providing technical support services to the school and community, (b) provides students with skills for a new economy, and (c) enables the schools to take greater advantage of the educational opportunities offered by technology. The Information Technology Management (ITM) program was developed through a partnership of an IT professional and a professor of education who here step back to analyse the clash of business and education cultures involved in initiating this new curriculum in approximately forty Canadian high schools.

In "Science for All Americans?" Margery D. Osborne and Angela Calabrese-Barton highlight the politics of curriculum policy and practice, nationally and locally. They examine the political implications of recent policy pronouncements and suggest an alternative science education politics and curriculum practice. Recent reform efforts in science education suggest that all students should attain some foundational knowledge of the substance and processes of science. Encapsulated by the phrase "science for all," these efforts fail to address the implications in defining such a canon or enabling its acquisition by students—they don't ask hard questions about the sources or functioning of such knowledge; they sit on all sides of conflicting beliefs about the function of knowledge in society without acknowledging any of them. The authors are concerned that many people see a "science for all" involving an "all" that becomes increasingly homogeneous. "All" is not a word that suggests heterogeneity, suggesting instead likeness and similarity, with the children who are "different" becoming more like the rest of us (whoever we are). Instead, they argue for rethinking assumptions and purposes of science education, and teacher roles, in ways that do not remake different children in others' images—but in ways that remake schooling and science in students' often multiple images. Through instances of their own teaching, they explore what it means to think about questions of difference in constructing a science curriculum and pedagogy "for all."

In "The Politics of Religious Knowledge in Singapore," Jason Tan follows the course of policymaking and unmaking in a highly centralized and seemingly authoritarian education system—the short-lived imposition of Religious Knowledge as a compulsory subject for upper secondary students. Religious Knowledge was the government's response to its concern that the society's moral values and behavior were threatened by modernization and undesirable "Western" beliefs and practices. It is a case of macropolitical analysis on a relatively small and thus manageable scale that suggests what other researchers might look for, to, or at in their own circumstances. Clearly illustrated are the management of participation or consultation as a legitimation strategy, the influences of extra-educational politics on education policy, and how governing bodies can limit dialogue by setting its terms and participants. Even conservative, top-down systems, however, are neither immune to external pressures nor able to resist change.

In "The Segregation of Stephen," Diana Lawrence-Brown deals with micropolitics in examining the very personal politics of special education placement and curriculum practice. Efforts underway internationally to include students with significant disabilities in general education classrooms are seeing mixed effects. Here a particular case is explored in its immediate social and historical contexts in 1990s western New York. Stephen is a student with multiple disabilities who was included in general education classrooms from second through sixth grades, and then transferred to a self-contained special education classroom away from his home district. Underlying policy, politics, and practice connections are explicated, including the ebb and flow of people and power relationships affecting the case. The impact on what Stephen does and does not have the opportunity to learn is highlighted. His perspective as well as those of his teachers are an integral part of the story.

In "They Don't Want to Hear It," Suzanne Miller and Gina DeBlase Trzyna examine how broader social and political dynamics enter into and influence curriculum practice as a multicultural literature class tries to avoid dealing directly with racism close to home. Against the background of recent ethnographic studies of English teachers with pluralistic goals for curriculum and pedagogy, the authors examine a critical incident in an eleventh grade English class in an urban high school. The class's struggle with issues of race and racism while studying Claude Brown's *Manchild in the Promised Land* erupted into a "major incident" when Derek, a black student, shared his personal, emotional response to the book and class discussion of it. Using interview transcripts and field notes from classroom observations as the primary data sources, versions of the event and its aftermath are shown from the very different perspectives of the teacher, six students, and the principal. Analysis reveals how "multicultural" took on differing meanings from their different perspectives. The negotiations among them were shaped by variously constructed notions of literacy, safety, cultural identity, and empowerment.

In "Curriculum as a Site of Memory," Nadine Dolby explores a case of the continuing "Struggle for History in South Africa" by juxtaposing the experience of an academic history class in an urban area of South Africa with a unit on apartheid against the ongoing, nationwide Truth and Reconciliation Commission hearings. She examines the views of the white students in the class in a prestigious girls' high school as they negotiate the two divergent stories of the past and try to make sense of their nation's history and their own place or role in it. The voice of the researcher and the voices of the young women are interwoven in this account of national politics, local practice, and personal meanings. Dolby's account illustrates how the personal is political, politics are personalized, and structural inequalities remain largely unacknowledged.

In "Understanding Shifts in British Educational Discourses of

Social Justice," Gaby Weiner provides a critical comparative analysis of 1940s and 1990s Labour educational rhetoric, policy, and practice. Of particular interest to her are how policies claimed to foster social justice (e.g., to reduce educational and social class disparities) affect working class and poor students, girls, students of color, and disabled young people. Despite the discourse of social reconstruction in the 1940s and of school effectiveness and "zero tolerance" of failure in the 1990s, it has been the already advantaged who have benefited from educational provision and change. While progressive in other areas, both new and old Labour educational policies have served more to maintain than to reform the social order. If anything, it appears that the number and diversity of disadvantaged groups has increased in the past fifty years.

In "National Standards and Curriculum as Cultural Containment?" Catherine Cornbleth examines both curriculum politics and policy activity and life inside classrooms to see how recent efforts to set state and national history standards and curriculum are playing out in local curriculum practice in California and New York elementary and secondary schools. Her analysis draws on and extends prior work to show that national standards and curriculum intended to serve purposes of cultural containment are unlikely to succeed. Instead of a single set of standards, official curriculum, or historical narrative, she suggests multiple possibilities for braided and reciprocal history that offer coherence through connections, not supposed or imposed commonalities. In so doing, she reverses the emphasis of prior chapters by using cases for illustration, rather than foregrounding them, as she highlights major themes in the volume as a whole.

References

Alterman, E. (1992). The triumph of the punditocracy. *Image*, July 19, pp. 14–23.

Appleby, J. (1992). Recovering America's historic diversity: Beyond exceptionalism. *Journal of American History, 79* (2), 419–431.

Ball, S.J. (1990). *Politics and policymaking in education.* London: Routledge.

Cornbleth, C. (1982). On the social study of social studies. *Theory and Research in Social Education, 10* (4), 1–16.

Cornbleth, C. (1990). *Curriculum in context.* London: Falmer.

Cornbleth, C., and Waugh, D. (1995). *The great speckled bird: Multicultural politics and education policymaking*. Mahwah, NJ: Erlbaum (Original edition, St. Martin's).

Conzen, K.N., Gerber, D.A., Morawska, E., Pozzetta, G.E., and Vecoli, R.J. (1990). The invention of ethnicity: A perspective from the USA. *Altreitalie*, 37–62.

Dewey, John. (1929). *The sources of a science of education*. New York: Liveright.

Eagleton, T. (1983). *Literary theory: An introduction*. Minneapolis: University of Minnesota Press.

Foucault, M. (1970). *The order of things: An archaeology of the human sciences*. New York: Pantheon.

Goodson, I.F., and Ball, S. (1984). *Defining the curriculum: Histories and ethnographies*. London: Falmer Press.

Gunn, G. (1992). *Thinking across the American grain: Ideology, intellect, and the new pragmatism*. Chicago: University of Chicago Press.

Kliebard, H.M. (1995). *The struggle for the American curriculum*, 2nd ed. New York: Routledge.

Massell, Diane. (1994). Setting standards in mathematics and social studies. *Education and Urban Society, 26* (2), 118–140.

McCarthy, C. (1995). The problem with origins: Race and the contrapuntal nature of the educational experience. In *Multicultural education, critical pedagogy, and the politics of difference*, edited by C.E. Sleeter and P.L. McLaren, 245–268. Albany: State University of New York Press.

Popkewitz, T.S. (1987). *The formation of school subjects*. London: Falmer Press.

Reid, W.A. (1990). Strange curricula: Origins and development of the Institutional categories of schooling. *Journal of Curriculum Studies, 22* (3), 203–216.

Schlesinger, A.M., Jr. (1991). *The disuniting of America*. Knoxville, TN: Whittle Direct Books.

Tyack, D.B., and James, T. (1985). Moral majorities and the school curriculum: Historical perspectives on the legalization of virtue. *Teachers College Record, 86* (4), 513–535.

Waller, Willard. (1932). *The sociology of teaching*. New York: Wiley.

2

&

A Tale of Two Cultures and a Technology: A/musical Politics of Curriculum in Four Acts

Vivian Forssman
and
John Willinsky

Prologue

"A plague on both our houses?" We may seem to invite the question, as we describe a partnership of business and education, two households both alike in dignity (as the prologue for *Romeo and Juliet* puts it) and caught in the passion of educational possibilities, set not in fair Verona but in rain-soaked Vancouver. Like Shakespeare, this tale offers a play of ideas. It is both dialogue and dialectic of cultural collaboration, whose action is powered by the tensions, the ancient grudge, the presumptions held by our two houses. Lacking the style of the bard, our feuds are not violent as the Capulet and the Montague families permit and there is no poison dram yet, for this story is still in progress. With our cast and chorus of education researchers, policy and curriculum makers, administrators, teachers, entrepreneurs, software developers, high school students and computers, some shall be pardon'd and some punished . . . and if you with patient ears attend, what here shall miss, our toil shall strive to mend.

As business and education, our houses came together with the shared protocol of the age, over a power lunch taken in a faculty club. We identified a common passion and purpose, the need for a curriculum that would be more responsive than the computer programming classes of the day, one that would meet the needs of the high tech, high touch world that we both worked in. We finished our salads, and then set out to establish a consortium of school district curriculum co-ordinators that would support our proposal to the Ministry of Education for funding. With moderate success in this first round of funding, we began. We built the Information Technology Management (ITM) program, a curriculum and service learning project that would enable students to support their school and community's technology needs consistent with the new world of work.[1] We began by working in the schools, alongside teachers and students, to develop and test the ITM Curriculum and Resource Guide as a product. Then, with the possibilities for group communication and collaboration that the Internet offers, this adventure evolved into a software development project, as we built a web-based learning product known as Studio A.[2] What began as a curriculum initiative became a company, Knowledge Architecture, with the business requirements and responsibilities of market development initiatives, strategic partnering proposals, venture capital spreadsheets, software development teams, customer support models and staff management plans. The company, a business-education partnership with the "sweat equity" of its partners, was more than the casual relationship that is typical between local businesses and a neighborhood school. This was a venture with a mission, perhaps in lieu of a business model, to provide the pedagogical scaffolding for technology, skills development, and service responsibility in schools.

Of the two of us, Forssman is business. She is an information technology professional with a career background in systems integration consulting. Her educational connection is nourished through three daughters making their way through the schools. Willinsky is education. He is professor, parent, and school teacher in language and literature, having once created a primitive computing device for a science fair as a child. Our chapter in the politics of curricular change touches on three critical aspects of the new educational context: education and business partnerships, educational philosophies of "Learning by Deweying," and computers in education. It is only fitting that this tale be told in two alternating voices. The meeting of business and education is first of all about learning from each other's cultures, while building a community that encourages and values distinct perspectives.

Act One / Inspirational Exasperation

In which the two citizens begin to approach the domain of the other out of a sense that something is terribly amiss in a most unproductive level of name-calling between them.

Scene I, What Lies in the (Network) Cards?

Willinsky: In the late 1980s, years before this partnership took shape, I set out to make something of business's constant complaints that educators failed to educate and that students were not adequately prepared for the demands of the workplace. In the simplest terms, I wanted business to put its money where its mouth was. This may well have been a bad attitude to bring to the table in hoping to form a partnership, I realize now, but it speaks well to the isolation and antagonism that had grown up between the two cultures.

More than that, I had the hubris to imagine that we might have an idea or two about reading and writing that might help business improve the literacy of its always inadequate workforce. In turn, I allowed that educators could stand to learn a thing or two about the literacy demands of the workplace so that we could better prepare students. I was proposing an exchange of lessons, with the deal sweetened, I naively assumed, by business's technological largesse that would result in computers for students.

After unsuccessfully trying to convince various businesses that education had something to offer, Lorri Neilsen of Mount St.Vincent University, with whom I was working at the time on what we called the Learning Connections project, secured an arrangement with the computer services company, Systemhouse.[3] Both researchers and high school students were soon learning a good deal about writing in the workplace. We gained a strong sense of the competitive excitement and collaborative devotion of the high-tech workplace, bidding on and delivering projects. We came to realize how readily e-mail created immediate and intimate forms of communication. We observed how much writing in the workplace is a form of just-in-time clip-text, as we ended up naming it, designed for use and re-use in different time-sensitive contexts.

More discouragingly, we learned how ill-prepared the schools were to take advantage of new technologies to extend connections and community, because of the lack of technical support. We used to joke about purchasing a permanent parking space at Doppler Computers, given how often we had to return networking cards, trying to find, in both a symbolic and literal sense, the right combination to bring everyone into the loop. The whole program became dependent on new protocols, the technical services, and community connections that supported the program. The roles, responsibilities and actions of the helpful student and teacher who turned their talents to solving the challenges of making new connections became a critical element of the program's success or failure.

After two years' work with the school and Systemhouse, the project came to an end, in the typical fashion of research-project funding. With the computers finally configured properly, the teachers returned to their regular programs, and the researcher and graduate students went off to produce papers and new grant applications. As it happened, the lasting effect of this initial foray in business-education partnerships came out of my meeting with Vivian Forssman, who wanted to explore how these connections between business and education could change both for the better.

Vivian and I decided that the best hope we had of forging a lasting connection between these two worlds—which students were expected to cross without much help—was to bring business and education people together around a table to solve a real educational problem: the need for an information technology curriculum in tune with the modern workplace. We envisioned a program where students would have an authentic learning experience, identifying problems, researching and solving them, interacting in groups, with "clients" to provide the technical support that was sorely missing in the schools. They would learn essential survival skills for high technology and knowledge work.

The gods fill the heads of those they are about to bring low with terrible ambition.

The first thing to fall, or at least wane, was my apprehension about the corrupting influences of business on anything educational. I had taught literature in a belief, so well characterized by George Sampson,[4] that we were preparing students *against* their vocation, with literature their very best protection. But the truth of it was, or so I imagine, apostate that I now am, that we were already in business, protecting our cultural capital so heavily invested in certain artful texts. As such, we may have been doing the students who were not going to join us in this trade a disservice for which we could only hope they would one day forgive us.

The cultural and educational politics of developing this new technology program was about negotiating a different stance for all of us, teacher, administrator, curriculum-maker alike, in our teaching attitudes with students and our perspectives of the world after school. It was a school-to-work transition that many of us had to make as teachers, realizing along the way that the counter-cultures of business and education share equal but different proficiencies and prejudices, all of which could be better understood by more frequent and better organized border crossings.

Scene II, Programming is No Education

Forssman: With all the gee-whiz high-tech hype and the hero-worship of Bill Gates, it seems paradoxical that there is now a national shortage in the U.S. and Canada of kids opting for education in computer science, an educational choice that presumably leads to productive careers in this hotbed of opportunity.[5] As an information technology (IT) professional involved in the hiring of new university grads, I was curious about the options students have for preparing to enter hi-tech workplaces. As a concerned parent, I found myself inquiring into the school on behalf of my own children. I observed that the use of information technologies in schools was immature and the only choice for aspiring nerds, techno-engineers and the computer-curious was learning to program with the arcane language of COBOL, nearly as dead as Latin.[6] It was no wonder that not many students were signing up.

When John Willinsky and I met and began our curriculum project in the early '90s, I was a harried career mother with a more-than-full-time job managing big network and software development projects for post office and telephone company clients at Systemhouse. I knew that the high-tech industry needed talents, people talents, project management talents. These were talents that no end of writing "go-to" code routines together in a computer class was ever going to develop. My own experience in the high technology sector spanned more than a decade and had evolved through the matching of business desires of my clients to custom-made technological solutions, a '90s career focused around project and product management coupled with technology marketing functions.[7] I had undertaken this high-tech, high-intensity work without COBOL.

The real skills to learn, as my own high technology career had taught me, were in recognizing the patterns of business and technical processes and then translating them into database or human-computer interface schema that would eventually result in some computer application that kept airplanes up or business losses down. This was accomplished by effectively interacting with technical gurus, contract managers and the much-respected "end-user," always using a *lingua techne* to communicate system architectures, organizational axioms and the so-called lifecycle methods of project management. Perhaps surprisingly to those that believe that technology is about machines, in fact, communications and interpersonal skills are critical to high technology work. Certainly software languages are a part of this discipline, but they should not be presumed to be the only entrance qualification for high technology work.[8] And as one of the few "skirts" in the boardroom and the mother of three daughters, I also knew of the never-ending need to develop skills that could make small contributions to a shift in the power and dominance of this still-male world of technology, as women and girls learned leadership in a new technological order.[9]

Something seemed terribly out of synch. The new wave of computer technology that was being implemented in the lab in my neighbourhood school seemed very vulnerable, lacking any systems architecture or apparent support mechanisms or training for the teachers, let alone imaginative, collaborative, knowledge-building applications. An active dialogue about skills development needed to be undertaken, because even as the schools upgraded their technology, the question of what and how they were teaching seemed to beg for participation from those of us that lived and worked in the business world.

Why, in 1994, when the Internet was settling into the office and women into the boardroom, were the computer science classes primarily boys-only, while the "data processing" classes were filled with girls seeking secretarial success in a '60s-style typing class, learning keyboarding skills of Microsoft Word, but risking the same pink-collared demise as Smith-Corona? Meanwhile, the telecommunications networks that we were implementing for corporate clients at Systemhouse had great potential as collaborative learning environments. At this stage, neither the school community nor business interests had even begun to quantify how we might multiplex[10] more than just the computers, bringing together the social value of connecting corporate return-on-investment with educational return-on-literacy through learning networks. All of these educational gaps were juxtaposed by an equal blindspot on the part of my high technology industry. This engine of economic growth with its growing labor shortages, had yet to articulate what it wanted from the schools, and what it could offer back to public education in terms of both technology and curriculum.

Although I had very limited knowledge of the purses, politics, and pedagogies that govern education, Willinsky soon had me thinking about the potential of introducing computer and network technologies along with related skills and methods into school settings, of helping kids prepare for the grind of my kind of "new economy" service and knowledge work. So I set up some meetings with senior education bureaucrats to get a sense of the opportunity and then proposed a market development plan to Systemhouse. The company figured that my proposal to enter the education market with network solutions and school-to-work skills consulting was "premature."[11]

You have to understand that business eyes public education with great suspicion. Except for the textbook publishers and school bus companies who have created a dedicated line-item stability in their relationship to the school, most businesses are wary of working with the educational market, not only because schools expect handouts, but because there is a perception that education lacks both capital and business acumen when it comes to planning and managing such things as technology. An example of this is how schools deal with the costing of computers. Business knows that the hardware and software amount to only 25–30% of the cost of introducing this technology into the workplace, while technical services and training cover the rest. Meanwhile, schools budget 100% for hardware and software and leave support to either the grace of God or over-worked teachers. It almost guarantees frustrations and business is reluctant to get involved.

Systemhouse's well-founded apprehension with my business proposal didn't dampen my enthusiasm for moving into the educational field, it directed my focus. I approached the West Vancouver School District superintendent as an independent consultant with a modest proposal, to develop and implement a secondary school program that would deliver high technology skills to the students, provide critically important technology services to the school district, and involve leading-edge curriculum concepts contributed by my new friends from the university. The Superintendent agreed to our proposal. I bid farewell to Systemhouse and the big company benefit plan, for we were officially in business as Knowledge Architecture Inc., curriculum entrepreneurs! Our celebration should have been tempered with the realization that curriculum and entrepreneurialism exist in very different and often conflicting worlds of public policy and bottom-line ventures. These differences were, although we didn't realize it at the time, the subject of our own studies.

I initially behaved like an overzealous business consultant in that cautious, ordered world of the school district office. First things first. We would need a project plan with a detailed schedule for implementing change that would have to be completed in a few months to assure prompt payment and customer satisfaction. No need to worry about minor issues. If no one in the school district had ever heard of quality assurance metrics or a Gantt chart, well, we would introduce the idea. I had no concern that my only experience with teachers was drawn from the report card review sessions on behalf of my own kids. I failed to notice the shudder of apprehension in Willinsky and others who wondered at a curriculum development process that was to be led by, of all people, a business manager.

Our onsite curriculum development process would be a real-time example of curriculum policy and practice, grounded in classrooms where teachers would become executive project managers, transforming kids into junior network managers and computer consultants. As a businessperson, I knew about networks and database environments, but not about the school reform visions of Howard Gardner (1991), the constructivist learning environments of Seymour Papert (1993), the authentic learning assessment theories of Grant Wiggins (1989), the learner-centered practices of Robert Marzano (1992), or the emergence of project-based learning as a discipline.[12] It just seemed obvious. These kids would learn plenty through authenticity, applying their late twentieth century "wired" acumen to providing essential services in the school. They would keep the computers and printers up and running while they learned about hardware, software, networks and the behavioral aspects of delivering services to irritable clients whose desktops were suffering from digital dysfunction.[13] While inspired by the demands of the new economy, our program forms a particular mode of *service learning* that we hope to see spread to other subject areas.[14]

The school district would save money that they didn't have by not having to hire in-demand network engineers. We would have an equal enrollment of girls and boys, contributing to the new order of gender equality. Teachers would have a built-in support system for performing all those technology-enabled paradigm shifts that the media and parents said they ought to try. We would create a stable technological environment as a framework for introducing collaborative, constructivist learning. Among the "Learning by Doing" theorists, we turned to Roger Schank, a cognitive scientist who has developed "teaching architectures" that support classroom-based apprenticeship (1994). Playing on the information technology "IT" theme, we worked at living up to slogans of "Kids Do IT," "Learning by Doing," "Learn IT, Teach IT, Do IT." The students would earn course credit, motivated by the responsibility of real work. Even the parents would be supportive of this tech-know utopia, knowing that Junior could buy her own snowboard with the promise of a part-time job these skills would guarantee.

Programming is not an education, but technology services delivered in the school by students for course credit is. Willinsky and I were about to embark on an educational experiment where project and service learning would be the subject of our research, the object of our product development, and the predicate (predicament?) of our business-education collaboration. Without fully anticipating the conundrums and complexities of innovation, we would test several axioms of socio-technical projects, such as those developed by Bruno Latour (1996) with his "actor-network theory."[15] We would discover our own de-programming in the process, the deconstruction of prior assumptions of the education and business communities. We would expose, critique and embrace the values of our differences, the differences of our values, while we tested a range of altered opinions, developing new and shared perspectives for educational innovation that involves technology and promotes "new economy" skill development.

Act Two / Getting It in Writing

In which the two citizens take the first steps to forging a working-at-the-table-together partnership to build a new program for the schools.

Scene I, Writing the Unread: A Curriculum Guide

Willinsky: Our idea was to build an Information Technology Management (ITM) program in grades 10–12 that would enable students to provide technical support for their school and community and learn skills that would serve them in this new economy. I had been in education long enough to know that a program was not real until it had a curriculum guide with at least three components. There were goals or "learning outcomes" as we currently call them, with its slight ambiguity around whether they are the outcomes of learning or learning as outcome. We also had a sequence of content and assessment activities. Vivian, for her part, was taken with the idea that we would set out a master plan of the program, structured by grade level, from 10 to 12. After all, documentation formed a critical phase of project management, establishing a record of accountability that could be traced and held to. But there are documents and documents, with each genre serving its own purposes rather narrowly.

For the team of teachers and industry people that we gathered to write the curriculum guide in the first year of the ITM program, we posed several challenges. The curriculum should be driven by the particular needs for service expressed by the school and community; it should be built on what students already knew instead of what they did not know; and it should be directed by the just-in-time learning demands of new projects.

Curriculum guides are most often written with at least the idea that they will guide practice. We were writing one that would describe the program as it was already underway and happening. Still we used the writing of the guide to establish the importance of process over specific technical content. Although we covered examples of what would be needed, we knew that the real challenge was communicating the process of managing projects with its elements of service-oriented teamwork, independent learning, and business communication skills. In the business world, this happens through mentoring and knowledge transfer by more senior project managers who establish performance standards and timelines with the team on the basis of meeting client expectations and budgets. In the school world, this kind of prescriptive process of learning by doing was a new idea.

The real need here was to meld cultures through documentary genres, that is, to create a cross of a business-style project management plan and a school-style curriculum guide. In order to have the course approved at the Canadian provincial level, we ended up with a document that looks a lot like a curriculum guide, which served our immediate needs of getting the program accepted into the schools. While it is as effective a curriculum guideline as any other, it misrepresents the program and how teachers and students dive into the process of providing services in ways that seem far removed from previous patterns of education. The critical concept within a service learning curriculum is this communication of process. For in this program, the teacher becomes a facilitator between students and the community, as well as the manager of time, resources and processes. The students adopt new roles such as instructing teachers and each other about how to use the web to gather materials or making presentations to say, the Language Arts class about proposing participation in a project's marketing plan through the development of brochures. If ever there was a need for a narrative- or case study-based curriculum guide, this would be it. New programs need all of the support they can garner in helping people to imagine the benefits of change, which in this case is extended school and community wide. Proving the program accountable by the conventional measures of learning outcomes, resources, and assessment activities, we missed the opportunity, at least in our first pass, of bringing change to the forms underwriting the programs themselves. But then perhaps we needed to know better what shape the program would take, creating more of an operators' manual, and we have just about arrived at this point, with this a chapter in that story.

Scene II, Feeding the Grant and RFP Addiction

Forssman: In presenting our product offering to Ministries of Education or school district superintendents, we were continually faced with their seeming inability to take action. While representing ourselves as either Knowledge Architecture education product entrepreneurs or university researchers, depending on the audience, we were always given a polite reception. But these agencies and individuals had neither established evaluative criteria nor funding for products or programs such as ours, and therefore were apt to reject our proposals on that basis, while warmly pumping our hand as they bid us out the door. It appeared that the only way to gain support for our product and program was through the process of competing for politically-motivated "innovation funds" posted by the provinces, through complicated Requests for Proposal (RFP) with their do-or-die requirements, partners, and deadlines. If there was ever more tangible evidence of a business-education partnership, it was in the shared pizza receipts, delivered long past dinner time, to a university professor and a technology industry proposal writer who would argue long into the night about the appropriate formatting of footnotes for responding to a Request For Proposal.

In British Columbia, innovation funds took the form of the 1994–96 Skills Now! Program; in Ontario, we surfaced through the 1996–97 Technology Incentives Partnership Program (TIPP); nationally, we became the flagship youth program for the Software Human Resource Council (SHRC), a federal skills development initiative funded by Human Resource Development Canada. This last contract placed us, like sacrificial lambs on the alter of skills development reform, where we found ourselves wrestling with educational, jurisdictional, and constitutional issues, a heady mix indeed, and one destined to seriously threaten the viability of our start-up educational technology company aspirations. We were challenged by SHRC to introduce our program in both official languages to Ministers of Education in at least seven provinces, while orchestrating a national trade show circuit. In a political climate of education reform inertia, this was close to impossible. In addition, we were to develop an Internet-based version of our program, to design a university-accredited teacher training program, and to provide regional classroom implementation activities, all on a minimal budget with a short timeline. The contract was canceled by SHRC halfway through its term. Our entrepreneurial naivete, coupled with our zeal for the project had led us to a dangerous precipice. We had contractually over-committed to what could be realistically achieved in thirty-six months. Our monthly status reports became a tool of torment, used by the funding agency to reinforce their perception of our ineptitude. The government agency reaction was to bail out of our contractual arrangement, rather than risk the consequences of reporting back the unforeseen complexity of systemic change to their own funding masters. Regrettably this reaction reinforces the conclusion that in domains of social reform such as educational change, political will often lacks forbearance.

All of these innovation-funding mechanisms seemed like a good idea at the time. Our enthusiasm for them was driven by the need to secure revenue sources to keep our vision of technology-enabled project and service learning alive. But in retrospect, there were serious flaws in relying on this source of revenue, not the least of which were the politics of paradigm shift parsimony. These contracts pushed us to deliver societal change in twelve months or less, and were tempered with sizable budget holdbacks and excruciatingly slow 120–day payment schedules. We conducted project evaluations as we went along which proved of little interest to the sponsoring innovation fund agency.[16] And when the grants expired, the projects ended where they started, with the hopes, expectations, and disappointments that have a habit of turning enthusiasts into cynics. In a recent survey of teachers' attitudes towards new technology, approximately 75% of teachers indicated that they wish to use technologies only when they have been shown to improve educational practice (Ungerleider, 1997). For all involved, how much more satisfying these projects might have been if the research and status reports, undertaken as part of the project deliverables, had been evaluated and published by the sponsoring agencies, integrated where appropriate into the agenda for curriculum reform and communicated back to the "early adopter" teachers as an affirmation of their significant efforts and contribution. And as a real contribution to the evolution of this kind of educational project, we need a means of systemic knowledge transfer. Research and status reports could inform project guidelines for future Requests for Proposal with various funding agencies, where we learn from others and move more confidently into curriculum reform.

Governments may pride themselves on creating a culture of educational innovation, exemplified by the grant programs we participated in. But a good part of the innovations' value, we now can see, is lost as insufficient attention is paid to sustaining what has proven to be most valuable about the idea. Participants begin to suspect that innovation is an end in itself, to demonstrate nothing more that an innovative culture. Don't worry about sustaining the value of this one as another one will come along. In addition to this end-in-itself approach, we also ran into the survival-of-the-fittest approach to innovation funding, in which one program among the many invested in proves the political favorite for sustaining funding into the future. The point, though is not about our set-backs, but how business, when it is drawn into working with education in development partnerships (as opposed to vendor-customer relationships), needs to understand that differences in culture are underwritten by differences in economy, in principles and practices.

Act Three / Threatening Cooperation

In which, having launched the ITM program within the schools, the citizens sought to expand the partnership and community into new realms that would sustain its hold on the imagination of educators if not the reality of education.

Scene I, The Gartner Group Has Us for Lunch

Forssman: We went into this partnership believing that we could deliver on the promise of bringing together our respective business and education communities. If we could build an educational program that merged knowledge economies, then leaders in both sectors would want to join in the development of this larger sense of community. We knew, however, that we needed to find a compelling basis for coming together, and who better to turn to than those who made it their business to know this new business. The information technology sector relies on a cabal of Massachusetts-based research companies, most notably Gartner Group,[17] to keep up-to-date on analysis of emerging technology trends, what works and what doesn't, the benchmarking and measurement of IT performance, the sorting out of fact and fiction, the hypes and hopes of technology. So if Gartner Group's research was good enough for Systemhouse, it would be great for kids who needed to learn, not just about IT, but about how IT is analyzed, as preparation for "being digital."[18] We imagined teenagers providing more than just a quick Windows fix for their school clients; we envisioned them participating in the ongoing debate of the pros and cons of object database strategies and virtual reality mark-up language while becoming junior pundits on converging technologies.

We proposed participation in our curriculum development initiative to a local Gartner Group research analyst, as a way of building industry validation of the technical topics that we wished to include in our syllabus. She was delighted to join in our workshops where we were conceptualizing the curriculum with teachers.

The next step was to further validate our program with a more significant, perhaps strategic relationship with this industry giant. Of course, such a vision was dangerous, for we risked losing the support of some teachers, educators who have adopted a deep suspicion of the corporate agenda as anti-intellectual and too narrow in its pursuit of education as "skills development." In Canada, Maude Barlow and Heather-Jane Robertson (1994) and Heather Menzies (1996) have been provocative in their challenge of so-called myths of skills shortages and failing international competitiveness as the basis for education reform led by corporate interests. David

Solway mordantly alludes to so-called systems of corporatism that are responsible for the intellectual ills of society: "The well-rounded educated person has yielded to the geek and the hacker, the long distance thinker to the nimble telecommuter, the prophet to the futurologist, and the old ideal of the autonomous individual to the new ideal of the corporate specialist" (1997, p. 93).[19]

Gartner Group today has a significant presence in the corporate learning business. But even if the company had been ready for a learning division back in 1995 when we initially approached them with our vision, we came to the negotiating table ill-prepared for the reception we received. We proposed that Knowledge Architecture would become education sector "subscribers" to the Gartner research. With appropriate intellectual property recognition and licensing agreements, we would then repackage and distribute this material, altered and simplified for our K–12 market, with the educational context appropriate to the spunky tastes of Negropointe's digital kids. We had hoped to become a "value-added reseller" of IT research for use as educational content. We started our proposal with an invitation to Gartner to provide sample material that we could distribute, free-of-charge, in professional development workshops to teachers.

Gartner Group threatened to sue us if we should ever distribute their material into schools. We quickly backed off, bruised by what we thought was a gross misunderstanding of purpose. Perhaps it was just the individuals we were dealing with at the time, or perhaps we had been poor communicators of our needs and intentions, or perhaps we underestimated the potency of turning commercial research material into learning resources. But what this incident served to demonstrate was a communications breakdown that all the fibre optics and digital switches would never address, that is the often conflicting and confusing agendas, interests, and messages that go back and forth between corporations and public education initiatives, perhaps exacerbated by our "middleman position" of trying to broker relationships on behalf of a larger community of interest.

We were reminded time and again that the pitch we were missing was a straightforward "what's in it for me" quantification, critical to winning the support and buy-in of corporate interests. We were advised that imagining a better trained high technology workforce whose literacy began far before students graduated with a university degree, was beyond the short-term vision of most managers slogging their way through a business plan or a distribution channel strategy. If only I had met Ken Kay a few years earlier. Ken is a high-tech strategist and lobbyist based in Washington, D.C. who has organized a group of technology CEOs into an initiative called CEO Forum.[20] Both Ken's efforts and Gartner Group's evolution indicates there is a growing awareness that the high technology sector has a major contribution to make in supporting both the adoption of technology and the development of "new economy" skills. The test will be whether this senior executive-level corporate commitment will be able to move hand-in-hand with both state curriculum machines and classroom teachers, to deliver the tools, technologies, and professional development necessary for program integration for the classroom and skills development for the kids.

Scene II, You Have to Have Conflict of Interest

Willinsky: With the development of ITM, I had entered into this Knowledge Architecture business arrangement with Vivian to make the program into a product. We had a contract with school boards to deliver and support the ITM program. I quickly realized that ITM had to work well enough, that it had to speak directly to teachers and students so that schools would subscribe to it, now and in the future. It was inspiring. We could not just watch it flop, knowing that flopping could also be written up and published. This was work rife with conflicts of interest over my role as researcher, partner, and university teacher. It was work that was based on a different sort of commitment. Here we were committed to getting the program right, to making it work for those it was supposed to serve, making it grow so that it created a community of users. This was not the way I had worked on other research projects, and it posed a conflict of interest in my role as researcher. I had a vested interest in getting it right this time, and it has made all of the difference.

This conflict was further complicated however, as the success of the ITM project attracted more federal grant money. The dynamics of projects operating with multiple economies is becoming increasingly common, as each funding participant looks for other stakeholders to join in the venture. In this case, ITM brought its achievements to be part of a successful bid with Canada's National Centres of Excellence funding program that was devoted to supporting "technology transfer" between the research community and industry. This was a very different arrangement, a different form of research funding that did speak to the government's expectations of seeing a more immediate return on its investment than is typically the case with research grants. It meant that the aim of my research, under the auspices of this new national research project was now to speed ITM's progress as a commercial product, as well as learn as much as we could about the role of new technologies in educational settings. In the sciences, of course, this theme of technology transfer was common enough, with the university securing patents for gene splicing or engineering processes. In education, it was unheard of, thus creating the uncomfortable dilemma. The university and I now faced a situation without a procedure, and only loosely associated precedents. It seemed to me, however, that this was the sort of thing that was bound to happen, given the pressure we are under to form partnerships and compete for research grants.

The university notified me in boldface type that, in light of my involvement in Knowledge Architecture and my research grant to facilitate the technology transfer, I was "in conflict of interest." I couldn't have agreed more. Knowledge Architecture's product development was clearly benefiting from the research, with minor financial support and "market-focused" understanding of teacher and learner expectations. Still, my work with the company had not involved university resources, and even my time fell under what was allowed for faculty "consulting" practices of one day a week. The connection with Knowledge Architecture had helped in some small way in securing the grant for the team of researchers, as recognition of the potential for commercialization of the work we were doing. Meanwhile the company was matching the research funds for the development of new components to the program, extending the university's limited research and applying these dollars towards the development of Studio A, which was designed to be a website as worksite that supported students doing service projects and managing the school's technology. The university looked into whether it could share in the (non-existent) profits of the company. This, too, proved a lesson.

After an extensive interview with the university's industry liaison office about ITM's educational qualities, I was told that my work did not represent "intellectual property," and that the university was not interested in staking a claim on the program. I made them promise not to tell my dean about this lack of intellectual property! We agreed to put a senior administrator in charge of the research account to measure the impact of the program and to give a more formal third-party review of budgetary allocations than is customary with research expenditures.

Is all of this really so new? Educators have long worked with businesses, such as publishers, to promote products intended to bring about curriculum change. And just as obviously, it does conflict with what we tend to think of as research standards of objectivity. One solution is to work at keeping the two activities separate. But I've begun to think about it more in terms of how to make a difference in education, how to best affect improvements, and how to make students and teachers feel better about the accomplishment of their daily trade. There is that strategic sense of taking advantage of the change underway, in the merging of interests between university and business, for greater business involvement in education. This needs to be carefully directed by both business people who are sensitive to the values within education and by educators who have a vision of school reform that extends beyond improving test scores, without failing to attend to that politic measure. My university ultimately informed me that such conflicts are not resolved; they are to be managed. How we manage to make sense of these conflicts seems part of redefining our positions as educators who would use all at our disposal, including research, teaching, and business partnerships, and the conflicts of interest among them, to shamelessly promote initiatives that we have become convinced could make a positive difference for the schools.

Act IV / To Be Continued . . .

In which the ITM program and an Internet product designed for students managing projects struggles to achieve continuing adoption in the schools when provincial seed funding is exhausted and efforts at professional development fail to fit in with the teachers' schedules and habits.

Scene I, Professional Development

Forssman and Willinsky, in chorus: For all the effort that went into the software development of Studio A, and notwithstanding all the conferences that proliferate with the topic of Internet learning, this program was about more than delivering to the students' desktop the technology of our "website as worksite." For all of the enthusiasm and pride students felt in supporting school and community, for all of the new economy skills development that were featured in this program, the critical success factors, as one of us liked to say, were the teachers. And critical they have been, in just that double sense. While much is made in the implementation literature on involving teachers in the process, whether it be to cooperate or to co-opt, their *buy-in* was required on another level in this meeting of cultures with its service learning and school-to-work elements (Fullan, 1991). This buy-in needed to take form in broader community participation and in a letting go of traditional classroom practices, as students worked outside the timetable to deliver their projects and services. As has been our theme throughout this case, what was at stake was the meeting of cultures. The challenge was to create professional development experiences for teachers who may not recognize this work as falling within the profession of teaching. We not only held workshops on project management, but set up job-shadowing experiences that sent teachers into high-tech workplaces for a couple of days, to give them a feel for how the world of work was changing, and the role that information technology was playing in that change. The teachers were keen to understand the demands of the new workplace; they and we were less certain about how to support the coming together of the two ways of working.

In the first two years of the program, we sent out mentors to work with the teachers participating in the ITM program. We had mentors that we hired from the information technology industry that had worked directly in the area of providing consulting and support services, and had an interest in education. We also had mentors who were teachers, enrolled in an education graduate program and interested in school change. These mentors took on specific responsibilities for the cultural challenges of implementation, working with the students and teachers in ensuring the ways in which the ITM program ran against the norms of the school did not lead to too many problems with the school principal and other teachers. The mentors were to work for one-to-two years with the classes, visiting each for roughly 20 hours a month.

The mentors built a wonderful rapport with the teachers and the students, helping the students provide a wide range of service projects, helping the teachers with community resourcing and project management. Projects were as varied as the interests of the students were. They included setting up and maintaining networks in the school, establishing small businesses to repair home computers, providing teachers with researched web links for particular course content, supporting the multimedia development of school yearbooks, website development for associations and cultural cen-

tres, student-run training for teachers in specific computer applications, maintenance of computers in a children's ward at a local
hospital and so on. The projects were so numerous that some we
only learned about when the program was written up in the
national newspaper.[21] But the mentors spent a lot of time schedul-
ing visits, and often ended up working directly with the students in
the role of the teacher, rather than mentoring the teachers. And
then from a business perspective, having mentors drive out to geographically dispersed schools in two provinces was expensive and
inefficient, especially in an age that was moving the delivery of services, from bookstores to insurance appraisals, online.

Didn't it make sense for us to explore this new technology for
providing teachers with anywhere, anytime support? Could we
augment this online approach through a system of telementors to
provide assistance? We set out to build a website, Studio A, that
would help students and teachers manage the ITM program. We
knew that almost all of the students' shortfalls in providing service
over the last three years had been about the management and
accountability they failed to maintain. Studio A was designed to
guide them through the processes, following a simplified industry
model. The resulting online "groupware" product uses the
metaphor of the studio, a place for creative work, and its neighborhood to provide desktop space on the web for each student and
teacher. The product was designed to provide a structured environment to help students manage and track their ITM projects, working individually or collaboratively with online tools and templates.

While we were able to create an innovative educational website for working and managing projects, rather than click-surfin',
we faced new challenges in reaching teachers and students who
had only begun to find their footing on the web. We were a long way
from imagining it might replace their binder as a way of doing
school, or the workshop for doing professional development. Here,
we naively said, come teach in a brand new way, with a different
sort of culture, one you have been rightly suspicious of, using an
unfamiliar medium. We succeeded in only pushing ourselves further into relying on teachers known as "early adopters" to take up
the program.

At this point, we have a mix of initial and new participants
who are using ITM and Studio A in their schools, but in order for
such a community-focused service learning initiative to take hold,
we need simpler ways of communicating, learning, and supporting
the processes of effective project management. We need tools and

processes that support connecting students with community agencies in need of student expertise. We need to better communicate the standards of the program, not just within the school, but to the community agencies who are "clients" of the program. The elements of the project management approach (goal articulation, task identification and allocation, role differentiation, time management, ongoing planning and formative assessment, open communications, and joint problem solving) require more modeling for successful classroom adoption.

And while there is plenty of momentum for getting schools wired, we are still a few years away from that much-anticipated environment where students have anytime, anywhere access to networked computers for effective participation in collaborative online workgroups. We are keen to shape the education which this technology will come to support, an education based on a blended or hybrid culture of learning and doing, of education and work, of independence and service.

In the meantime, we are working with educators to refine Studio A's ability to provide a place where students can find support for project-based learning directed at service to their school and community, not just in information technology but across the curriculum. This calls for a web environment that begins with the students and their learning needs, rather than with the course and its materials. Instead of promoting visually exciting and bandwidth-depleting content approaches, web environments first and foremost should enable community building and collaboration, a "social and application scaffolding" for students who are engaged in projects and for teachers who are building communities of practice along a myriad of bottom-up themes. Curriculum makers and administrators need to create opportunities, incentives, and assessment models for building and serving in collaborative communities, where teacher and learner are working together to build lasting resources.

The talk of wired schools is not enough unless there is consistent Internet application access through email addresses, a policy agenda that would provide universal equity in connecting educators and learners to the Internet. Every teacher and learner needs to be a "cybercitizen," with full capability to research, publish and work individually or in project teams on the web before a model of community-connected, team-based service learning can effectively take place. While these requirements are greater than serving only the interests of service learning, they are intrinsic to the model of community-making, which is what service learning is about. What we have learned through the uniting of our two cultures and a technology is that this is about addressing authentic community problems with skilled, willing, and responsible students. It is about working with community agency representatives who have the time and willingness to work with students. It requires leadership by teachers who wish to facilitate a student-centered, learning environment based upon project management, and it relies on resources and a means of inter-participant communication that is best delivered through web collaboration environments.[22]

By encouraging a wider community of both teachers and learners, we can engage in new models of teacher development support with the qualities of learning networks. Teacher development can then become what it must be—ongoing, peer-supported, just-in-time, asynchronous learning that fits within a framework of theory, practice and participation. Yet the professional development called for is as much on our side, as developers of the program. We need to consolidate the lessons we have acquired up to this point. We need to understand that the real challenge of the new technologies is to understand the range of educational opportunities which they make possible, so that teachers can realize more of what they have always wanted to realize with their students. To make our contribution to that process, we now understand that the promise of our program initiative lies in its extension of the educational culture of the school to encompass aspects of the new world of work, where people think, support, propose, reflect, build, create, teach, and perform.

Epilogue

Enter Forssman and Willinsky, bearing a torch, a computer modem, and a roll of paper covered in yellow stickies, otherwise known as a project plan.

The old divisions between school and business are changing, just as notions of *student* and *teacher*, *work*, and *career* are changing. This play of ideas, with its struggles and hopes, is intended to expand the politics of the curriculum to encompass the meeting of cultures, the building of community across traditional boundaries. Our curriculum project became a company, then a calling, and along the way has challenged many presumptions, both our own and those held by the communities we serve. Just as the politics of curriculum have evolved to be inclusive of language, culture and canon, so too it must include the attitudes and workprocesses of the new economy "working to learn, learning by doing" culture. The tools of this culture are computers and networks; the processes are no longer related to line management tasks, but rather revolve around projects with a defined start and end date. Curriculum must maximize the educational advantage of these new technologies, processes and alliances. If we are going to use the same tools, and tools that so readily expand the circles of communication, then the opportunities for a convergence and connection of practices is within reach.

The new cultural form of this expanding learning community is bound to have its awkward, stumbling moments, given how selective we tend to be in finding the educational excitement and advantages of each new aspect. Although the technology continues to grab hold of people's attention, much as it does today in theater and films and "edutainment" games, we are keenly working at creating and telling of a new sense of community rather than a new sense of computer-hype. We may stumble, but we shall not fall, even as bureaucrats and funding agencies withhold their ducats while equivocating over policies and strategies that embrace this new cultural form.

We are still a long way from coming forward to take a bow. This dialogue and dialectic of cultural collaboration needs to expand into projects and communities of many schools, many districts. As the prince instructed Romeo and Juliet's distressed families at play's end, "Go hence, to have more talk of these . . . things."

Notes

1. Economic futurist, Rifkin argues that work as we know it is coming to an end with automated technologies replacing workers in both the manufacturing and service sectors of the economy (1997). His hope for the young finding meaningful work is in the Third or Civil Sector which falls between marketplace and government. This sector includes social services and nonprofits, as well as educational institutions and organizations: "The Third Sector is the bonding force, the social glue that unites the diverse interests of the American people into a cohesive social identity" (p. 32). And in response, he asks for schools to teach about this sector and to have student engage in forms of "service learning" that will "expand opportunities for students to become more involved in their communities" (p. 33).

2. ITM and Studio A: http://www.knowarch.com. Go into Visitors entrance and then to Front Office to find research and evaluation reports.

3. Systemhouse is a systems integration company that provides technology services ranging from software development to the integration of hardware and application software and more recently as an outsourcer, managing the information technology assets of large companies. "Established in 1974 in Ottawa, Canada, MCI Systemhouse has grown to become one of the world's leading systems integrators." *http://www.systemhouse.mci.com.*

4. The British educator of English teachers, a Western Canonite hellbent on saving young English minds from the corrupting influences of the common culture.

5. Vice President Al Gore announced on January 12, 1998 a series of Administration actions to help meet the growing demand for workers with information technology skills. "The initiatives I am announcing today will help ensure that America has the best information technology workforce in the world," the Vice President said. "Information technology is the engine of the new economy, and it is critical that American workers are prepared to take advantage of these new high-skill, high-wage jobs." According to Labor Department projections, the demand for computer scientists, engineers, and systems analysts will double over the next 10 years—an increase of more than one million high-skill, high-wage jobs. Today, many employers report difficulty in recruiting enough workers with these skills. Kirk Winters, *ED Initiatives*, Office of the Under Secretary, U.S. Department of Education.

6. In 1993, the debate raged as to whether IBM or MAC computers should be the de facto standard in schools. Parents and teachers would come to meetings displaying vendor evangelism, but with virtually no discussion of how these computers would be used to enhance learning. Networking the computers was only just beginning to be thought about. Up until 1996, in many states and provinces the curriculum for computer science or information technology was based on early 1980's COBOL programming and systems analysis and design content.

7. That experience included exposure to several facets of the industry hardware, data-processing services, telecommunications networks and software development with employers that included Hewlett-Packard Inc., an online financial services company, the data networking division of a telephone company, and MCI.

8. As part of our program delivery in B.C. in 1995–96, we ran a series of workshops to evaluate and encourage secondary-post-secondary articulation in information technology subject areas (Provincial Laddered Career Program). Most post-secondary instructors, lecturers, and professors

expressed their frustration with the lack of standards and expertise for teaching programming languages at the secondary school level and felt that students usually had to "unlearn" high school-taught programming languages in order to proceed with effective code writing.

9. Feminist discourse on technology and science has brought new perspectives to questions about the social structuring of science and technology, from the socio-scientific models of Ursula Franklin (1990) to the identity politics of Sherry Turkle (1995) and on to the cybersexuality debates of Donna Haraway (1991).

10. Telecommunications colloquialism referring to "multiplexer technology," the bringing together of multiple data circuits into a bigger digital circuit.

11. Premature by perhaps only a year or so. In 1996, MCI Systemhouse competed and won a strategic initiative to implement network infrastructure and perform network management services connecting all learning institutions within British Columbia (Provincial Learning Network). However, MCI Systemhouse may still have the last word on the premature nature of this market, because as of January 1998 the project had suffered from a range of competing interests and still did not have government funding to proceed.

12. "Project-based learning (PBL) is a model for classroom activity that shifts away from the classroom practices of short, isolated, teacher-centered lessons and instead emphasizes learning activities that are long-term, interdisciplinary, student-centered, and integrated with real world issues and practices. . . . Students apply and integrate the content of different subject areas at authentic moments in the production process, instead of in isolation or in an artificial setting. PBL helps make learning relevant and useful to students by establishing connections to life outside the classroom, addressing real world concerns, and developing real world skills. Many of the skills learned through PBL are those desired by today's employer, including the ability to work well with others, make thoughtful decisions, take initiative, and solve complex problems." http://www.irl.org/challenge2000/PBLGuide/WhyPBL.html.

13. The online version of ITM is Studio A: http://www.knowarch.com. Go into Visitors entrance and then to FrontOffice to find research and evaluation reports.

14. Advocates of "service learning" tend to define it by example, occasionally drawing on underlying common goals. These include meeting actual community needs, time to reflect on what has been learned, engages a new sets of skills, as set out in the National and Community Service Act of 1990. We follow that model by presenting an instance that qualifies as, but does not pretend to define, service learning. The manner of its creation

and the method of research undertaken with it set its distinction. New York and Vermont require community service for graduation, while a province such as British Columbia has a thirty-hour work requirement.

15. While Bruno Latour's story of the prototyped and abandoned French public transportation system has more technology elements than a curriculum project, it is an apt metaphor for technological dreams gone wrong as a result of innovation issues and political risks (1996). While Latour's story involves different technologies and social issues than that of introducing computers, service learning, and industry partnering into schools, some of his axioms would have been useful warnings. For example: "The only way to increase a project's reality is to compromise, to accept socio-technological compromises" (p. 99) might have been a warning to reduce the expectations of technology adoption in schools.

16. See note 11.

17. Gartner Group is an information technology research firm, a leading provider of IT advice to leading corporations. In January 1998, Gartner Group announced "a nationwide initiative to deploy strategic information technology (IT) programs in colleges and universities. The goal: to help alleviate the IT skilled-labor shortage facing U.S. employers in both the private and public sectors." *http://gartner5.gartnerweb.com.*

18. Negropointe builds his vision of the future around the thesis that "the control bits of the digital future are more than ever before in the hands of the young" (1995, p. 231).

19. There were teachers in the ITM program who complained about Knowledge Architecture's "calls for 'stuff' that the students have done," as one teacher put it, ". . . to push their product to more schools and districts to strengthen their position with the Ministry." The students appeared delighted to have their "stuff" recognized, to see it accepted (Depres, 1996).

20. The CEOs from Bell Atlantic Corporation, Compaq Computer Corporation, Apple Computer and the National School Boards Association was founded in the fall of 1996 to "help ensure that America's schools effectively prepare all students to be contributing citizens and productive workers in the 21st Century." The CEO Forum reports that while there have been increases in the number of computers in the classroom as well as increases in access to the Internet, only 3% of the nation's schools are currently maximizing educational technology in America's classrooms. "The CEO Forum has made a four-year commitment to keep us all on track by assessing where we are and where we need to go." *http://www.ceoforum.org*

21. Studio A Press Coverage, http://www.knowarch.com.

22. Larry Wolfson, a graduate student whose research has focused on the classroom dynamics and community interactions of the ITM program,

has written the Community Service Learning Project Management Curriculum Guide, a resource that provides tactical approaches to address each of these issues.

References

Barlow, M. and Robertson, H.J. (1994). *Class warfare: The assault on Canada's schools*. Toronto, ON: Key Porter Books.

Depres, B. (1996). *"Moving to another level of working and learning": Evaluation of year two information technology management (ITM)* Vancouver: Knowledge Architecture. http://www.knowarch. com/index/front_office/evaluation/year2.htm.

Franklin, U. (1990). *The real world of technology.* Toronto, ON: CBC Massey Lectures.

Fullan, M. (1991). *The new meaning of educational change*. New York: Teachers College Press.

Gardner, H. (1991). *The unschooled mind: How children think and how schools should teach*. New York: BasicBooks, HarperCollins

Haraway, D. (1991). *Situated knowledges: The science question in feminism and the privilege of partial perspective*. New York: Routledge.

Latour, B. (1996). *Aramis or the love of technology*. Cambridge, MA: Harvard University Press.

Marzano, R.J. (1992). *A Different kind of classroom: Teaching with dimensions of learning*. Washington, DC: ASCD.

Menzies, H. (1996). *Whose brave new world: The information highway and the new economy*. Toronto, ON: Between the Lines.

Negropointe, N. (1995). *Being digital*. New York: Vintage Books.

Papert, S. (1993). *The children's machine: Rethinking school in the age of the computer*. New York: Basic Books.

Rifkin, J. (1997). Preparing students for "the end of work." *Educational Leadership, 54*(5), 30–33.

Schank, R. (1994). *Engines for education*. The Institute for Learning Sciences, Northwestern University (www.ils.nwu.edu).

Solway, D. (1997). *Lying about the wolf: Essays in culture and education*. Montreal, QE: McGill-Queen's University Press.

Turkle, S. (1995). *Life on the screen*, New York: Simon and Schuster.

Ungerleider, C. (1997). *West Vancouver Teachers' Association teacher computer technology use survey.* Unpublished paper, University of British Columbia, Vancouver, BC.

Wiggins, G. (1989). Teaching to the authentic test. *Educational Leadership, 46*(7), 41–47.

Wolfson, L. (1998). *Community service learning project management guide.* Unpublished paper, University of British Columbia, Vancouver, BC.

3

ᘒ

Science for All Americans?
Critiquing Science Education Reform Efforts

Margery D. Osborne
and
Angela Calabrese Barton

Recent reform efforts in science education suggest that all students should attain some foundational knowledge of the substance and processes of science. Encapsulated by the phrase "science for all" these are described in the report "*Project 2061*" (AAAS, 1993) and subsequent documents (Goals 2000, 1994; NRC, 1996). Such an ideal, however, fails to address the implications in defining such a canon or enabling its acquisition by students under either a version of society in which canonical knowledge is important for societal functions to occur or one in which such knowledge is key to enacting societal change. In other words, they do not ask the primary curriculum questions, "Whose knowledge?" or "Knowledge for what purpose?" Visions of "science for all" and derivative articulations of science education are inherently conflicted—because they don't ask hard questions about the sources or functioning of such knowledge, they sit on all sides of conflicting beliefs about the function of knowledge in society without acknowledging any.

We argue that an important piece of the current reform efforts in science education about making science accessible to all Americans ought to be how science, power, and privilege intermingle in the context of learning and doing science. This in turn should be viewed in the context of how such knowledge of science relates to the construction of different models of society and societal change. The connections among curriculum document, practice, and context must be made explicit and recognized as a problematic with different answers depending upon different articulations of political purposes.

Background

The "science for all" reform effort has been hailed by contemporary science education researchers as critical to the education of women and minorities (Anderson 1991; Roseberry 1994). The proposed reform stresses the importance of making the rules, structures, content, and discursive practices of science explicit and accessible to all students with the direct goal of creating a scientifically literate citizenry. In this framework, to be scientifically literate means that one is able to "grasp the interrelationships between science, mathematics and technology, to make sense of how the natural and designed worlds work, to think critically and independently, to recognize and weigh alternative explanations of events and design trade-offs, and to deal sensibly with problems that involve evidence, numeric patterns, logical arguments, and uncertainties" (AAAS, 1993, p. XI). In one sense this reform effort mirrors the egalitarian tradition in American democracy by claiming that all citizens have the right as well as the responsibility to be aware of scientific concepts and it should enable a progressive vision of democracy, in which all voices count. It differs from traditional versions of science teaching which were based more on finding and educating future scientists. Yet, we argue that although such a vision might be important, it operates on three assumptions which should be addressed if a "science for all" is to become more than a slogan.

- First, *Project 2061* assumes that schools function as meritocracies. Schools, however, have played a historical and social role in reproducing race/ethnicity, class, and gender inequalities in part through disciplinary studies and pedagogy (Anyon, 1984; Harding, 1991; Oakes, 1990; Reyes and Valencia, 1993). Documents like *Project 2061* perpetuate the illusion that if all children learn science, all children will be equal.

- Second, the reform documents maintain a deficit model of minority knowledge: minorities are *lacking* in important knowledge. By favoring only white, male, middle-class cultural values, it implies that minorities and women are inferior (Apple, 1992).
- Third, it assumes that students will choose to adopt these values when their own are shown inconsistent and (implicitly) inferior. When students do not it is assumed they are at fault and *not* the instruction or the content of instruction (Foley, 1991; Apple, 1979).

These three assumptions neglect to acknowledge that science and its practices reflect power differentials in our society and that science education is nestled in the politics of assimilation and meritocracy (Barton and Osborne, 1998). The politics behind the construct of difference is a legitimization of the dominant society under such assumptions. Acknowledging these assumptions allows a potential for revisioning both science and school practices. Without acknowledging these assumptions the reforms require minority students to silence their cultural and linguistic heritage and to embrace a way of knowing which has effectively defined minorities and women as socially and intellectually inferior (Davidson, 1994). The national science education reform initiative, *Project 2061*, states that "teachers should . . . make it clear to female and minority students that they are expected to study the same subjects at the same level as everyone else and to perform as well" (AAAS, 1989, p. 151). This message implies that minority students and females need to work and act like their White male counterparts, not that either science or instruction will be modified to accommodate them. Although it can be argued that this is a call for teachers to engage all students, not just the White middle-class males, in the academic rigors of science, it can also be read as a call for teachers to encourage, if not require acculturation. In the very effort to create inclusive science education communities, policy, practice, and curriculum become connected in the politics of assimilation with schools and teachers as agents (Calabrese and Barton, 1995).

It seems to both of us that we need to ask a terribly important question: Who are we thinking about when we dream of a science for all? What is a "science for all" like? Wouldn't a "science for all" look different from the education we are now trying to enact? We are suspicious that many people see a "science for all" involving an "all" that becomes increasingly homogeneous. "All" is not a word that suggests heterogeneity. It suggests, instead, likeness and similarity, the children who are "different" slowly becoming more like all of us (whoever we are). We would like to pose an argument that answers to such questions do not involve thinking of ways to enable marginalized students—or any students—to engage in present educational forms. Rather, an education for marginalized children involves rethinking foundational assumptions about the nature of the disciplines, the purposes of education and our roles as teachers. It does not mean remaking those children into our own images. It involves remaking schooling and science in their often multiple images.

In our society the question of what to do with difference in our classrooms has been a perennial one. As teachers we know that every child is different, behaviorally and in background, interests, and ability. Sometimes we celebrate that difference but other times that difference is an impediment—it gets in the way of our teaching (Ball, 1993; Lensmire, 1993; Osborne, 1997, 1998). A central question in teaching which extends from our worrying generically about how to get through another day to our pondering how are we going to teach particular science concepts is "What do we do about difference?" Such a question should be similarly important when envisioning the construction of a "science for all." In the following, through stories of our own teaching we will explore what it means to think about the question of difference when constructing a pedagogy and curriculum within the ideal of a "science for all."

Responsive Science Teaching in a Political Context

Other writers have suggested such re-thinking about education in general and in fields other than science (for example: Delpit, 1988; 1992; Gates, 1992; hooks, 1994; McIntosh, 1983; Weiler, 1988; West, 1993). We would provide an image of what it might mean to do this remaking in science. Science can be shaped and responsive to our experiences of the phenomena of our surrounding world as well as the realities of children's lives. Such investigations are not foolish or trivial. They use science and they connect with the real lives and concerns of children. And they also make and remake science. Such science is true to the vision of the disciplines and teaching described by John Dewey (1902/1956) as well as Paulo Freire (1970) for it connects to children's experiences in the most authentic way imaginable.

In the following we will tell four stories to juxtapose images of a "science for all" in ways which give our critique substance. These involve students which one of us (ACB) worked with closely for several years at homeless shelters in a northeast urban area and the other of us (MDO) taught in first, second, and third grade at a public school in Michigan and, later, at a summer science camp in Illinois. One of us (ACB) conducted research to understand how the marginality of homeless children influences their engagement in science, including their understandings of science and of themselves as active participants in science, and the role that informal science education settings can play in the lives of homeless children. Such children experience achievement difficulties resulting from irregular school attendance, and the lack of resources for educational daycare, tutoring, and instruction in sports, fine arts, and school subjects. These inequalities have led homeless children to feel that their own life experiences are somehow inferior to those of "normal children" (Polakow, 1993; Quint, 1994). The other (MDO) researched how teachers' practice is shaped by the demands of context, subject matter, and ideological commitments.

The methodologies employed in this study consist of interactive ethnography (Hollingsworth, 1994; Maher and Tetreault, 1993) and teacher-research (Cochran-Smith and Lytle, 1993). These methodologies, as we use them, fall into the categories of "action research" and "interpretive design." Our research seeks to politicize and deconstruct knowledge, power and relationships among students, teachers, researchers, and science (Fine, 1994; Gitlin, 1994; Noffke and Stevenson, 1995). Hence, we have chosen to share our research findings as stories. Presenting our research as narrative allows us to convey the context of our study (Tobin and McRobbie, 1996), express its temporal dimensions (Stanley and Wise, 1993), and acknowledge our influence on our study as "narrators" (Packwood and Sikes, 1996). This last point is most significant in our research presentation because in the settings we study, we are both teacher and researcher.

Learning About Digestion: Reading K'neesha's
Experiences with School Science (written by ACB)

Following K'neesha into school science is not an easy thing to do. She had been to three different schools in the first four months of the school year. Three weeks into her stay at her new school in the city she changed schools again when she was labeled "learning disabled." Her new school was an alternative school within the district. The alternative status meant that it was especially designed for children who required special attention for emotional or cognitive difficulties. In K'neesha's case, she attended the school because her teachers thought she would benefit from more individual attention. As far as K'neesha was concerned, she was attending this school because she was "stupid."

The alternative school placed a strong emphasis on reading, writing, and math along with social and emotional counseling. Although science was taught daily, K'neesha's science experience was often replaced by "pull-out" activities and counseling. For example, when K'neesha's class was studying human digestion, K'neesha missed parts of two classes over the six-day unit for remedial reading and writing. When she was in class, she often doodled in her notebook while her teacher, Mr. Kradlen, talked about human digestion. A glance through K'neesha's science notebook reveals a few science words such as "digestion" and "stomach" or pictures such as the mouth leading to the esophagus, interspersed with her own pictures of people or her signature practiced hundreds of times.

During the unit, Mr. Kradlen often stood at the board and drew pictures of the digestive system while lecturing. He would always pause during his lecture to answer any questions. In fact, I never observed him ignore a raised hand. If there were points in his lecture he felt were particularly difficult or confusing, and students did not have questions, he would ask them questions, in attempts to get them critically thinking about the material. K'neesha never had questions, nor was she ever directly questioned by her teacher. As he informed me, he understood she had learning difficulties, and he did not want to embarrass her since she already seemed to be a quiet student.

During this six-day unit, his seventh-graders were introduced to concepts like mechanical and chemical breakdown of food as well as the various organs. They also learned about how the body makes and stores energy. Mr. Kradlen made several efforts to connect the unit on digestion to the students' lives and bodies. The very day he started the unit with his students, he had his students eat crackers and predict the process of digestion in small groups. He also had his students eat M&Ms and compare the rate of chemical breakdown to mechanical breakdown in their mouths. K'neesha, although missing part of this class due to remedial reading and writing, actively involved herself in eating the crackers and candies upon her return. K'neesha wrote nothing down on her observation sheet, but she did tell me later that she thought it was "gross" to put the crackers and candies in her mouth and "let them dissolve without chewing them." She also said that she thought that it made spit drip out of her mouth, and that not chewing the cracker made it taste bad.

The crackers and candy activity was not the only way Mr. Kradlen tried to involve his students in active and personally relevant learning. When he talked about food and energy, he asked his students questions about how they felt around 11 a.m. on days they had not had breakfast. He also asked if it made a difference what they ate for breakfast. He used these questions to get the students to link food consumption and energy levels with their personal lives.

The end of the unit was clearly demarcated with a paper and pencil test where the students were required to answer a combination of multiple choice and short answer questions. These questions focused squarely on the material covered in class, and required the students to have mastery of the organization of the digestive track, the role of the various parts of the system, and the relationship between food and energy. Mr. Kradlen was careful to stress that he wrote questions his students with reading and writing "problems" could handle, but that still tested and challenged their understanding of the science. He also pointed out that he asked "thought" questions rather than "regurgitation" questions to further refine his students' scientific literacies.

Both Mr. Kradlen and the school science program as a whole portray a concerted educational effort to ensure that K'neesha would succeed in science. Her school had materials—in fact, many materials—for the children to do science. And, her teacher was endeared to hands-on activities, like the crackers and M&Ms, that he thought children would enjoy. K'neesha's teacher cared about her: He recognized her quietness and her reading and writing needs, and made decisions he thought were best for her because of those needs. Finally, he believed that if he provided his students, including K'neesha, with enough opportunities to experience science, and if he held high enough standards for success, that he would help his "alternative" students "make it in the science world." In short, K'neesha was in a school that worked hard to provide her with the resources and opportunities to excel academically. Yet even with all of these efforts, K'neesha officially failed the unit on digestion. According to school policy, failing the unit meant that she did not complete her assignments or the exam in a manner which indicated that she had mastered the science content.

Here is a clear case where a minority girl in urban poverty was given equal access to resources, and where she was given extra opportunities to develop her skills and knowledge so that she might enter into the circle of science in personally relevant ways. Yet, K'neesha officially failed to move appropriately towards the content and processes by which she was measured. She also continued to feel alienated from a powerful influence in society. From many perspectives, K'neesha did not become part of the "all" in "science for all."

This story suggests to us that to create a more inclusive science the particular qualities—cultural, gendered, and classed—of children need to be examined in order to create a space where children like K'neesha can participate. It would appear that the institutional and disciplinary settings (i.e., formal school science settings) with their inherent hierarchies are co-opted by children during the social and contextualized construction of personal identities and roles (Foucault, 1980; McCarthy and Crichlow, 1993; Thorne, 1993). This does not always act to the child's particular advantage. In our teaching of girls and minorities we attempt to recognize this and to teach science in a way that values the lived experiences, ways of knowing the world and social identities held by all students, especially women and minorities. We recognize that students' concepts of "science" also help to constrain roles and expectations. Thus, our efforts are focused on moving ourselves and our students beyond these assumed roles and perceptions to help girls and minorities become empowered and liberated through developing multiple understandings and critiques of science.

In our teaching we are purposely attempting to construct a practice which is "inquiry based": in which teaching and learning are guided by questions and interests of children (Dewey, 1902/1956). We have defined science as a process rather than as particular content and have started with the belief that science can be constructed out of any pursuit—if questions are asked, science can be done. Therefore our task has been to help children to ask questions, hear questions in the things they do and say and finally figure out ways that we can address those questions. We have been teaching science from a social constructivist philosophy in which the children explore the science together and through conversation come to construct meaning (Vygotsky, 1978). In this teaching we rely on the children to speak about both what they are doing and thinking and about the sources and motivations for their theory making. Our teaching is dependent upon the outside experiences the children bring to class as much as upon the experiences they have in class. We try to hear, validate, and work from and with these experiences.

We believe that hearing, validating, and working from and with children's lived experiences is central to answering, from a pedagogical standpoint, the question of difference which drives this chapter. In the following we present our own attempts to construct inclusive spaces in school science. Our attempts are formed through our understandings of how science class is positioned within knowledge and power hierarchies and the subsequent role that science class plays in how girls and minorities negotiate social identities. We use these insights to create a forum where feminist conceptions of science and science teaching and learning are explored as a viable and liberatory alternative to contemporary science teaching methods for children. Investigating the ways in which the urban, minority children we work with perceive science and themselves in relationship to science, we discover how these images and relationships change as students are encouraged to explore the meaning of science in the context of their lived experiences. In particular, we attempt to show how responsive science settings allow the possibility of constructing spaces in which a multiplicity of roles can be tried on and a "destabilized" vision of science "played" with. When we enable children to participate in science in a responsive manner we open the door to a potential for creating a space in which the children can re-create the science in ways that address their perceptions of science and their everyday experiences as well as their own needs and beliefs about themselves.

Exploring Gravity in Third Grade (written by MDO)

"Kristin are you ready? [*Kristin has been drawing a picture on the board that she wants to use to present an idea to the class.*] Can you show us what you drew?"

> *Kristin:* Well, see, on the Moon here, a man can walk and he can jump up and down, but on the Moon there's no gravity, so if he went to the bottom of the Moon and just stood there he wouldn't fall because there he could just . . . he would not fall because there is no gravity and gravity makes you fall.
>
> *Timmy:* No, gravity makes you stand!
>
> *Teacher:* Hand up, Timothy . . .

Kristin has been a delicate problem in this third grade science class since we started our first unit on machines. At the beginning of those discussions Kristin turned out to be very knowledgeable— more so than Timmy or Yong Sun or Jin, three little boys who seemed to know *everything* in science. This was I think due to her spending weekends working with her father rebuilding cars. I spent a lot of time in those classes reaffirming her knowledge and encouraging her to share it with us in class. I made sure that she had enough room to speak whole thoughts without interruption, and then often I would organize ensuing discussion so that people were talking in response to what Kristin had just explained to us. I made sure that the (apparent) antagonisms between Kristin and some of the little boys like Jin and Timmy were suppressed. I wanted Kristin to have a chance to exercise a knowledgeable voice in my science class. Often this was difficult because Timmy, Jin, or Yong Sun would just *assume* that they knew more.

Things are different in these classes on gravity and the planets. Here, while Kristin still wants the floor and wishes to keep her ideas focal, they are wrong. They are based on partial knowledge and misunderstandings cobbled together by Kristin as she tries to present and defend her ideas. This day's conversations had started out with the children wondering about where the gravity on Earth comes from. I wished them to connect the idea of gravity with that of mass so I asked whether or not there was gravity in space, guessing (correctly) that children would say there was none. Then I asked about gravity on the Moon. Kristin's statements derive from her understanding that the Moon is in space and since space has no gravity, neither will the Moon. But she also has seen pictures of people walking on the Moon. She wishes to explain that and still retain the idea that the Moon is without gravity. The children argue until I stop the class and have them write in their notebooks what they think gravity is.

In this class, when I invite the children to share their ideas, I hope that through the gathering of multiple ideas wrong ones will be identified. This process of critique is potentially hegemonic from a perspective of the discipline—what constitutes "right" science and why?—and from the perspective of the personal relations between the children. Should Timmy or Jin argue Kristin down? What are the repercussions of this? I feel though, a disquieting sense of hegemony to one side and anarchy to the other.

I call the class together to listen to Jin read the definition of gravity given in the science textbook: "The force of one object pulling on another object, gravity pulls things toward the Earth." I start asking different children what they thought that definition meant. I start with Amina.

> *Amina:* Um, that means that, well I don't understand the first part, the force of one object pulling on another object . . . um, um, *oh!* one object is pulling on another object, this is an object [pen], so if I jump off with the pen gravity pulls both things down at one time.

I move back a step: "Where is gravity coming from?" Timmy answers: "Gravity is coming from down in the Earth." I repeat his answer and he adds that then gravity can also be on all the different sides of the Earth. So I ask him if the Earth is also pulling on him.

> *Timmy:* No, *gravity* from the middle of the Earth.
>
> *Teacher:* Gravity's pulling on you?
>
> *Timmy:* Yeah.
>
> *Jin:* I think gravity pulls birds down 'cause, well, 'cause when they're flying and they're trying to pull it down and then they're still flying and it makes them more tired and it makes them have to go down.

Kristin and the boys start to seriously argue in a way in which no progress on ideas is being made so I interfere: "I don't understand, what's the point of what you're arguing about?" Kristen responds (with Jin breaking in repeatedly): "Well, I think that anything could fly up in the air if there was no gravity . . . [*Jin interrupts*] . . . but Jin said 'but not a truck' because it's too heavy because the gravity . . . [*Jin interrupts again*] . . . and the people on the Moon, they don't quite fly but they jump up really high but they do come down." Jin corrects her: "No, they wear really heavy boots that make them stay on the ground. If they don't wear those boots like, I think if you're on the Moon, then I think things weigh six times less, I'm not sure but it was much less, so, so if like, if you have, if we were running right now and we were on the Moon then we would be floating because our shoes are not heavy enough!"

> *Teacher:* Is there gravity on the Moon?
>
> *Jin:* No.

Teacher: There's no gravity on the Moon? But you do have a weight on the Moon?

Jin: Yeah 'cause if you have boots or like heavy boots like six pounds or something really heavy, well not six pounds but like really heavy, then, then you'll stay on the ground and but you can still hop really high you can still jump really far and high the boots just make you stay on the ground.

Kristen: How?

Teacher: How do they make you stay on the ground if there's no gravity?

Jin: 'Cause they're heavy.

Teacher: But if there's no gravity what difference does it make how heavy they are? If there's no gravity doesn't everything just float?

Jin: Some boots make you stay on the ground.

Teacher: But you said there's no gravity.

Jin: I know, that's why they made gravity boots!

Teacher: You mean the boots have their own gravity?

Timmy: Yeah they give it out, that's what I just told him, they're gravity boots.

Jin: That's what I'm trying to say!

Timmy continues, his enthusiasm mounting: "The gravity boots can make you stick on the ground where there's no gravity. That's why they have them but they have to jump or else it's too hard just to walk in the gravity boots, but if they jump they can't float away, the gravity will bring them back down but they'll jump!" The children in the room are *very* interested. The room is full of huge round eyes. The children are very excited by this statement. Personally I am pleased and amused by such an imaginative solution to the logical trap I have ensnared them in. I do have rather a sinking feeling in my stomach, however; I still think I have all the cards.

I ask another question which I hope will turn the conversation from examining the effects of Timmy and Jin's idea to deeper assumptions. "Can I ask a question? Why does the Earth have gravity?" Daniel answers: "Maybe it was made that way." Meanwhile

Amina draws a picture. I ask her to explain it. "Now this part . . . just pretend it's flat . . . the Moon has no gravity, some people think it does but it doesn't. These lines are the people [on Earth] and the Moon, it has nothing but bumps on it and that's why the Moon has no gravity."

> *Teacher:* So in order to have gravity you have to have living things is that what you are saying?
>
> *Amina:* Yeah, I don't think I should say this, but whatever one you believe in, God, well, God, he thought that there should be, well, I don't know, but maybe this, but maybe it's just because the Moon doesn't have to have gravity because there's nothing, why should it have gravity because there's nothing on it that *should* have gravity.
>
> *Teacher:* Oh so the Earth *needs* to have gravity *because* there are living things?

This is very true; would the concept of gravity exist without us needing it? Mightn't there be another way to visualize the whole relationship that doesn't require a concept like gravity? Amina's linking this to her concept of God and God's plans is a part of common teleological argument; arguments which hinge on a higher authority or a greater purpose—stated or unstated. In traditional science the higher authority is one of Eurocentric rationality. It doesn't have to be that way either and our rationality is at best multiple and conflicted. Concepts such as gravity or God arise because our articulations of reality are partial and incomplete. God and gravity are different because our abstractions are different. When Amina talks about God as an explanation no one challenges her right to talk about this just as no one challenged Timmy's and Jin's gravity boots explanation. Rather, they listen to how she is using it, and then present their ideas.

I ask children to take the floor with their theories, knowing that sometimes they are wrong. I try to validate their voice by making them central, by enabling their voices and their ideas to become focal to our discussion. I avoid allowing the new ideas which arise through these discussions to become associated with particular "owners." I keep all ideas (even scientifically acceptable ones) problematic. I try also to remain mindful of how all this makes children like Kristin or Amina feel and how it might effect their sense of self and developing voice (Gilligan, 1982). I try to validate a child like Kristin as a person and learner yet help her, and the class, understand that her notions about gravity on the Moon, and in general, are wrong.

In such responsive science teaching the possibility of constructing spaces in which a multiplicity of roles can be tried on and a "destabilized" vision of science "played" with occurs. While respecting the religious sentiments of Amina, the imagination of Timmy or Jin and the developing voice of Kristin, these children enact different roles in the classroom and simultaneously challenge the nature and definitions of acceptable science. Enabling children to participate in science in a responsive manner opens the door to a new environment in which the children can re-create the science in ways that address their perceptions of science and their everyday experiences as well as their own needs and beliefs about themselves.

Braids in Summer Science Camp (written by MDO)

Two summers ago the group of second grade girls I taught in summer science camp represented a large number of different backgrounds—Korean daughters of graduate students; white middle class children with parents who were musicians and who went river rafting in Colorado on vacations; white working class girls of fundamentalist religious background; some from blended marriages; two low socioeconomic status African American children on scholarships. Jennifer, a child of intense religious views, chose not to participate in the questioning I was leading the girls through as they compared their experiences with kite flying. She did not participate in the "science" side of anything we did. She led the class in turning our "science" into arts and crafts, turning the empirical testing of kite tail design into a workshop on braiding. She polarized the group; her friends were torn between friendship for her and their interest in the group's inquiry.

I responded by changing the curriculum to accommodate—I provided many different materials for braiding and then crafts; I asked questions about the qualities of materials in light of what the children wanted to do with them. I asked the children repeatedly to think and articulate ways they thought what we were doing was science. The science became hidden beneath the "crafts" but it was still there as we examined the properties of materials, testing and assessing them. We designed things and tried to realize them. Such an evolution in the science we were doing happened by responding to the children's wishes rather than forcing them to choose science or their own desires.

Working to help children ask questions, hear questions in the things they do and say, and find ways that we can address those questions, I place girls' empowerment central in my practice. The girls in my classes, however, are occasionally unresponsive and so I change how I teach or the content of my teaching to try to involve them. As the girls in this story co-opt the science discussions to begin their own explorations of braiding and materials they enlarge our definitions of science to include the aesthetic and emotional/social. Jennifer, however, imposes her own form of social oppression not unlike that described by Lyotard in *The Postmodern Condition* as he defines the "terror" imposed by discourse communities:

> By terror I mean the efficiency gained by eliminating, or threatening to eliminate, a player from the language game one shares with him. He is silenced or consents, not because he has been refuted, but because his ability to participate has been threatened (there are too many ways to prevent someone from playing). (Lyotard, 1984, p.64)

I tried to address this by my role in providing multiple opportunities and pathways of engagement. I suggest, though, that such terrorist activity might have been addressed explicitly although I can only speculate on the outcomes. In such science where curriculum decisions are driven by the needs and desires of the children, social role playing can take on very important dimensions which transcend the personal and individual. The teacher's role is in mediating these, in finding compromises. Such "solutions" can only be partial. They are unsettling to the teacher when depicted as "frozen," snapshots out of time: I was very unhappy with this class for example. Such social roles, however, as Foucault points out in *The History of Sexuality* (1978) are to be played with and when played with act to destabilize all relations. Certainly what is destabilized here are definitions of science. As the classes progressed, social roles changed as did the children's relations to one another. Other children began introducing materials to the arts and crafts, making our explorations much more science-like and restoring more of a negotiated equilibrium between children in which the dominance of one child was reduced.

Inventing Recycled Paper: Doing Science with
Children at a Homeless Shelter (written by ACB)

I believe I learned a very important lesson at the shelter. As part of our environmental theme, I wanted to help the children invent ways of making recycled paper. Besides, it was near the winter holidays, and I wanted the children to have their own paper to make cards and gifts to send if they desired. In their informal conversations of the past few weeks, the children had been talking about the kind of things they wanted to get and give for the holidays. Most of these things were dream items—such as a "car for my mom"—as most of the children rarely possessed more than pocket change.

Before I arrived at the shelter, I planned to have the children collect leaves, twigs, dirt, and other natural items from around the block. I brought with me a stack of old newspapers, string, fabric, and office paper, for the recycled paper, as well as popcorn, juice, and graham crackers for snack. Although I planned for the children to invent their own recycled paper, I had also planned their inventions around the ingredients I thought the children might use and how they might go about using them through the kinds of things I brought and had the children talk about. After all, I had made recycled paper successfully with several other children in the past. When the children began mixing their choice of ingredients for recycled paper, three boys separated themselves from the rest of the group. In their bowl, instead of mixing the materials from outside with the newspapers and other materials, they instead were mixing popcorn and the graham crackers that I had brought for snack along with some leftover flour from an activity a few weeks earlier. They mixed their concoction to a thick paste, spread it into a thin sheet on a large rectangular pan where they were to have put their recycled paper to dry, then asked if they could bake it.

While their concoction was baking I asked them about what they were doing. Jason informed me that they had decided to make "edible paper." When they were done, they cut their product up into tree shapes, ate some of them, and made plans to give the rest of them out as edible Christmas cards.

I was fascinated with the boys' choice to make edible paper. I was also fascinated by the kinds of questions the boys were asked by their peers, and the responses they gave, when their peers learned about their covert actions. In this conversation, Jason, as the spokesperson for the boys, indicated that they examined and discussed the sample pieces of recycled paper I brought for the children. The boys understood that there was a particular way to make recycled paper, and based on their analysis of the sample pieces, they described what that process was. The boys also described what it was they wanted to do different from the planned activity.

For example, Jason was asked why he made the edible paper. His response was that he "didn't want to make ordinary paper," that he "saw how you could do it" and had "different ideas for something [he] wanted to try." He also said that when they "took a close look at the paper" they knew it could be "done different ways," and that the purpose of recycled paper was to "make it from what you already got, using materials that already served a purpose." In making this point he picked up the sample paper I made and pointed to the pine needles embedded in it, then compared that to the popcorn kernels in his own paper. Finally, Jason also told how if he gave away "edible cards" then "people could eat it," and that it would be "like a two-way present."

In some ways the very act of making recycled paper promoted the material separation of the "haves" and the "have-nots": We were making recycled paper so that the children could have cards to give away as gifts. In addition, possessing food and the times and places for eating it were strictly restricted by the shelter. In fact, as the teacher, I, like the students, was conscious of this positioning through their stories about "dream gifts." I wanted to recognize this reality, as it seemed particularly salient during the holiday season, and because I did not want to actively participate in how such material differences separate children through the have and have-not status. Besides recycled paper was "in," and making and giving recycled paper could be read as an environmentally friendly and even politically correct act just as it could also have been read as an act of poverty. Jason's imaginative subversion of this gift-making by causing it to also be about having food in inappropriate places and times could only be admired.

Yet, Jason's actions pushed me to consider my whole analysis on another level. He addressed his desire to give a particular kind of present (rather than a prescribed one). He challenged rules about where food can be used and eaten at the shelter. Finally, he challenged the marginalization created by definitions of acceptable science through challenging the production, uses, and nature of science. Science no longer was something done by scientists far away in labs or by teachers who tell the students how to do the science through explicit directions or persuasion. Science became the active intersection between the knower and the social, political, cultural, and physical conditions and contexts embracing—but also being acted upon by—the knower.

Such acts of invention are socioculturally inscribed—science/technology and inventive acts occur as individuals interact dialectically with materials, desires, values and social goals in a distinctive way to generate something (Foucault, 1975; Haraway, 1997; Schon, 1983). Even when the agent is a single individual, invention remains a social and political act because the self is contextualized (Weber, 1949). In short, human agents always act dialectically—in the contexts of their interconnections with others, with things, and with the socioculture (Buber, 1970; Geertz, 1973).

Jason's and his friends' activity was much more than simply mucking about with food, and my choices were about much more than collapsing material separations between haves and have-nots. Jason chose to center his desires and dreams in a way that critically valued yet critiqued both school-based and home-based knowledge. Jason's actions promoted a critical rereading of the science in his life and his life in science. This critical reading politicizes and destabilizes the boundaries that define science, repositioning the traditional power-knowledge relationships which influence how students learn to label valued knowledge—knowledge about self, others, and science. By valuing their choices and agency around materials, processes, and purposes, the boys and traditional science were re-positioned and effectively redefined.

Reconstructing "Science for All"

The complex dilemma of constructing a "science for all" can be explored through issues raised by K'neesha's school science experiences and the stories we have described of our teaching. Our stories suggest that if science education is to become inclusive of all children, science educators need to work to expand the vision of science education beyond an embodiment of White middle class culture but this process is neither simple nor without conflicts. The possibilities of science for all raised by our stories do not answer the problems of K'neesha's experiences in school but they do give our thinking about them a richness. The story of Jin and Timmy suggests that students' concepts of "science" constrain roles and expectations, shaping power and privilege in science class by defining social identities. Most compellingly this is illustrated as a process constructed through interactions in the class that are deeply intertangled with the subject matter. The stories of Kristen and Jennifer illustrate the complexities involved in teaching when children co-opt institutional and disciplinary settings (i.e., formal school science or science camp settings) with their inherent hierarchies during the social and contextualized construction of personal identities and roles. The story of Jason and his friends challenges what it might mean for us as feminist scientists and educators to teach science in a way that values the lived experiences, ways of knowing the world and social identities held by all students, especially women and minorities. Finally, all three stories question how can we move beyond these assumed roles and perceptions to help girls and minorities become empowered and liberated through developing science understandings. Arguing that we need to encourage all science students to explore the natural world through their own ways of knowing and understanding and then through comparison and critique develop an understanding of the traditional science model is neither a simple or prescriptive statement.

We do believe, however, a reform movement designed to promote "science for all" is detrimental when it is located in the politics of assimilation. Although the argument is strong for enculturating all students into the culture of science so that their career paths in science will be open, we believe that this action promotes elitism at the expense of equality. It also promotes a static image of science rather than the shifting and contextual image emergent in our stories. The essence of an inclusive science lies in a desire and ability to value a multiplicity of cultural experiences, values, and expectations. Following from this, the life experiences of all children need to be incorporated into the science class. Life experiences recounted in science class can promote an understanding of science less abstract, broaden the definition of science with which students come to class, broaden the forms of science practiced in class, and connect theories of school science to intuitive understandings. By valuing the life experiences of all children, teachers and students, in the struggle to create an inclusive science, can begin to "stand up" to the institutions of science and education by creating spaces from which to make explicit and problematic cultural biases in the teaching and learning of science (Barton, 1998). To accomplish this teachers, administrators, and curriculum writers need to develop cultural sensitivity and a critical perspective in order to find creative ways to explore the natural and physical world across cultural barriers. We believe that this critical exploration must move beyond cursory glances at "cultural difference" in science learning; they must involve theoretical and practical explorations of the meaning and production of culture in science class as well as knowledge-power relationships maintained by the institution of science. This involves a recognition by all that traditional science embodies and reflects cultural assumptions itself: it is not "a-cultural."

None of the children in our stories have engaged in science in ways devoid of culture. All have brought their histories, values, beliefs, and emotional social selves to our science. As teachers we would not, could not, deny this or ignore it. Our acts and theirs effectively re-write science. We believe that participation in science by all children would increase if science was taught in a way that reflected human life and experience. An inclusive science would be more conducive to minority students' participation because it rejects traditional scientific practice as the only way, and postulates other viable ways of obtaining scientific understandings. Students will have the opportunity to explore personal, individual development of hypotheses and interpretations of results. Facts, procedures and theories will still exist, but they will be publicly acknowledged as value-laden. They will become guiding or reference points instead of potentially marginalizing truths. This will also mean that students will be expected to approach the construction of knowledge from multiple perspectives including those that have been marginalized or utterly rejected: they will not feel they have to chose between their home culture and the culture of science and school. It will mean that they will not feel mastered by the material nor themselves be master of it. Finally, they will experience science in the classroom as they experience the world: holistically, interactively, passionately, and intellectually.

As feminist science teachers we wish to encourage such critical empowerment through understanding, liberation (Barton and Osborne, 1995), and our belief that science is constructed, through discourse, as a set of knowledges, and can act as an expression of identity. This provides us with the means to re-construct science and science education so that girls and minorities can find a place or create a new place for themselves within it. Such goals, however, are in conflict with the constraints and demands of an entrenched, established discipline and become the terrain in which science becomes remade. The children's engagement in our science takes on the form of destabilizing activities, challenging and breaking/remaking the grand narrative of science. This makes it into a "science for all," or at least a closer approximation.

Conclusions

As educators, we often pretend power relationships do not exist or matter in school settings. From national policies like desegregation, to classroom-based activities like group work, we are asked to create the illusion that power relationships are absent or at least negotiable. Our stories about children such as K'neesha remind us that all children are not equal partners in the process of schooling and they do not stand at equal levels to construct knowledge in classroom settings.

In the context of science education, assuming that equal "levels" should be attained, that acquiring the same knowledge and understandings by all is a goal, could be self-defeating. As we attempt to infuse our teaching practices with the notion that all knowledge is constructed socially we recognize that the question of knowledge construction is not just an epistemological position. It needs to involve serious reflection about identity and experience as these relate to science education and as balanced against an individual child's purposes, both within science and their larger culture.

To uncritically accept the knowledge base of science is to perpetuate relationships of power and domination (Barton, 1997; Barton and Osborne, 1995). Current reform initiatives—even those aimed at enabling students to negotiate their way into the culture of science—if not concerned with helping students critically examine science, may contribute to students choosing to remain outsiders to science and to the culture of science by posing either/or choices about ways of knowing and hence identity. Despite the doors that a social constructivist position on subject matter opens (Atwater, 1996; Eisenhart, Finkel, and Marion, 1996), the otherness created by alternative cultural ways of knowing remains unexplored in traditional pedagogy (Barton, 1997; Brickhouse, 1994, Stanley and Brickhouse, 1995). The borders of science that need to be traversed in school settings require that students who have been marginal to dominant cultures take a step towards involvement. This involves acknowledging the unequal power relations of "knowledge" and "authority" in science (Gore, 1993; Foucault, 1980), and that they willingly examine other culturally defined identities and ways of knowing but it does not mean that they do so uncritically (Barton and Osborne, 1995).

Our research in informal science education settings indicates that science education ought to be about more than passing on the disciplinary knowledge of science. Science with children is an incredibly complex social site marked by multiple interacting layers of power arrangements and social and institutional forces which shape and define the boundaries of what is possible. For example, Kristin, Jin, and Timmy had found ways to use science time to further their social role playing. This suggests just how much science education is about issues of power and relationships on a personal as well as an institutional level. As Weiler (1988) claims, "teaching extends beyond subject matter knowledge; the centrality of teaching lies in a recognition of the values of students' own voices, subjective experiences of power and oppression, and the worth of their class and ethnic cultures" (p. 148). Envisioning science as a social construction locates the learning and doing of science within social relationships on a day-to-day level, not just historically. Allowing these relationships and the questions and concerns they provoke to guide the science creates opportunities for self and social empowerment (McLaren, 1989). This was clearly the case with Jason and his friends.

In the *Post-Modern Condition*, Jean-Francois Lyotard suggests two contradictory societal roles for knowledge which in turn support conflicting models of social structuring.

> One can decide that the principle role of knowledge is as an indispensable element in the functioning of society, and can act in accordance with that decision, only if one has already decided that society is a great machine.
>
> Conversely, one can count on its critical function, and orient its development and distribution in that direction, only after it has been decided that society does not form an integrated whole, but remains haunted by a principle of opposition. (Lyotard, 1984, p.13)

Such views presuppose a functional rather than passive role of knowledge in society—either actively contributing towards its homogeneity and continuity or playing a fundamental role in its fragmentation and reconstruction. These ideas of knowledge also suggest an active role for knowledge in the creation and maintenance of power differentials in society although the outcomes for such differences in each model are radically different.

Working with girls, minorities, and children in poverty is not easy in general and trying to construct science with these children that connects with their lives and empowers them in a liberating manner has compound difficulties. These children's lives and needs are complex. The manner in which the children in this paper explore science allows spaces to fit science into this entanglement rather than keeping it unconnected and separated as so much traditional schooling and science would do. Race, class, and gender, however, are not only dimensions of our social structure that reflect forms of power and privilege, they are also ways to think about our social processes and the way we live our lives. We argue that relationships are not always smooth or of an actor's choosing; they are constructed in contexts where actors have certain access to power and resources depending not only upon their relationships in the educational structure, but also their location and identity in the larger society. Attempting to consider the multiple layers that emerge and are formed in educational settings, this focus becomes important for understanding the complex problems and issues that emerge in connection with pedagogy and curriculum in classrooms.

In looking at our stories, pedagogically, in the construction of science curriculum, and in our relationships with children, we want to recognize that these are linked and all must be altered before the marginalized can engage in science. Indeed our concepts of the role of disciplinary knowledge in society must alter to incorporate change, evolutionary and revolutionary. Underlying our discussion of approaches to dealing with diversity is a questioning of what those courses of action imply about attitudes towards difference. Do they imply that difference is something to be "fixed," changed, or that difference should be worked within and maybe finally respected or even advocated? Don't they suggest that difference is fundamentally at the root of the democratic processes of our society?

Our stories cause us to think about what doing something about diversity means to us and to society. Respecting diversity (rather than trying to fix it, for instance) implies that our assumptions about the norms of society as reflected in the discipline of science will change. This implies that our ideas about subject matter and assumptions about good behavior, homelife, interests, and goals will evolve and enlarge. We suggest in answer to such concerns a rethinking of science, the discipline, in trying to construct a "science for all." We echo the classic writing of Peggy McIntosh (1983) in saying that we can't describe what such a new science might be. As our stories and this final quote from Lyotard (1983) suggest, it must be emergent through the acts of its creation:

The postmodern would be that which, in the modern, puts forward the unpresentable in presentation itself; that which denies itself the solace of good forms, the consensus of a taste which would make it possible to share nostalgia for the unattainable; that which searches for new presentations, not in order to enjoy them but in order to impart a stronger sense of the unpresentable. (p. 81)

References

American Association for the Advancement of Science. (1989). *Science for all Americans*. Washington, DC: Author.

American Association for the Advancement of Science. (1993). *Benchmarks for scientific literacy*. New York: Oxford University Press.

American Association of University Women (1992). *How schools shortchange girls*. Washington, DC: National Education Association.

Anderson, C.W. (1991). Policy implications of research on science teaching and teachers' knowledge. In M. M. Kennedy (ed.), *Teaching academic subjects to diverse learners*. New York: Teachers College Press.

Anyon, J. (1984). Intersections of gender and class: Accommodations and resistance by working class and affluent females to contradictory sex role ideologies. *Journal of Education* 166(1), 25–48.

Apple, M. (1979). *Ideology and curriculum*. London: Routledge.

Apple, M. (1992). The text and cultural politics. *Educational Researcher*, 21(7), 4–11.

Atwater, M. (1996). Social constructivism: Infusion into the multicultural science education research agenda. *Journal of Research in Science Teaching* 33, 821–838.

Ball, D.L. (1993). Halves pieces and twoths: Constructing representational contexts in teaching fractions. In T.P. Carpenter (ed.), *Rational numbers*. New York: Lawrence Erlbaum.

Barton, A.C. (1997). Liberatory science education: Weaving connections between feminist theory and science education. *Curriculum Inquiry*, 27(2), 141–163.

Barton, A.C. (1998). *Feminist science education*. New York: Teachers College Press.

Barton, A.C. and M.D. Osborne (1995). Science for all Americans? Science education reform and Mexican-Americans, *The High School Journal*, 78(4), 244–252.

Brickhouse, N. (1994). Bringing in the outsiders: Reshaping the sciences of the future. *Curriculum Studies*, 26, 401–416.

Buber, M. (1970). *I and thou*. New York: Scribner.

Calabrese, R. and Barton, A.C. (1995). Mexican-American male students and Anglo female teacher: Victims of the policies of assimilation. *The High School Journal*, 78(3), 115–123.

Cochran-Smith, M., Lytle, S.L. (1993). *Inside/outside: Teacher research and knowledge*. New York: Teachers College Press.

Davidson, A.L. (1994). Border curricula and the construction of identity: Implications for multicultural theorists. *Qualitative Studies in Education* 7(4), 335–349.

Delpit, L.D. (1988). The silenced dialogue: Power and pedagogy in educating other people's children. *Harvard Educational Review, 58*(3), 280–298.

Delpit, L.D. (1992). Acquisition of literate discourse: Bowing before the master? *Theory into Practice*, 31, 296–302.

Dewey, J. (1902/1956). *The child and the curriculum*. Chicago: University of Chicago Press.

Eisenhart, M., Finkel, E., and Marion, S. (1996). Creating the conditions for scientific literacy: A re-examination. *American Education Research Journal*, 33, 261–295.

Fine, M. (1993). Passions, politics and power: Feminist research possibilities. In M. Fine (ed.) *Disruptive voices: The possibilities of feminist research*. Ann Arbor: The University of Michigan Press.

Foley, D. (1991). Reconsidering anthropological explanations of school failure. *Anthropology and Education Quarterly*, 22(1), 60–86.

Foucault, M. (1978). *The history of sexuality*. New York : Pantheon Book.

Foucault, M. (1980). *Power/Knowledge: Selected interviews and other writings. 1972–1977*. New York: Pantheon Books.

Freire, P. (1971). *Pedagogy of the oppressed*. New York: Continuum.

Gates, H.L. (1992). *Loose canons*. New York: Oxford University Press.

Geertz, C. (1973). *The interpretation of cultures: Selected essays*. New York: Basic Books.

Gilligan, C. (1982). *In a different voice: Psychological theory and women's development*. Cambridge, MA: Harvard University Press.

Gitlin, A. (1994). *Power and method: Political activism and educational research*. New York: Routledge.

Goals 2000: Educate America Act. (1994). Pub. L. No. 103–227 (33/31/94), Stat. 108.

Gore, J. (1993). *The struggle for pedagogies: Critical and feminist discourse as regimes of truth.* New York: Routledge.

Haraway, D. (1997). *Modest witness@second-millennium. Femaleman-meets-oncomouse: Feminisms and technoscience.* New York: Routledge.

Harding, S. (1991). *Whose science? Whose knowledge? Thinking from women's lives.* Ithaca: Cornell University Press.

Hollingsworth, S. (1994). *Teacher research and urban literacy education.* New York: Teachers College Press.

hooks, b. (1994). *Teaching to transgress: Education as a practice of freedom.* London: Routledge.

Lensmire, T. (1994). *When children write: Critical re-visions of the writing workshop.* New York: Teachers College Press.

Lyotard, J.F. (1984). *The postmodern condition: A report on knowledge.* Minneapolis : University of Minnesota Press.

McIntosh, P. (1983). *Interactive phases of curricular re-vision: A feminist perspective.* Working Paper 124, Wellesley, MA: Center for Research on Women.

Maher, F. and M. Tetreault. (1993). Doing feminist ethnography: Lessons from a feminist classroom. *Qualitative Studies in Education,* 6 (1): 19–32.

Maher. F.A. (1987). Inquiry teaching and feminist pedagogy. *Social Education,* 51, 186–192.

McCarthy, C. and Crichlow, W. (1993). *Race, identity, and representation in education.* New York: Routledge.

McLaren, P. (1989). *Life in schools: An introduction to critical pedagogy in the foundations of education.* White Plains, NY: Longman.

National Research Council (NRC) (1996). *National science education standards.* Washington, DC: National Academy Press.

Noffke, S. and Stevenson, R.B. (1995). *Educational action research.* NY: Teachers College Press.

Oakes, J. (1990). *Lost talent: The underparticipation of women, minorities, and disabled persons in science.* Santa Monica, CA: Rand Corporation.

Osborne, M. D. (1997). Balancing individual and group: A dilemma for constructivist teachers. *Journal of Curriculum Studies* 29 (2), 183–194.

Osborne, M.D. (1998). Responsive science pedagogy in a democracy: Dangerous teaching. *Theory Into Practice.*

Packwood, A. and Sikes, P. (1996). Postmodern narrative. *The International Journal of Qualitative Studies in Education,* 3, 335–346.

Polakow, V. (1993). *Lives on the edge.* Chicago: University of Chicago Press.

Quint, S. (1994). *Schooling homeless children: A working model for America's public schools.* New York: Teachers College Press.

Reyes, P. and Valencia, R. (1993). Educational policy and the growing Latino student population: Problems and prospects. *Hispanic Journal of Behavioral Sciences,* 15(2), 258–283.

Roseberry, A. (1994). Interpretive perspectives on scientific discourse. Presented at the American Educational Research Association, annual meeting, at New Orleans, LA.

Schon, D. (1983). *The reflective practitioner: How professionals think in action.* New York: Basic Books.

Stanley L. and Wise S. (1993). *Breaking out again: Feminist ontology and epistemology.* New York: Routledge.

Stanley, W. and Brickhouse, N. (1995). Multiculturalism, universalism and science education. *Science Education,* 78, 387–398.

Thorne, B. (1993). *Gender play: Girls and boys in school.* New Brunswick: Rutgers University Press.

Tobin, K. and McRobbie, C. (1996). Cultural myths as constraints to the enacted science curriculum. *Science Education,* 80(2), 223–241.

Vygotsky, L. (1978). *Mind in society: The development of higher psychological processes.* Cambridge MA: Harvard University Press.

Weber, M. (1949). *The methodology of the social sciences.* Glencoe, IL: Free Press

Weiler, K. (1988). *Women teaching for change.* South Hadley, MA: Bergen and Garvey Publishers.

West, C. (1993). *Race matters.* Boston: Beacon Press.

4

ε**ल**

The Politics of Religious Knowledge
in Singapore Secondary Schools*

Jason Tan

My focus is on the short-lived government imposition of Religious Knowledge as a compulsory subject for upper secondary students in Singapore, a multi-ethnic, multi-religious country. The move to introduce Religious Knowledge arose out of concern on the part of senior cabinet members that the moral values of the wider society were under threat from modernization and undesirable "Western" values. Six options—Bible Knowledge, Islamic Religious Knowledge, Buddhist Studies, Confucian Ethics, Hindu Studies, and Sikh Studies—were made available in 1984. However, barely five years later, in 1989, the government announced that Religious Knowledge would no longer be a compulsory school subject from the following year onwards, and would instead become an optional subject to be conducted outside of official curriculum hours. It would be replaced by a common Civics and Moral Education course for all secondary school students starting in 1992.

In the first section, I outline the demographics and political system in Singapore, thus setting the stage for the subsequent discussion

---

* This chapter is a revised and updated version of my "The rise and fall of religious knowledge in Singapore secondary schools," which appeared in the *Journal of Curriculum Studies*, 29 (5), 1997, 603–624.

of the various stages in the policymaking and planning processes. The following sections deal with (a) the initial broaching of the idea of a compulsory Religious Knowledge subject; (b) the implementation of the Religious Knowledge curriculum; and (c) the official decision to relegate Religious Knowledge to the status of an optional subject. In the final section I reconsider the key issues in the Singapore case.

Among the several interesting issues posed by the short-lived experiment in introducing Religious Knowledge in Singapore are questions surrounding curriculum knowledge (Cornbleth, 1990: 99, 118–119, 133–135), for instance, how is knowledge selected and organized? Who controls the selection and organization process? How is knowledge treated? What knowledge is made available to whom? Who benefits from a particular selection, organization, treatment, and distribution of knowledge? How does the State affect curriculum policymaking? The Singapore case is especially interesting in view of the often controversial debates relating to the provision of religious education in various countries (Tulasiewicz and To, 1993). The discussion about religious education in a multi-cultural society is also timely in view of the rise of religious and ethnic conflict around the world (Friedman and Isserman, 1998; Lake and Rothchild, 1998).

The Singapore case illustrates:

- the intensely political nature of decision making about curriculum knowledge, and also the strengths and limitations of adopting a top-down technocratic approach to curriculum;
- the importance of treating curriculum as a "contextualized social process" (Cornbleth 1990: 13) instead of as a mere technocratic document or plan;
- the way in which the introduction of Religious Knowledge as a form of crisis management, despite the objections of educators, in turn sowed the seeds for the eventual dismantling of the programme within a few years.

The entire episode provides a vivid illustration of how the best of technocratically laid plans are unlikely to have much success without the concomitant provision of a supportive structural and socio-cultural context. As Fullan and Stiegelbauer (1991: 95) point out, policymakers frequently make "hyperrational" assumptions when introducing changes. By failing to come to grips with the realities of the people who are the main participants in implementing changes, policymakers will not succeed in their change efforts.

Demographic and Political Background

Demographics. There are three main ethnic groups in Singapore: the Chinese (pop. 2,350,391), the Malays (pop. 415,300), and the Indians (pop. 190,003), comprising 78.7%, 13.9%, and 6.4% of the population respectively (Department of Statistics 1997: 61). There are also other minorities such as Eurasians, Filipinos, and Thais. Each of the three major ethnic groups is further composed of different language groups, thus making for a multilingual mix in addition to the ethnic diversity.

There is also diversity along religious lines. Malays are the most homogeneous ethnic group in terms of religious affiliation, with almost all Malays identifying themselves as being Muslims. In contrast, the Chinese and Indians are much more heterogeneous in this respect. Also, about one in six Chinese claims no religious affiliation. Most of the major religions in Singapore are closely affiliated with particular ethnic groups. For instance, the majority of Buddhists are ethnic Chinese while the majority of Hindus are ethnic Indians. The one major religion with the most heterogeneous ethnic composition is Christianity (Department of Statistics 1997: 220).

Political Structure and Operation. The ruling People's Action Party (PAP) has governed Singapore ever since it won the 1959 general elections. Singapore has been described as an "administrative state" (Chan, 1975), characterized by "the centralization and accumulation of power in key political and bureaucratic centres, the shrinkage of the political arena, and the disappearance of open politics and any overt display of independently organized power" (Chan, 1989: 81–82). Policymaking in the public arena is highly elitist in nature, with most, if not all, policies being formulated by the Cabinet, which is the supreme policymaking body within the government (Quah and Quah, 1989). There is a heavy emphasis on economic rationality, in which government decisions are based in large part on the views and opinions of technocrats (Chua, 1994). Many of these technocrats have in the past been awarded Singapore government scholarships to pursue their undergraduate education at prestigious universities such as Oxford and Cambridge and have been recruited directly into the top ranks of the government administrative service upon their return to Singapore. This governing style extends naturally to the realm of education policymaking (Wong, 1991). Various professional organizations may provide input into policy formulation but only within the officially predetermined policy frameworks (Chan, 1976; Quah and Quah, 1989). The PAP governing philosophy regards lobbying efforts on the part of various interest groups as detracting from speedy and efficient policy implementation (Chan, 1975).

In addition, the PAP has pursued numerous highly interventionist policies in such areas as public housing, family size, fertility trends, and marriage patterns. The basic tone throughout official discourse is one of the-ends-justify-the-means utilitarianism, in which "all aspects of social life are to be instrumentally harnessed" in the relentless pursuit of economic growth (Chua, 1995, 59). A local social scientist has remarked that the government is unable to speak meaningfully to the public apart from the language of competitive economics (Chew, 1976).

The Introduction of Religious Knowledge

Prior to the introduction of Religious Knowledge as a compulsory subject, various secular based moral education programmes had been implemented. The PAP government instituted a compulsory ethics programme in all primary and secondary schools. This was replaced by a Civics programme in 1967, which was in turn replaced in 1974 at the primary level with Education for Living, a combination of civics, history, and geography. Both Civics and Education for Living were taught in either Chinese, Malay, or Tamil, as part of the belief that value transmission was best carried out in the "ethnic language." All the teachers of these two subjects were concurrently teaching one of the three languages, and no formal training was conducted for Civics teachers (Ong, 1979, 3).

No religious instruction, rituals, or ceremonies were permitted in government schools (that is, schools that are administered and funded entirely by the government). However, government-aided church schools[1] (run by various denominations such as Presbyterians, Methodists, Anglicans, and Catholics) were allowed to conduct religious instruction lessons for one lesson period a week outside of the official curriculum time and also to have brief prayer sessions at the start or close of each school day. These schools could also run religious clubs for students, such as the Legion of Mary. In addition, several privately-run *madrasahs* (Islamic religious schools), which received only nominal financial aid from the government, were allowed to conduct classes in Islamic Religious Knowledge.

Since coming to power in 1959, the PAP political leadership has expressed grave concern over the maintenance of "traditional cultural values" against the onslaught of modernization and undesirable "Western" influences. The local population is periodically urged to avoid the perceived "moral decline" in the West.[2] Several local academics have commented on the way in which the officially preferred "traditional values" have been chosen on purely utilitarian and instrumental grounds, as those that can best serve the twin goals of economic growth and social stability (Gopinathan, 1980; Koh, 1980). At the same time as the government urges the maintenance of "traditional cultural values," it is also concerned with the task of integrating an ethnically, linguistically, and religiously diverse population.

The chain of events that led eventually to the decision to introduce Religious Knowledge was set in motion at the end of the 1970s. In 1978 then-Prime Minister Lee Kuan Yew had commissioned then-Deputy Prime Minister Goh Keng Swee, who was concurrently serving as Education Minister, to prepare a report on educational reform in primary and secondary schools. Goh had in turn commissioned then-Minister for Communication to chair a committee to review moral education programmes. Both reports,[3] which were published in 1979, were highly critical of the Civics and Education for Living programmes (Goh, 1979; Ong, 1979).

Among the problems pointed out were those relating to textbook adequacy and choice of subject matter. In addition, the *Report on Moral Education* pointed out that neither teachers nor students were treating the programmes seriously because they were non-examinable.[4] At the same time, this report pointed out that religious studies helped to reinforce the teaching of moral values. It observed that many teachers in mission schools were able to teach Civics and Education for Living more effectively because of their "strong religious background" (Ong, 1979: 7). The Ministry of Education was therefore urged to allow government-aided church-run schools "greater flexibility in implementing religious instruction programmes" (Ong, 1979: 12). Furthermore, Lee's views on "the ideal Singaporean" as someone who could "live, work, contend and co-operate in a civilised way" (Ong, 1979: 8) were endorsed wholeheartedly.

The release of both reports triggered a flurry of action on the part of the Ministry of Education. First, in 1979 the Ministry approved the inclusion of Bible Knowledge and Islamic Religious Knowledge as examination subjects in the secondary school termi-

nal examinations. The following year it established three committees to explore the possibility of introducing Muslim, Hindu, and
Buddhist studies in schools. In his response to the *Report on Moral
Education*, Goh stressed the need for "an intellectual basis which
will bind the various moral qualities we deem desirable into a consistent system of thought" (Ong, 1979: iii). One of the members of
the committee that had drafted the Report on Moral Education recommended the expertise of a local Jesuit priest who had a "distinguished academic record in theology and philosophy" (*ibid*.: iii).
This priest was commissioned to design a secular moral education
programme based on the recommendations of the earlier *Report on
Moral Education*. The Being and Becoming programme, as it was
termed, was designed for primary and lower secondary students
and was pilot tested in 1981. That same year, the government introduced another secular based programme, Good Citizen, at the primary level. The latter programme was designed by the newly-
established government-run Curriculum Development Institute of
Singapore.

The decision to implement Religious Knowledge instruction
was announced formally by Goh Keng Swee in January 1982. He
painted a bleak picture of profound moral crisis in Singapore,[5] and
warned that Singapore needed to avoid the "decline in moral standards" taking place in the West. Goh warned that the government
could not afford to wait for the Being and Becoming programme to
be extended to cover all secondary schools and to assess its effectiveness (*The Sunday Times*, January 17, 1982). He bore personal
testimony to back up his assertion that a secular moral education
programme was inferior to one based on religious knowledge.
According to Goh, the material success of many of his former classmates at a local Methodist boys' school, as well as the fact that none
of them had been imprisoned for criminal breach of trust, bore testimony to their trustworthiness, which in turn was a product of
their exposure to Christian values in school. Goh neglected to mention, however, the recent widespread media publicity given to the
prevalence of social snobbery at that same school.

One is struck immediately by the incongruity of appealing to
material instincts to evaluate the worth of religious education or to
justify the introduction of religion. It is evident as well that not only
was the government directly influencing curriculum policy through
the issuing of mandates, it also was dominating the entire course of
the debate by framing the definitions of issues, problems, and solutions, while at the same time establishing the fundamental para-

meters for any subsequent public debate. It should also be noted that hardly any public debate or consultation took place prior to Goh's announcement about the new subject.

Curriculum Policy

Upper secondary students (in Secondaries three, four, and five) were to choose one of five options: Buddhist Studies, Bible Knowledge, Hindu Studies, Islamic Religious Knowledge, or World Religions.[6] Every school, regardless of its religious affiliation, would have to offer any option that was requested by at least twenty parents. The choice of options was left entirely to parents. Those parents not wishing their children to take Religious Knowledge at all would have to seek exemption directly from the Ministry of Education. Although the subject was to be compulsory for upper secondary students, they could decide whether or not to be examined in the subject during the national secondary school terminal examinations. However, in order to provide an incentive for students to do so, students would be allowed to use the examination grades obtained in the subject for entry into pre-university classes (the stage of schooling immediately following secondary school). In addition, the Minister of State for Education assured students that Religious Knowledge was "a relatively easy subject" (*The Straits Times*, January 18, 1982), thus providing further evidence of the paradoxical appeal to utilitarian concerns in promoting the study of religion.

The government stated its hope that Religious Knowledge would build on the foundation provided by the secular moral education programme at the primary and lower secondary levels. An Education Ministry report stated that religion had been the "basis of individual and public morality for the past few thousand years" (*The Sunday Times*, January 17, 1982; see also *Parliamentary Debates*, 54, October 6, 1989: cols. 622–623 for a restatement of this belief). The programme was being introduced at the upper secondary levels because

> . . . for moral education to be effective at the higher levels of our secondary schools . . . [it] cannot be taught simply as a collection of bits and pieces of good advice or moral platitudes. At that age . . . children . . . will not simply accept what they are told. It must be related to what is called a 'unifying intellectual basis' which will place desirable moral

values within an 'intellectually acceptable conceptual framework' (*Parliamentary Debates*, 53, March 20, 1989: col. 511).

In addition to the original five options, Confucian ethics was added in February 1982 and Sikh Studies the following year. Thus, students in most schools had a total of six options at the beginning of 1984: Buddhist Studies, Bible Knowledge, Confucian Ethics, Hindu Studies, Islamic Religious Knowledge, and Sikh Studies.[7] The belated addition of Sikh Studies was undertaken in response to a request by the Sikh Advisory Board (*The Straits Times*, February 18, 1982), and may be viewed as an attempt to buttress government claims to neutrality and even-handedness with respect to religion.

The case of Confucian Ethics is interesting in that it was introduced at the specific request of the then-Prime Minister just after the initial announcement regarding Religious Knowledge had been made in January 1982. Goh Keng Swee claimed that Confucian Ethics was "completely secular"[8] and that it would provide students with a "cultural ballast against the less desirable aspects of Western culture" (*The Straits Times*, February 4, 1982). He pointed to the content of two books—*Enemies of Society* by Paul Johnson and *The Culture of Narcissism* by Christopher Lasch—as evidence of the "state of confusion" in the West (*The Straits Times*, December 28, 1982).

In response to charges that the promotion of Confucianism was a ploy to legitimize and institutionalize the government's own authoritarian rule, a crucial if somewhat tenuous distinction was made between Confucian political ideology and Confucian ethics. Confucian doctrine as a political ideology was deemed as not relevant to Singapore, while Confucian doctrine as a code of conduct governing the behaviour of "an honourable man or gentleman" was what Singapore needed: "Confucius believed that unless the government is in the hands of upright men, disaster will befall the country. By the way, in this respect, the PAP also believes the same thing" (*The Straits Times*, February 4, 1982).

In addition, Confucian ethics was directly relevant to "a country that is trying to achieve fast economic growth in the 20th Century, using modern science and technology." The rapid economic growth of the "Gang of Four"—Taiwan, Hong Kong, South Korea, and Singapore—was attributed to the Confucian ethic. According to Goh, there was a direct parallel between the Confucian ethic in these Asian countries and the Protestant ethic in the United States, as both of them demonstrated the importance of character in achieving success. One sees here once again the use of instrumental reasoning in the discussion of ethics.

Several objections had been raised to the introduction of a compulsory Religious Knowledge subject by various educators and Members of Parliament during public forums and Schools Council[9] meetings as well as in Parliament (*The Straits Times*, February 11, 1982, September 6, 1982). During a Schools Council meeting with Goh, some school principals questioned whether over-enthusiastic teachers might seize the chance to evangelize among their students. Goh replied that it was the principals' responsibility to "detect something untoward in their schools" (*The Sunday Times*, January 17, 1982). During a Parliamentary debate session, a Member of Parliament expressed similar apprehension about religious conversion. In his reply, the Minister of State for Education replied that teachers would be selected only from among those who belonged to "established churches in the case of Christians," and not from among "members of fundamentalist sects (which have a record of evangelical excesses)" (*ibid*.: Col. 373).[10] Teachers of Islamic Religious Knowledge, Hindu Studies, and Buddhist Studies would have to be approved by the Islamic Religious Council of Singapore, the Hindu Advisory Board, and the Singapore Buddhist Federation respectively.

Furthermore, strongly worded assurances were given that parents need not fear that their children would be subject to attempts at religious conversion on the part of over-zealous teachers. First of all, worship practices or religious objects or attempts at proselytization would be strictly forbidden. Secondly, teachers would be restricted to using only prescribed textbooks—"it's like studying Shakespeare," quipped the Minister of State for Education. In addition, examination questions would only test students' factual knowledge, and would not solicit their opinions (*The Straits Times*, January 18, 1982). This last statement stood in stark contrast to the government's assertion that older students "will not simply accept what they are told." Also interesting was the government's asserting on the one hand that religious knowledge needed to be taught by "someone with conviction" and with "an exemplary lifestyle" (*The Straits Times*, January 18, 1982),[11] while on the other hand cautioning that over-zealous teachers would not be tolerated.

The Jesuit priest who had earlier designed the Being and Becoming programme was one of several critics who warned that religious knowledge alone would not produce "moral students." He warned that the only way of achieving direct changes in students' behaviour was through inculcating religious faith, and not mere knowledge about religion (*The Sunday Times*, January 17, 1982).

The official rebuttal to this criticism focused on the government's claim that Singapore was a secular state,[12] and that the State, being mindful of the religious sensitivities of a multi-racial, multi-religious population, could therefore not be involved in religious propagation. In an inimitably technocratic fashion, a rather tenuous distinction was drawn between "religious instruction" and "religious knowledge." The former aimed to "implant in the individual full religious conviction and practice" (*Parliamentary Debates*, 54, October 6, 1989: col. 623), and was "a matter for the individual and his own conscience and [not] a matter for the state to provide" (Tay 1983: 84). The latter was to be restricted to "informing students about the religion, its founder or its origins and the universal moral teachings and main beliefs of the religion" (*Parliamentary Debates*, 41, March 3, 1982: col. 373).

Other critics warned that it was precisely because Singapore was a multi-cultural nation that students needed to undertake a comparative study of all the major religions, instead of narrowly focusing on one religion, in order to better promote inter-religious understanding and tolerance (*The Straits Times*, February 17, 1982). It was also pointed out that the introduction of various options could lead to a polarization along ethno-religious lines (Chiew, 1983: 257). Goh noted the objections raised, but insisted that the programme should proceed as planned. "Bold measures" were needed instead of a "timid, cautious approach" to tackle the serious problem of moral decay (*The Sunday Times*, January 17, 1982).

Implementation of the Religious Knowledge Curriculum

Now that the decision to proceed with the teaching of Religious Knowledge had been publicized and legitimized, the task of designing curriculum materials and training teachers had to be undertaken. At a press conference in February 1982, Goh Keng Swee outlined a six-point plan for the implementation of the Confucian Ethics curriculum (*The Straits Times*, February 4, 1982). The plan serves further to illustrate the top-down, technocratic implementation style used by the Singapore government. The first step involved setting up a conceptual framework of which aspects of Confucian doctrine should be taught. Secondly, the syllabus needed to be designed, "and this was a job for professionals." The next two steps involved drafting a synopsis of the syllabus and holding a public debate on the synopsis. However, the public debate would *not* be for the purpose of discussing whether or not to teach Confucian Ethics, but instead would focus on which aspects of doctrine to include in the syllabus. The fifth step involved the writing of textbooks and teaching materials, and, finally, teachers would be selected and trained.

Right from the initial announcement about Religious Knowledge in January 1982, there was no doubt that the government would remain in firm overall control of the policymaking process from start to finish. Having identified the need for Religious Knowledge, it would also define what constituted legitimate "religion" and "religious knowledge" to be taught to students. For instance, Taoism was not on the list of options. Secondly, it would also steer the content of textbooks in directions consonant with its own governing philosophy. This meant also that the content in the various Religious Knowledge options would have to be homogenized (see Kuah, 1991 and Tamney, 1988: 119–124, for detailed analyses).

Thirdly, the government had firm control over resource allocation and the delegation of tasks such as the writing of curriculum materials and textbooks, as well as the power to prescribe which particular textbooks could be used. For instance, it decided not only which particular individuals would be invited as consultants, but also which organizations would be enlisted in the search for advice on doctrinal matters as well as the arrangements for teacher training. It seemed confident that despite the objections of critics, the adoption of a rational, technocratic approach to curriculum planning and implementation would be sufficient to ensure the success of the entire scheme.

Despite, and perhaps because of, the top-down approach of the government, the implementation of the Religious Knowledge programme was by no means smooth and efficient. For example, some school principals resorted to drafting teachers without prior consultation into Buddhist Studies training programmes in order to fulfil their quota of teachers to be sent for training. Their move was in direct contradiction to the Ministry's policy of recruiting teachers with enough personal conviction and commitment to serve as worthy examples for students. This policy aroused complaints from Christian teahers who had been forced to teach Buddhist Studies

(Kuah 1991). The issue of teacher quality and preparation had been the subject of criticism in the *Report on Moral Education 1979* (Ong, 1979), but the lessons had obviously yet to be learned.

The entire Religious Knowledge saga illustrated several key points: (a) the intensely political nature of curriculum policy-making. For instance, it was clear that decisions about what knowledge to include in the subject were not wholly impartial and rational as the policymakers made them out to be, but instead were closely intertwined with questions of power; (b) the importance of viewing curriculum as a social process embedded in a structural and socio-cultural context, and not merely as a technocratic document or plan; and (c) the importance of creating enabling conditions for curriculum change in order better to promote curriculum reform.

I mentioned earlier that one of the original options to be made available was World Religions. There were multiple problems involved in syllabus drafting, textbook writing, and teacher training that led the government to abandon that option. First, there was disagreement among the various religious bodies as to which religions should be included in the syllabus. The Ministry of Education, with the help of a lecturer on comparative religions, finally decided to cover nine major world religions: Buddhism, Christianity, Confucianism, Hinduism, Islam, Jainism, Judaism, Sikhism, and Taoism. The next problem revolved around what particular aspects of the various religions to include in the syllabus. The Ministry of Education was unable to find "any academic, either in Singapore or overseas, who was brave enough to try and write a textbook" (*Parliamentary Debates*, 53, March 20, 1989: col. 513). Yet another problem was that of finding teachers who could teach the subject "in a fair and unbiased" manner (*ibid.*: col. 513). The then-Minister for Education confessed early on that "other than a person who has a degree in divinity, I don't think any ordinary graduate of . . . [the] National University of Singapore can handle this subject" (*The Straits Times*, December 28, 1982).

Even as these various problems and dilemmas were being played out, the introduction of Confucian Ethics as a Religious Knowledge option attracted a disproportionate amount of media attention. The senior political leadership repeatedly trumpeted Confucian doctrine as a vital asset in the promotion of economic growth and social stability.[13] Goh Keng Swee visited the United States in May 1982 to confer with a number of leading Confucian scholars. A large amount of publicity was given to the visit to Singapore in the third quarter of 1982 by eight Chinese-American Confucian scholars from prestigious universities in the United States. They had been invited by the Ministry of Education to act as consultants to the Confucian Ethics programme. The scholars gave public lectures and seminars, met with Members of Parliament and Cabinet ministers, and appeared on television forums in order to publicize Confucianism.

Their presence was evidently intended to boost the legitimacy of the policymaking process and the resultant programme by endowing it with an aura of professional objectivity and respectability. As a further gesture of official support for Confucianism, a government-funded Institute of East Asian Philosophy was established in 1983 to promote the study of East Asian philosophies (Kuo, 1992). None of the other Religious Knowledge options came remotely close to receiving such official patronage and orchestrated media fanfare. This biased treatment would seem once again to be evidence that the government was not, as it claimed, neutral and even-handed in the religious sphere. It was prepared to utilize multiple means to influence curriculum policymaking, such as mandates, resource allocation for capacity building, exhortation, and influencing public opinion and debate.

Soon after the launching of Confucian Ethics, Lee Kuan Yew had predicted that more Chinese parents would opt for Confucianism than for Buddhist Studies (*The Straits Times*, February 8, 1982). However, despite the tremendous government support given to Confucianism, Confucian Ethics remained the least popular option among Chinese students. The percentage breakdown of choices of Secondary three (the third year of secondary school) students in 1989 was as follows: Bible Knowledge (21.4%), Buddhist Studies (44.4%), Confucian Ethics (17.8%), Hindu Studies (2.7%), Islamic Religious Knowledge (13.4%), and Sikh Studies (0.4%).

Ironically, a major contributing factor to the lower popularity of Confucian Ethics was the perception among many parents that it was easier to pass Buddhist Studies than Confucian Ethics (*Parliamentary Debates*, 54, October 6, 1989: col. 604). The government had obviously been caught in yet another double bind. It had used the pull of pragmatism—being able to use Religious Knowledge grades for entry to pre-university classes—to encourage students to be examined in the subject in their terminal examinations. The students and parents had responded in kind by making the instrumental choice as to which option promised "easier returns" in the competitive education system.

The Scaling Back of Religious Knowledge

Even as the Religious Knowledge programme was being implemented in secondary schools, alarm bells were already beginning to sound in official circles. In 1985 the government lodged complaints with the Catholic Archbishop of Singapore about articles in the *Catholic News* that were critical of government policies (*The Straits Times*, October 12, 1989). In May 1987 sixteen individuals were arrested by the Internal Security Department for being involved in a Marxist conspiracy to overthrow the PAP government and establish a communist state in Singapore. Several church groups had allegedly been infiltrated by this group of individuals, who reportedly disseminated writings about class differences and worker exploitation in Singapore (Quah, 1987; Tamney, 1992a).

The government expelled a regional ecumenical organization, the Christian Conference of Asia, from Singapore in December 1987 on the grounds that its monthly publication had included articles on liberation theology (Tamney, 1992a). In his National Day Rally address that year, Lee Kuan Yew issued a stern warning to religious groups not to get involved in politics, but to restrict themselves instead to humanitarian activities such as providing relief for the destitute. The examples of Sri Lanka and India were cited as cases where the mixing of religion and politics had had "unhappy results" (*The Straits Times*, August 17, 1987). The government's concern over the possible threat posed to its legitimacy and authority by religious groups led it in 1990 to enact a Maintenance of Religious Harmony Act that prohibited religious organizations from becoming involved in political issues.

In February 1988, three National University of Singapore sociologists released a report on religions and religious revivalism in Singapore that had been commissioned by the Ministry of Community Development (Kuo, Quah, and Tong, 1988). Their report documented the dramatic growth in Christianity, especially in Protestant evangelical charismatic groups, and drew attention to the links between socio-economic status and English-medium education and receptivity to Christianity. The increasing scale of Christian evangelical activities was causing concern among local Muslim leaders. At the same time, a Buddhist revival was taking place.[14]

The report also pointed out the contributory role that the Religious Knowledge curriculum had played in religious revivalism and evangelistic activities among Buddhists and Christians. The government was urged to ensure that teachers maintained a clear distinction between their professional and religious roles. Also, the authors asserted that the government had not been impartial in matters of religion as manifested, for instance, in the choice of specific religions as course options and the choice of particular ideological stances within the various theological traditions of each religion. They urged the government to assess the long-term impact of the Religious Knowledge programme on current and future religious developments in Singapore.

To complicate an already complex situation further, the 1980s also saw the increasing rise of ethnic consciousness in Singapore (Hussin, 1992). There was a host of issues revolving around ethnicity: educational disparities along ethnic lines, recruitment of Malays into the Singapore Armed Forces,[15] the imposition of ethnically-based quotas in public housing, and the impact of different fertility rates among various ethnic groups on future economic growth. The various ethnic minorities were increasingly apprehensive over what they perceived as government efforts to promote ethnic assertiveness among the Chinese community through such measures as the annual "Speak Mandarin" campaign, the promotion of Confucianism, and plans to encourage 100,000 Hong Kong Chinese to emigrate to Singapore.

The findings of the report on religion and religious revivalism had a direct impact on government policy. The recent incidents involving the alleged Marxist conspiracy, with direct implications for State authority and legitimacy, very likely fuelled government concern as well. The then-Minister for Education informed Parliament in March 1989 that his Ministry was reviewing the Religious Knowledge programme. He outlined three alternative courses of action.

The first option was to scrap the subject completely and replace it with the pre-1979 civics programme. But the latter programme had already been found wanting. Another option was to replace the current options with a course on comparative religion. However, attempts to design a World Religions option had failed dismally so far. Finally, Religious Knowledge could be offered as an optional subject outside school hours but could not be used for admission to pre-university classes. In a tacit acknowledgement of the prevalent pragmatic mindset, he conceded that this proposal would likely lead to a drastic reduction in the number of students taking the subject.

He proposed holding public consultative sessions with such groups as parents, teachers, principals, religious leaders, community leaders, and academics in order to arrive at "a better and more rational solution" (*Parliamentary Debates*, 53, March 20, 1989: col. 514). The government was much more cautious now, preferring to seek greater public consultation than when it initiated the Religious Knowledge programme. Such consultation would also serve to boost the legitimacy of any decisions made. The drop in support for the PAP in the 1984 general elections had led to various government attempts to boost its legitimacy by establishing several feedback mechanisms for the general public (Chan, 1989). The public consultation in the case of the review of Religious Knowledge should be viewed in this socio-political context.

The Government Parliamentary Committee (GPC) on Education[16] conducted an informal public hearing as well as dialogue sessions with various religious organizations and teachers' unions. In addition, the Minister for Education held four meetings between May and August 1989 with principals and teachers, academics, members and resource persons of the GPC, heads of religious organizations, community leaders, and the general public. Several main viewpoints emerged during these meetings. The first viewpoint argued for the retention of Religious Knowledge in its current form. The second was that Religious Knowledge should be taught as an optional subject during school hours. Yet another viewpoint was that Religious Knowledge should be replaced by a study of the major religions in Singapore (*Parliamentary Debates*, 54, October 6, 1989: cols. 575–577, 584–585).

The GPC recommended to Parliament that Religious Knowledge should no longer be compulsory, but should instead be taught as an optional subject outside official school hours. It suggested that teaching only a few religions was unfair not only to the excluded religions, but also to free thinkers. Making Religious Knowledge compulsory was also inconsistent with the secular nature of the government and the State. Furthermore, teaching students only one specific religion might accentuate religious exclusivism and hamper nation-building. Teaching Religious Knowledge might also heighten religious proselytization (*Parliamentary Debates*, 54, October 6 1989: cols. 585–586).

The GPC further recommended that a new Civics curriculum be introduced for the first three years of secondary school. Students in the final year of secondary school should be allowed to concentrate on examinable subjects. Although the new subject would be non-examinable, measures (none were specified) should be taken to ensure that teaching periods were not used for make-up or remedial lessons for other subjects. One sees here the inherent irony of surrendering to the utilitarian mindset in one instance, while recommending measures to counter it in another.

The government conceded that it had erred in making Religious Knowledge compulsory. It also conceded that its promotion of Religious Knowledge had violated its officially secular stance. In a *non sequitur* argument, both the Minister and the Senior Minister of State for Education said that the teaching of religious values and beliefs (which was avowedly not the aim of the Religious Knowledge subject in the first instance) should be left to the parents and should not be the responsibility of the schools. However, the Senior Minister of State insisted that the original rationale for introducing the subject—to have students learn about a major religion so as to reinforce the moral education they had received in their earlier school years—remained valid (*Parliamentary Debates*, 54, October 6, 1989: cols. 579, 622–625).

The Minister for Education announced in Parliament in October 1989 that beginning in 1990 Religious Knowledge would no longer be compulsory, and that from 1995 onwards it could no longer be used for entry to pre-university classes (*Parliamentary Debates*, 54, October 6, 1989: cols. 580–582). A Member of Parliament commented that this change in policy would mean that Religious Knowledge would "die a natural death" (*Parliamentary Debates*, 54, October 6, 1989: col. 601). Several other Members protested the removal of Confucian Ethics on the grounds that it was not a religion and therefore should not suffer the same fate as the other five options (*Parliamentary Debates*, 54, October 6, 1989: cols. 599–601, 619–621). However, their objections were overruled by the Minister for Education on the grounds that Confucian Ethics had to be treated on a par with the other components in the Religious Knowledge package (*Parliamentary Debates*, 54, October 6, 1989: col. 634).

In place of Religious Knowledge, a new compulsory Civics and Moral Education programme would be designed for all secondary school students. After two years of syllabus construction, textbook writing, and teacher training, the first batch of students would be taught the new subject in 1992. The new subject would incorporate factual knowledge about the main religions in Singapore, as well as elements of the Shared Values that were first promulgated by the then First Deputy Prime Minister in 1988 as part of a proposed National Ideology (Goh 1988, Singapore Government 1991).

Discussion

The short-lived experiment with Religious Knowledge as a compulsory subject in Singapore secondary schools constitutes a fascinating and illuminating case study for individuals interested in the politics of curriculum policymaking and curriculum change. First of all, it is evident that curriculum cannot simply be viewed as a technocratic document or plan, but instead as a "contextualized social process" (Cornbleth, 1990: 13). Throughout the entire Religious Knowledge saga there were complex intertwining relationships between the various players such as the Ministry of Education, foreign consultants, teachers, principals, parents, students, members of the religious, and the senior political leadership.

There was also evidence of the ways in which the education system mediated State and socio-cultural pressures, and of interactions between the various layers of context. For instance, even as the government was introducing the subject in order to produce moral beings, it constantly appealed to instrumental considerations in the policymaking process. Utilitarian considerations in turn influenced the decisionmaking processes of students and parents in ways that worked counter to the expectations of the senior political leadership.

Central to the Singapore case also are considerations of curriculum knowledge: How is knowledge selected and organized? Who controls the selection and organization process? How is knowledge treated? What knowledge is made available to whom? Who benefits from a particular selection, organization, treatment, and distribution of knowledge? How does the State affect curriculum policymaking?

The Singapore case demonstrates the intensely political nature of decision making about curriculum knowledge and dispels any notion that curriculum knowledge and decisions about that knowledge are wholly or even largely neutral and objective. Throughout the entire episode the Singapore government was employing a top-down, technocratic approach to curriculum decision making and planning. It exerted control over curriculum in several ways by:

- maintaining hegemony over policy debates by defining the problems and issues as well as delimiting the range of possible solutions. The initial 1982 announcement about Religious Knowledge was not preceded by widespread public consultation. Even the review of Religious Knowledge was carried out as a result of government initiative;

- controlling the resource allocation and capacity building process. The government dominated the syllabus design, textbook writing, and teacher training processes. It imposed a distinction between "religious knowledge" and "religious instruction," and defined also what constituted legitimate "religion" and "religious knowledge." The textbook writing and teacher training were carried out by the government-run Curriculum Development Institute of Singapore. Various consultants, both local and foreign, as well as several local religious bodies, were invited to assist in the curriculum development and teacher training processes in order to boost the prestige and legitimacy of the programme. Nevertheless, the consultants and religious bodies clearly had a subordinate role within the government's predetermined scheme of things. Not only did the government decide which particular individuals or organizations to consult, it even prescribed particular "desirable values" for consultants to advocate. These "desirable values" were to be those deemed consonant with the government's ideas of good moral beings, who would contribute to economic growth on the one hand, while not threatening the existing social and political status quo. For instance, Goh Keng Swee mentioned that an ideal Singapore son who happened to be a policeman would arrest his father for speeding. "Now, that is the sort of ethic we should teach in Singapore. It is up to the scholars to find it somewhere in Confucian literature" (*The Straits Times*, December 31, 1982);
- the constant use of exhortation in order to justify and legitimize its own actions. For instance, the citizenry was constantly warned of the moral decline underway in the West and of the need for Singapore to take urgent action to avoid a similar fate. In order to make a convincing case, the writings of prominent individuals in the West expressing concern over social trends in the West were cited as well.

Another lesson from the Singapore case concerns the limitations of adopting a top-down technocratic approach to curriculum policy making and planning. The introduction of Religious Knowledge was a form of crisis management to stem what was perceived to be serious moral decay. The *Report on Moral Education 1979* (Ong, 1979) had pointed out the need for such measures as adequate teacher training and teacher commitment and conviction. Several educators and academics had also pointed out such potential problems as proselytization and heightened religious antagonism. In addition, the growth of Christianity among the highly-educated had already become evident in the 1980 population census figures (Khoo, 1981: 34). Furthermore, Islamic revivalism had been underway in Singapore and elsewhere in Southeast Asia since the 1970s (Hussin, 1990).

However, the government brushed these considerations aside and proceeded with the programme. Perhaps it was confident that a rigid control over syllabus production, textbook content, and teacher training would minimize such potential problems. The government seemed to be trying to harness Religious Knowledge as a means of socializing students into accepting its own socio-political agenda. Ironically, however, when the 1988 government-commissioned report indicated that the programme was in fact contributing to an ongoing religious resurgence, and when some evangelistic groups appeared to pose a threat to the government's political legitimacy and authority, the government decided to scale back the programme.

The government was rushing headlong into a new curriculum initiative without being able simultaneously to identify or create a favourable context for the fostering of the initiative (Fullan and Stiegelbauer 1991: 96). Quite predictably, the implementation process was fraught with numerous contradictions and tensions, which in turn sowed the seeds for the eventual review of the programme within a few years of its inception. The entire episode illustrates vividly how the best of technocratically-laid plans are unlikely to have much success without the concomitant provision of a supportive structural and socio-cultural context.

Epilogue

One of the main themes in the compulsory Civics and Moral Education programme that was implemented in all secondary schools in 1992 is "Unity in Diversity." This particular theme aims at fostering "cultural and religious appreciation" (Curriculum Development Institute of Singapore 1991: 1). Approximately half of the upper secondary component for this particular theme is devoted to religion. Students are provided with factual knowledge about

Buddhism, Christianity, Confucianism, Hinduism, Islam, Sikhism, and Taoism. The modules deal with the origins, major tenets, rituals, festivals, and symbols of these faiths. The earlier problems that the Education Ministry had claimed to face with the provision of a World Religions option in Religious Knowledge appear to be have been resolved rather rapidly once the decision to scrap Religious Knowledge had been taken.

One sees in the new modules a persisting attempt at maintaining a distinction between "religious knowledge" and "religious instruction." In addition, the approach is extremely factual and teachers are supposed to adopt a balanced treatment of the various religious faiths. Unlike the earlier, more exclusive approach in which students had to choose a particular religion to study, there is now a conscious desire to provide all students with a knowledge of the major faiths in Singapore with the hope of developing genuine interreligious understanding and harmony. Once again, the government has maintained its technocratic control of syllabus design, textbook writing, and teacher training. However, this control does not always extend into the micro-world of schools and classrooms. For instance, since Civics and Moral Education is not examined in the secondary school terminal examinations, the long-standing questions about the priority awarded the subject by both teachers and students may be raised yet again.

In 1997 the government launched a National Education initiative at all levels of the education system. One of its major objectives is to ensure that all young citizens are aware of the importance of interracial and interreligious harmony. Government leaders have claimed that this initiative is necessary because young people are ignorant of Singapore's recent history and may therefore take material prosperity and social stability for granted. Besides involving all teachers and students, both formal and informal curricula are being harnessed as well. There are echoes here of the sense of national moral crisis that precipitated the introduction of Religious Knowledge. It will be interesting to observe how successfully this latest government-dictated programme, which is on a scale far surpassing that of Religious Knowledge, will fare in Singapore schools.

Notes

1. There were 30 government-aided church-run primary schools out of a total of 193 government and government-aided primary schools in 1998. The corresponding figures for secondary schools were 29 and 147

respectively (Ministry of Education, 1998: 1–26). These government-aided schools receive heavy financial subsidies from the government and follow the same national curriculum as government schools.

2. For instance, in 1994 the Prime Minister Goh Chok Tong drew public attention to the concern voiced by former United States Secretary of Education, William Bennett, about the rise in violent crime, illegitimate births, and divorces in the United States over the past three decades. Goh warned also of the need for Singapore to avoid "this change in the moral fabric" in the United States and the United Kingdom (*The Straits Times*, August 22, 1994: 24).

3. In line with the elitist governing philosophy with regard to policy-making, the *Report on the Ministry of Education 1978* was produced by the Education Minister together with a team of 12 civil servants. The *Report on Moral Education 1979* was produced by the Minister for Communication, together with five PAP Members of Parliament and two civil servants.

4. A Member of Parliament has lamented the long-standing tendency by both schools and students to treat moral education lessons lightly. In fact, some schools even use the officially designated lesson period to conduct supplementary classes for other subjects (*Parliamentary Debates*, 54, October 6, 1989: Col. 588).

5. Goh claimed that, when he was Defence Minister, he noticed that wallets or watches disappeared if left unattended for more than 10 seconds in army camps. "So one day I told the Prime Minister that the schools are turning out a nation of thieves and that something must be done about this in our education system" (*The Sunday Times*, January 17, 1982).

6. It is strange that no mention at all was made of Taoism, which claimed over 580,000 adherents, or 38.2% of the majority Chinese community in 1980. Tamney (1988: 118–119) points out that this was probably due to the official perception of Taoism as being associated more with folk religion than with morality.

7. World Religions was never made available to students. The reasons for this omission will be mentioned later in my chapter.

8. Ling (1989: 697) points out that in fact two forms of Confucian cult along the lines of folk religion exist in addition to the non-religious veneration of Confucian philosophy. In a similar vein, Tan (1994: 68–69) writes that the secularistic version of Confucianism favoured by the Singapore government was only one of several interpretations of classical and neo-classical Confucian writings.

9. The Schools Council was established in February 1981 to promote regular dialogue between the schools and the Ministry of Education. It consisted initially of 13 Ministry of Education officials and 20 school principals. Its proceedings were open to the press.

10. This statement casts further doubt on the government's claim to neutrality in the religious sphere.

11. The *Report on Moral Education 1979* had emphasized the same point (Ong 1979: 6). The Secondary Teacher Christian Fellowship recommended that "only committed teachers should teach religious education" (*The Straits Times*, March 12, 1982).

12. This claim had been asserted on several occasions in the past (Ling, 1989: 694–695). However, Tamney (1992a: 204–205) points out that the government was violating its supposed neutrality in the religious sphere by banning such groups as the Jehovah's Witnesses and the Unification Church.

13. Wong and Wong (1989) provide evidence that it is in fact very difficult to establish any direct causal relationship between Confucian values and Singapore's economic development.

14. No mention was made of the Islamic revival taking place in Singapore (Hussin, 1990).

15. The then-Trade and Industry Minister remarked that Malays could not be assigned certain posts in the Armed Forces because the government "did not want them to be placed in a position where their emotions for the nation might be in conflict with their emotions for their religion" (*Parliamentary Debates*, 49, March 17, 1987: cols. 378–379).

16. Government Parliamentary Committees were created in 1987 in response to rising public sentiment in favour of a system of checks on the PAP government. The various committees consist of Members of Parliament assisted by lay resource persons. They scrutinize parliamentary legislation and propose ways of improving the functioning of the various ministries (Chan, 1989: 85).

References

Chan, H.C. (1975). Politics in an administrative state: Where has the politics gone? In C. M. Seah (ed.), *Trends in Singapore* (Singapore: Singapore University Press), 51–68.

Chan, H.C. (1976). The political system and political change. In R. Hassan (ed.), *Singapore: Society in transition* (Kuala Lumpur: Oxford University Press), 30–51.

Chan, H.C. (1989). The PAP and the structuring of the political system. In K. S. Sandhu and P. Wheatley (eds.), *Management of success: The moulding of modern singapore* (Singapore: Institute of Southeast Asian Studies), 70–89.

Chew, S. (1976). The language of survival. In R. Hassan (Ed.), *Singapore: Society in transition* (Kuala Lumpur: Oxford University Press), 149–154.

Chiew, S.K. (1983). Singapore in 1982: Economic slowdown and normative change. In *Southeast Asian affairs 1983* (Singapore: Institute of Southeast Asian Studies), 249–262.

Chua, B.H. (1994). Arrested development: Democratisation in Singapore. *Third World Quarterly*, 15, 655–668.

Chua, B.H. (1995). *Communitarian ideology and democracy in Singapore* (London: Routledge).

Cornbleth, C. (1990). *Curriculum in context* (London: Falmer).

Curriculum Development Institute of Singapore (1991). *Civics and moral education pupil's workbook 3A* (Singapore: Longman Singapore).

Singapore Department of Statistics (1997). *General household survey 1995 release 1: Socio-demographic and economic characteristics.* Singapore.

Friedman, M. and Isserman, N. (Eds.). (1998). *The tribal basis of American life: Racial, religious, and ethnic groups in conflict* (New York: Praeger).

Fullan, M.G. and Stiegelbauer, S. (1991). *The new meaning of educational change*, 2nd ed. (New York: Teachers College Press).

Goh, C.T. (1988). Our national ethic. *Speeches*, 12(5), 12–15.

Goh, K.S. (Chairman). (1979). *Report on the Ministry of Education 1978* (Singapore: Ministry of Education).

Gopinathan, S. (1980). Moral education in a plural society: A Singapore case study. *International Review of Education*, 26, 171–185.

Hussin, M. (1990). Islamic revivalism in ASEAN states: Political implications. *Asian Survey*, 30, 877–891.

Hussin, M. (1992). Singapore's quest for a national identity: The triumphs and trials of government policies. In Ban Kah Choon, A. Pakir and Tong Chee Kiong (eds.), *Imagining Singapore* (Singapore: Times Academic Press), 69–96.

Khoo, C.K. (1981). Census of Population 1980, Singapore. Statistical Release 9: Religion and Fertility (Singapore: Department of Statistics).

Koh, T.A. (1980). Cultural development in the global village. In *Southeast Asian affairs 1980* (Singapore: Institute of Southeast Asian Studies), 292–307.

Kuah, K.E. (1991). State and religion: Buddhism and nation-building in Singapore. *Pacific Viewpoint*, 32, 24–42.

Kuo, E.C.Y. (1992). Confucianism as political discourse in Singapore: The case of an incomplete revitalization movement. Working Paper No. 113, Department of Sociology, National University of Singapore.

Kuo, E.C.Y., Quah, J. S. T. and Tong, C. K. (1988). Religion and religious revivalism in Singapore. Report prepared for the Ministry of Community Development, Singapore.

Lake, D. and Rothchild, D. (Eds.). (1998). *The international spread of ethnic conflict: Fear, diffusion, and escalation* (Princeton, NJ: Princeton University Press).

Lee, K.Y. (1972). Traditional values and national identity. Mimeograph of speech delivered at the Singapore Teachers' Union 26th anniversary dinner.

Ling, T. (1989). Religion. In K. S. Sandhu and P. Wheatley (Eds.), *Management of success: The moulding of modern Singapore* (Singapore: Institute of Southeast Asian Studies), 692–709.

Ministry of Education. (1998). *Directory of schools and educational institutions 1998* (Singapore: Ministry of Education, Author).

Ong, T.C. (Chairman). (1979). *Report on moral education 1979* (Singapore: Ministry of Education).

Parliamentary debates, official reports, 41, March 3, 1982; 49, March 17, 1987; 53, March 20, 1989; 54, October 6, 1989.

Quah, J.S.T. (1988). Singapore in 1987: Political reforms, control, and economic recovery. In *Southeast Asian affairs 1988* (Singapore: Institute of Southeast Asian Studies), 233–252.

Quah, J.S.T., and Quah, S. R. (1989). The limits of government intervention. In K. S. Sandhu and P. Wheatley (eds.), *Management of Success: The moulding of modern Singapore* (Singapore: Institute of Southeast Asian Studies), 102–127.

Singapore Government. (1991). *Shared values*. Cmd. 1 of 1991 (Singapore).

The Straits Times, Singapore, January 18, 1982, February 4, 1982, February 8, 1982, February 11, 1982, February 17, 1982, February 18, 1982, March 12, 1982, September 6, 1982, December 28, 1982, December 31, 1982, August 4, 1983, August 17, 1987, October 12, 1989, August 22, 1994.

The Sunday Times, Singapore, January 17, 1982.

Tamney, J.B. (1988). Religion and the state in Singapore. *Journal of Church and State*, 30, 109–128.

Tamney, J.B. (1992a). Conservative government and support for the religious institution in Singapore: An uneasy alliance. *Sociological Analysis*, 53, 201–217.

Tan, T.W. (1994). Moral education in Singapore: A critical appraisal. *Journal of Moral Education*, 23, 61–73.

Tay, E.S. (1983). Some issues on education. In *Issues facing Singapore in the eighties* (Singapore: Ministry of Culture), 71–99.

Tulasiewicz, W. and To, C. (1993). *World religions and educational practice* (London: Cassell).

Wong, J. and Wong, A. (1989). Confucian values as a social framework for Singapore's economic development. Paper presented at the conference on Confucianism and economic development in East Asia (Taipei, Taiwan).

Wong, K.Y. (1991). Curriculum development in Singapore. In C. Marsh and P. Morris (eds.), *Curriculum development in East Asia* (London: Falmer).

5

è🙚

The Segregation of Stephen*

Diana Lawrence-Brown

Efforts are underway internationally to include students with significant disabilities in general education classrooms. Here I explore a particular case in its more immediate social and historical contexts. Stephen is a student with multiple disabilities who was included in general education classrooms from second through sixth grades, and was then transferred to a self-contained special education classroom out of his home district. Underlying policy, politics, and practice connections are explicated, including the ebb and flow of power relationships affecting the case. The impact on what Stephen has the opportunity to learn is highlighted; his perspectives as well as those of his teachers are an integral part of the story.

Following an introductory section on inclusion, I introduce readers to Stephen and his educational experience, and explore the micropolitical aspects of his placement in a self-contained special education class where low expectations, learned passivity, and segregation predominate. It is argued that expectations are not only low, but are unjustifiably low. Low expectations constrain achievement (Good, 1981; Rist, 1970); learned passivity and segregation are likely to perpetuate negative stereotypes and limit opportunities to form

---

*I wish to thank Catherine Cornbleth, S. G. Grant, and Gillian Richardson for their helpful comments and suggestions on earlier versions of this work.

meaningful relationships (e.g., Cole and Meyer, 1991). This combination seems likely to increase the probability of an adult life characterized by segregation, stigmatization, and reduced quality of life.

Recurrent Issues for Individuals with Disabilities

Two problems recurrently faced by individuals with significant disabilities are: (a) low expectations by teachers and significant others and (b) lack of opportunity to form the meaningful, freely-entered relationships which are a cornerstone of a person's quality of life. The impact of teacher expectations is well-known and well-documented: high expectations facilitate high levels of achievement, while low expectations tend to limit achievement (e.g., Good, 1981; Rist, 1970). While low teacher expectations can be a problem in any educational setting, this is particularly problematic in self-contained special education classrooms. Teachers faced with groups made up entirely of students with significant disabilities may find it very difficult to maintain high expectations in their teaching.

Case studies of students with significant disabilities were compiled by Bogdan (1982) in the infancy of the development of inclusive placements (i.e., in general education classrooms). "Timmy" was a fourteen-year-old student who had been placed in self-contained special education classrooms from kindergarten through age eleven and then transitioned to a general education classroom; he provided the following explanation of what it had been like to be in a self-contained special education class:

> A lot different from the [general education] class. They treat ya differently. When I was in special ed., they treated me like I was somebody else. They didn't treat me like a regular person, [but] like a four-year-old. (p. 348)

Low teacher expectations and their limiting impact on achievement may contribute to an understanding of research indicating inferior educational outcomes for most students with disabilities in segregated special education classrooms compared to outcomes for similar students placed in general education classrooms (Lipsky and Gartner, 1995; McLaughlin, Warren, and Schofield, 1996).

A second recurrent problem is that meaningful, freely given relationships can be elusive for individuals with significant disabilities. Such personal relationships are dependent on opportunities for like-minded individuals to spend time together and to get to know each other. They develop between people who find that they enjoy each other's company and then choose to spend time together. However, people with significant disabilities may have very few of these opportunities. They often find themselves surrounded by people who are present not because they like a particular person and want to spend time with him or her, or as a result of everyday classroom groupings, but because they are either staff or other people with similar disabilities[1] in the same program (Strully and Strully, 1985). This is particularly true for individuals who no longer live with their families. It is difficult for most of us to envision ourselves in a position where the people available to us are others involuntarily placed in a group with us based on shared weaknesses, or staff paid to be present in order to remediate those shortcomings. Yet this has often been an unintended outcome of segregated services, whether they are in self-contained classrooms or residential or vocational facilities for individuals with significant disabilities.

Concerns such as these have prompted parents and other advocates to find ways to provide individuals with disabilities with the services and supports they need in more natural and less limiting environments. These efforts have been facilitated by the development of strategies to modify curricula and include diverse learners in general education settings, e.g., partial participation (Baumgart et al., 1982) and cooperative learning. Such advances have enabled students with significant disabilities to receive an appropriate education in general education classrooms. Research (see Lipsky and Gartner, 1995 and McLaughlin, Warren, and Schofield, 1996 for reviews) increasingly indicates "improved student outcomes (academically, behaviorally, and socially) for both special education *and general education students*," (p. 5, emphasis added) and that there is little evidence of superior outcomes as a result of segregated placements (Cole and Meyer, 1991; Lipsky and Gartner, 1995; Morrow, 1996; Rogers, 1993). McLaughlin, Warren, and Schofield (1996) report largely positive findings for inclusion as well (the exception being some studies of academic outcomes for students labeled learning disabled).

Critical Perspective on Education

In the dominant view of special education, students are viewed as having special needs due to pathological conditions (Skrtic, 1995). Differential diagnoses are considered both objective and useful. Special education is seen as a benevolent and humanitarian system designed to benefit students with disabilities. Reform is interpreted as fine-tuning the existing system.

In contrast, a critical view of special education (e.g., see Squibb, 1981) is utilized for this analysis. Although pathological conditions exist, students' needs are viewed as becoming special when they do not fall within the organization's standard instructional practices. This perspective is helpful for understanding widely divergent policies and procedures across school districts and regions for students with very similar disabilities. Even the same student might be offered an inclusive placement in one district but not in the next district into which he or she moves (with no corresponding change in the student's needs or abilities).

The aim of this critical perspective is to understand the origins of special education and whose interests it serves, and to contribute to equity and empowerment for individuals with disabilities (Stanley, 1986). Squibb's analysis seems fitting to special education in the United States and elsewhere, that "some of our aims, objectives, and practices may be derived not from an objective view of the special child, but from values and attitudes which originate in the wider social situation" (p. 50).

Consider, for example, new categories of disability that have been promulgated as special education has grown. It might be argued that these have arisen from a more refined understanding of disability, enabling us to differentiate more precisely the true nature of various types of disability. Others would argue that increased differentiation of categories serves a social function. Sleeter (1986), for example, outlines the use of the learning disabled category in the 1960s to explain school failure of middle class children in a less stigmatizing fashion than labels such as mentally retarded, slow learner, emotionally disturbed, or culturally deprived, that were more often applied to lower class and minority children.

Squibb (1981) points out that "the greater the range and sophistication of the devices used to test for a handicap, the more widely will that handicap be discovered" (p. 47). He posits that the percentage of students with disability labels would be reduced simply by eliminating the diagnostic and remedial systems associated with the application of such labels. He goes on to provide incidence data illustrating the dramatic increase in the percentage of students labeled as disabled in the U.K. between 1961 and 1976, stating:

it is difficult to believe that the affluent 1960s and early 1970s did in fact see an *actual* increase in . . . handicaps or a fundamental change in the special education needs of the handicapped. . . . At least the figure suggests that by increasing the structures we increase the number of handicapped children. (pp. 47–49)

Squibb (1981) also points to the over-representation of minority children in special education as an indication of the subjective, social nature of the labeling process, and argues that it says more about our society and schools than about minority children.

Consistent with the recognition that pure objectivity is impossible for any researcher, and with recommendations for qualitative researchers that the author's place in the text be provided openly (Lincoln and Denzin, 1994), I attempt to clarify my position. My vision for education is of a system that values and accommodates diversity in many forms, including diversity of ability (e.g., gifted or disabled), race, language, ethnicity, socioeconomic status, learning styles, and multiple intelligences. I see extensive inclusion of students with disabilities in general education classrooms as an integral part of this larger vision. In the words of York-Barr and others (1996):

Inclusive schooling . . . extends far beyond mere physical proximity to providing students and adults the support required to belong and achieve in classroom and school communities. Inclusion is both a process for and outcome of understanding, acceptance, and valuing of differences . . . a process and an outcome for achieving social justice and equity in our society (Sapon-Shevin, 1992; Wlodkowski and Ginsburg, 1995). (p. 92)

I believe that segregated educational placements are inherently unequal, that every child has the right to be educated in regular classes, and that segregated programs should be reserved for circumstances where extensive inclusion efforts have failed. I see many parallels between recent efforts to integrate individuals with disabilities and historical efforts for racial integration in the U.S. I do not believe that special education classes should be eliminated entirely; it has been my experience that when one solution (to anything) is mandated for everyone, it is sure to become the worst experience for some. However, my reading of the research and my own experience lead me to believe that inclusion should be the rule rather than exception.

Historical and Definitional Issues
Surrounding Inclusion

One factor that impedes discussion of inclusion is that consensus about its definition does not exist among educators. An historical perspective may provide a better understanding of its current usage.

The concept of inclusion could not come about until exclusion had first taken place. While students with severe disabilities were often considered ineducable and were rarely educated in public schools in the U.S. prior to the adoption of the Education for All Handicapped Children Act of 1975, students with mild disabilities, who now constitute the vast majority of students labeled as disabled, seem not to have been excluded from general education classrooms until the development of self-contained special education classrooms (Lawrence-Brown, 1998). Historically, self-contained special education classes are a relatively new idea; they did not become widespread outside of large cities until well after World War II (Tyack and Cuban, 1995; Winzer, 1993). The institution of special education classrooms tended to follow the institution of graded classrooms and the phasing out of one-room schools. While one-room schools were organized in a way that accommodated a wide range of ages and ability levels, graded classrooms increasingly were not. According to Tyack and Cuban (1995), "batch processing of pupils created a category of organizational deviant: the 'retarded,' or slow student who was not promoted" (p. 90).

Although a common perception of segregated special education classes is that they were developed for the benefit of students with disabilities, a look at the words of some early proponents of special classes provides a different perspective. J. E. Wallace Wallin (1914) anticipated many current objections to segregated classes when he observed:

> grouping many abnormal children together threw their idiosyncrasies and their abnormalities into conspicuous relief; it made them feel they were a group apart and inferior or different; their parents objected to the stigma of special class placement; students had no occasion to mingle with normal children and were robbed of the opportunities to learn imitatively by association with their normal fellows; and many had to travel long distances to special classes (Wallin, 1914, p. 391 as described by Winzer, 1993, p. 328).

However, Wallin stressed, advantages offset these shortcomings: segregated classrooms allowed closer grading of pupils and were altogether more economical and efficient. "Great relief" was afforded to the normal pupils and the regular grade teachers by the removal of the "flotsam and jetsam," the "hold backs and the drags" (Wallin, 1914, p. 390), the "unassimilable accumulation of clinkers, ballast, driftwood, or derelicts" (Wallin, 1924, p. 94). These sentiments were echoed by Annie Dolman Inskeep (1926), a "specialist in the teaching of atypical children" (title page) who described her charges as "those who clog the wheels of normal progress" (p. x).

Special classes, while housing increasing numbers of students, were still by no means the norm. In 1931, it was estimated that 10 million students with disabilities were in the schools, of whom only 1 million were receiving any sort of special education (White House Conference, 1931). Even Arnold Gesell, a prominent supporter of special classes, assumed that they could never be provided in all communities and acknowledged that "special adjustments" could be made to enable students with disabilities to be educated in general education classes (Safford and Safford, 1996, p. 80).

These changes came about much more quickly in urban areas than in rural areas. In rural areas, one-room schools persisted until at least the late 1940s, due at least in part to a lack of transportation. This situation prevented the development of both graded schools and segregated special education classes (Robinson and Robinson, 1976; Soltow and Stevens, 1981), as both (by definition) required the school to have more than one room. When transportation became more available, especially after World War II, most school districts consolidated and bused their students to centralized schools. Although the timing of the adoption of graded schools and segregated special education classes was different in urban and rural schools, the pattern seems to be similar, with the development of graded schools being followed by the development of segregated special education classes.

Legislative and Judicial Safeguards

In 1975, Public Law 94–142, the Education for All Handicapped Children Act,[2] was adopted in the United States, guaranteeing the right of all students with disabilities to receive a free, appropriate education in the least restrictive environment (or LRE). As federal legislation, the Education for All Handicapped

Children Act did not guarantee the right of students with disabilities to education *per se*; constitutionally, education is the responsibility of the states. P.L. 94–142 is civil rights legislation (based in the Fifth and Fourteenth Amendments to the Constitution[3] and Section 504[4] of the Rehabilitation Act of 1973); if states elect to provide education they may not discriminate on the basis of disability. As with segregation on the basis of race, segregation on the basis of disability has been recognized as inherently unequal (Biklen et al., 1987; McDonnell and Hardman, 1989; Rogers, 1993).

In the 1970s, especially after the passage of P.L. 94–142, increased efforts began to identify occasions when students with disabilities could be successfully integrated with nondisabled peers. This was termed "mainstreaming." Students typically were pulled out of special education classes on a part-time basis, often for nonacademic programs such as gym, music, and lunch. When mainstreaming in academic areas was attempted, the student was generally expected to function without support (an example of such support would be oral testing and presentation of content for students with reading disabilities). The special education class remained the primary placement. Resource rooms eventually enabled some students to receive special education services on a part-time, pull-out basis, with general education as the primary placement. Still, the student's time in the regular classroom was generally expected to be accomplished without accommodations for his or her disability.

In the 1980s, the emphasis in special education reform shifted again, this time toward making students with disabilities true members of general education classrooms, rather than occasional and somewhat exotic visitors. Both the number of students included and their range of and type of disability increased. For the first time, students with severe mental and physical disabilities became active members of general education classrooms. The term "inclusion" became popular during this period as well. The initial intent seemed to be to provide a term differentiated in meaning from mainstreaming, where students remained members of special education classrooms and received little support in general education settings. As the term became popular, however, its usage became more casual. In some instances, "inclusion" now is used to refer to any amount of time that any student identified with a disability spends in a regular classroom, whether or not they are members of that classroom, and without reference to the degree or type of support needed or provided. In other cases, the student might not even be in a general education classroom, but merely have his self-contained classroom relocated from a special education school to a regular school, or from a regular school out of his neighborhood back to his home school.

For purposes of this paper, inclusion is defined more narrowly as educating a child with a significant disability

> in the school and classroom he or she would otherwise attend . . . bringing the support services to the child (rather than moving the child to the services) and requires only that the child will benefit from being in the class (rather than having to keep up with the other students) (Rogers, 1993, p. 1).

Rationale for Inclusion

Cases of inclusion of students with significant intellectual disabilities[5] in general education classrooms in the U.S. provide an illustration of the phenomenon of micropolitics in special education placements, made through a decision-making process that asserts its objectivity. Grounds for inclusion are plentiful, ranging from research on positive outcomes for students both with and without disabilities (e.g., Cole and Meyer, 1991; Lipsky and Gartner, 1995) to recognition through legislation and the courts of the presumptive legal right of students with disabilities to education in integrated settings (Yell and Shriner, 1996). Students with all disabilities recognized by federal special education law have been successfully included in regular classrooms, according to the National Study of Inclusive Education (1994). Inclusion takes place across the United States, and across a wide range of districts (large and small, urban, suburban, and rural). Golomb and Hammeken (1996), citing U.S. Department of Education statistics, report that in Vermont, 89% of students with disabilities are placed in general education classrooms. Yet in most areas, inclusion remains the exception to the rule of segregated placements for students with significant intellectual disabilities (Golomb and Hammeken, 1996).

Educators naturally worry that inclusion of students with disabilities will detract from the educational experience of students without disabilities. A growing body of research has addressed this concern. Staub and Peck (1994), for example, found no evidence that students without disabilities progress more slowly, lose teacher time and attention, or learn undesirable behaviors in classrooms that include students with significant disabilities . A number of studies document benefits to students without disabilities, including personal, social, and moral development and increased appreciation of human diversity (see Lipsky and Gartner, 1995 for a review).

Yet regulations and research have been insufficient to secure inclusive placements for most students with disabilities. The average percentage of students with disabilities placed in general education classrooms in the United States is only 40% and the range extends down to 6% in Arizona (Golomb and Hammeken, 1996). Even in locales where inclusion is happening, it often takes places only in some of the schools in a district, at some grade levels (National Study of Inclusive Education, 1994). Some districts include no students with significant disabilities.

It has been my observation that such uneven adoption of inclusive practice seems to be related to a number of factors. Inclusion often gets its start in a district at the insistence of parents knowledgeable of the legal rights of their children. It may spread to other children from there, either at the insistence of other parents, or as staff begin to see its value and become more knowledgeable about and more comfortable with the idea and its implementation.

Many districts do not extend inclusive opportunities to all students with disabilities in the district. Who is deemed "appropriate" varies from district to district. One district decides that inclusion is appropriate only for students with mild disabilities, while others reserve inclusion for students with severe disabilities. Some districts include students with learning difficulties, or physical disabilities, or emotional problems, while in other districts the same students would be placed automatically in segregated special education classrooms. Thus, uneven adoption of inclusive practice is attributed to characteristics of students, but seems more dependent on local resistance to inclusion of certain students. Squibb (1981) takes an even stronger view: "The actual barriers to integration [of individuals with disabilities] . . . are social, political, and economic, rather than physical or psychological [characteristics of individuals]" (p. 50).

Micropolitics as a Feature
of Change Efforts in Schools

Educational decision-making can be seen as a politicized process, including placement decisions for students with disabilities (see Smith, 1982, for a detailed description of this process). Squibb (1981) describes such decisions as

influenced by factors extraneous to the case. The relationships and interactions of the members of the case conference will depend on many social factors such as external
status, past experience, knowledge, qualifications, etc. The
outcome of the conference may be seen as a function of the
various structures which impinge upon it. Important
among these will be the ideologies held by the members,
their view of the world, of the nature of man, of the purpose
of education and of the child. As all these are basically political views (in the broadest sense), then the decision which
results can be seen as a political decision. (p. 43)

In this chapter, I describe some of the micropolitics encountered by advocates of inclusion of students with significant disabilities in general education classrooms. Although it utilizes as an
example a specific case that I have studied in depth as a researcher,
it is more broadly based on my overall experience as an educator.[6] I
find the underlying issues to be quite typical of change efforts in
general, and expect that it will "ring true" for many readers, even
those without a special education background.

It would be surprising to find a leader of change efforts who
has not encountered the micropolitical realities of reform. Hoyle
(1988, p. 256) describes organizational micropolitics as "strategies
by which individuals and groups . . . seek to use their resources of
power and influence to further their interests."

Micropolitical strategizing is naturally frustrating and possibly even dangerous to reformers. For example, Lutz (1988)
describes the case of an administrator who was hired with the
express purpose of serving as an educational change agent. The
intended reform was ill-received by the faculty, who marshaled
arguments against him such as "not listening" to them, despite
repeated efforts on his part to involve them in the process. He was
called before his superior with the accusation: "How did you ever
get the idea that you should reorganize the school?" (p. 341).
Threatened with termination, he eventually resigned.

The negative impact of micropolitical struggles on adults, who
at least benefit from the experience gained and move on to other
projects, is likely to be short-lived. The real losers are our students.
Students may not even be aware of the struggle, but they are surely
the losers as we fail to provide more effective schools. In fact, we
usually find ways to blame them (see below), or alternatively, their
parents (e.g., see Erwin and Clapp, 1967). In the case of students

with disabilities, it's even easier to blame the victim. We simply reassure ourselves and their parents that they are not "appropriate" for the classrooms that nondisabled students attend.

Hoyle (1988) describes micropolitical interests as likely to be defended in terms of "professional" arguments that are considered more legitimate than personal or territorial claims. The language of appropriateness is perhaps the most oft-cited reason for exclusion of students with disabilities from regular classrooms, i.e., some children are "appropriate" for inclusion, while others are not. This is problematic because the onus for the success or failure of inclusion is placed upon students, who exercise little power over critical placement and programmatic decision-making.

A Case Study of the Micropolitics of Special Education Placement

Some of the micropolitics involved in educational decision-making are illustrated through a case study of Stephen,[7] a student who is labeled "multiply disabled" by the special education services committee in his district because he has difficulties with learning, communication, and motor skills. I worked with Stephen in his inclusion program (see note #6); it is through this role that I learned the historical background of inclusion at his school and the details of his inclusion program. My knowledge of his special education program and experience comes from a case study that I conducted as a doctoral student.

Case Study Methodology

During the 1997–1998 school year, I spent time with Stephen at his new school. A series of three one-to-one interviews were conducted with him, and he was observed in ten different classes, over a period of seven weeks. His current special education teacher also was interviewed. An analysis of documents was undertaken, including his Individual Education Plan and worksheets that were assigned to him in the special education classroom.

All interviews were audiotaped and then transcribed. Data analysis was completed using Seidman's (1991) suggestions for reducing transcribed text and identifying themes, along with Spradley's (1980) domain analysis procedure. Domains identified for focused observations were types of staff expectations and goals for the class in general, types of staff expectations and goals for Stephen in particular, rationale for expectations and goals, kinds of opportunities to form relationships with peers, and results of opportunities to form relationships with peers.

I am aware of my preference for general education class placement for most students with disabilities, and consciously looked for evidence that was not in line with my expectations (Peshkin, 1988). I drafted a research memo regarding my subjectivity, including an outline of what I expected to see. In light of my substantial experience as a special education teacher, it seemed unlikely that I would not see some of what I expected to see. Although my expectations were substantiated by the data in some instances, in other instances I was positively or negatively surprised by what I saw. For example, I expected to see predominantly life skills instruction, and was surprised at the amount of academic instruction. I expected to see an acceptance of childish behaviors (e.g., playing with toys intended for younger children, being rewarded with stickers), but was surprised to find that behavioral expectations were largely age-appropriate. I concluded that, while I had seen some of what I expected to see, I had also managed my subjectivity at least to the extent that I was able to be surprised.

The themes of low expectations, learned passivity, and segregation emerged from repeated readings of transcripts and field notes, marking interesting passages, organizing excerpts into categories, and searching for patterns and connections within and between categories (Seidman, 1991). Further consideration of these themes led to the conclusion that expectations are not only low, but are unjustifiably low. Low expectations constrain learning (Good, 1981; Rist, 1970); learned passivity and segregation are likely to perpetuate negative stereotypes and limit opportunities to form meaningful relationships (cf. Cole and Meyer, 1991). This combination seems likely to lead to an adult life characterized by segregation, stigmatization, and reduced quality of life.

Stephen

Stephen is a teenage boy who lives with his mother in Hartdale, a primarily working class community in the northeastern United States. Stephen's mother's job in a nearby factory is typical of many Hartdale wage earners. Like other local boys his age, Stephen has a penchant for video games and the region's professional football team. His best subject was social studies; he does not enjoy gym. Motor activities in general are difficult for Stephen. Balance and coordination are troublesome and his muscle tone is low, making ambulation and other motor tasks (from riding a bike to using a pencil or keyboard) difficult.

Stephen's speech is very difficult to understand. The most obvious communication obstacle for him is articulation; however, he also experiences difficulty with word-finding and labeling. For example, he tried unsuccessfully for years to learn to label numbers, letters, and colors. Stephen also requires some assistance with self-help tasks (e.g., opening lunch containers). He occasionally uses acting out behavior (e.g., pushing materials off his desk) when he doesn't want to do something.

Stephen was in a general education classroom from second grade through sixth grade.[8] His program typically included a mixture of regular classroom activities (often adapted to facilitate his successful participation), occupational, physical, and speech therapy services, community-based instruction, and daily living skills instruction. His program also included pre-vocational skills instruction, e.g., helping with attendance in the school and eventually helping out in a local governmental official's office.

Beginnings of Inclusion in Hartdale

Despite the presumptive legal right to regular class placement, this was not an option for students with significant disabilities in Hartdale until Stephen's second grade year. Up until that time, they had been routinely placed in segregated special education classes. The only decision involved was what type of special education class, and where. As noted previously, this is not an unusual practice.

Even after the inclusion program was started, it was limited to students with the most severe intellectual disabilities. Most students with significant disabilities were still sent to special education classes; all of these were located outside of the district. Space was limited in the school building, and had never been allotted to special education classes. Therefore, the district contracted with a regional service provider for these classes.

Inclusion in Hartdale got its start through the efforts of the district's special education coordinator. She had been on staff for over twenty years, and was known as a no-nonsense woman who got what she wanted. Although she was willing to work with administration, her comment to a novice coordinator was that a special education coordinator should not allow administration to "push [her] around." She had tenure in the district, and had further back-up from special education law requiring the board of education to implement recommendations of the placement committee or lose federal funds. No administrators were members of the placement committee. Administrators seemed to consider special education decisions as outside the realm of their responsibility; it was not uncommon to hear, "That's a [special education services committee] decision."

Further incentive for inclusion came from a parent of a child with significant disabilities. She was knowledgeable of her child's right to be educated in the regular classroom, and was unwilling to consent to special class placement.

The special education coordinator gained the tentative support of a few general education classroom teachers, partly through promises of a full-time aide. Two students with significant disabilities were subsequently enrolled in regular primary level classrooms.

Special education support was to be provided for students and general education classroom teachers via the school's existing resource room teachers, but was subsequently described as sporadic. General education teachers reported that little time was available for the inclusion students in the schedules of the resource room teachers. A collaborative team approach was not in place, and the primary responsibility for the inclusion students fell to the regular classroom teachers and the aides.

Opportunities to Learn in the
General Education Classroom

Stephen became a member of a regular classroom in his second grade year. Although his teachers held modified educational expectations for him, he seemed to thrive in the general milieu of age-appropriate expectations inherent to the general education classroom. Stymied though he is by many traditional academic tasks, Stephen was provided the opportunity in the regular classroom to acquire and communicate his understanding of complex concepts. For example, he earned a "B" in fifth grade social studies after tests were modified for him to an oral, multiple choice, matching, and true/false format. He demonstrated his understanding of orally presented literature such as *The Trumpet of the Swan* and *Caddie Woodlawn*. A "Student Evaluation" report to parents from his fifth grade teacher included the following comment:

> Stephen is doing well in reading. He participates and is
> involved. Please continue to read to him from the novel,
> *Sign of the Beaver.* [In] writing, Stephen is working on [dic-
> tating] his second friendly letter. . . . He is also working on
> poetry. (Student Evaluation Report, 12/1/95)

In light of these accomplishments, it may surprise some readers to
learn that Stephen's IQ tests in the moderately mentally retarded
range. In consideration of some of the things he cannot do, it may
even be an accurate summary statistic. However, its helpfulness for
teaching and learning processes seems questionable.

In Stephen's fifth grade year, staff who had worked with him
over the years at Hartdale were asked to comment on his progress.
One staff person noted the inclusion program's somewhat rocky
start:

> [During] the first year for inclusion in Hartdale . . . nobody
> knew the meaning of this or their appropriate jobs. In [the
> following year] many of Stephen's IEP goals were met.
> Stephen gained in occupational therapy, socially, and per-
> sonally. (Evaluation of Inclusion Program, April 1996, p. 4)

Other staff members commented more specifically on what he had
the opportunity to learn both academically and socially, especially
emphasizing the impact of being included with nondisabled peers:

> I truly believe that socially Stephen has benefited much by
> being around more capable students. (Evaluation of Inclu-
> sion Program, April 1996, p. 3)

> Stephen advanced a great deal, not only physically but men-
> tally. His confidence was boosted significantly. He became
> more well-rounded because he had [nondisabled] peer role
> models. He accomplished many of his IEP goals for the year
> and accomplished some goals that seemed impossible for
> him. (Evaluation of Inclusion Program, April 1996, p. 2)

Respondents also speculated on the impact on Stephen had he been
placed in a special education class. For example:

> As I've watched Stephen's progress, I believe a special edu-
> cation classroom would result in him drooling, weakening,
> and loss of social gains. Stephen learns orally as many indi-

viduals do and he needs to understand this is his way of learning. The students, staff, and community have noticed Stephen's gains. This will help and further Stephen's continuous entry into the community and a job. (Evaluation of Inclusion Program, April 1996, p. 4)

Stephen made friends in my room, went to his first birthday party, made science projects—[but] best of all thought he was not handicapped. These things wouldn't have happened as easily if he was separated again in another school. (Evaluation of Inclusion Program, April 1996, p. 2)

Others noted the impact that Stephen had on people without disabilities:

The students have learned to be more sensitive, caring, and respectful of handicapped children. (Evaluation of Inclusion Program, April 1996, p. 3)

As well as Stephen being able to facilitate himself—others will understand as well. This may also help motivation in others. (Evaluation of Inclusion Program, April 1996, p. 4)

The class and school love him and are always looking out for him. (Evaluation of Inclusion Program, April 1996, p. 1)

It was the impact that Stephen and the other inclusion students had on people without disabilities that surprised me most about being involved with inclusion. In addition to the affective benefits noted previously, students without disabilities in inclusive classrooms seemed to enjoy academic benefits as well. In Stephen's case, for example, inclusion successively brought a cadre of support staff into the general education classroom, including therapists, the special education teacher, and the aide. Informal modeling of special education and therapeutic strategies was available to the regular classroom teacher (and vice versa).[9] Although the priority for support staff was Stephen, their frequent presence in the general education classroom allowed for informal consultation about other students as well. Similarly, the priority for the aide was Stephen, but this person also worked with other students in the classroom who needed help. A spillover effect of these supports to students was apparent. For example, a resource room student was able to avoid removal from the regular classroom to a special education class placement.

The Segregation of Stephen:
Administrative Instability and Power

After the inclusion program at Hartdale had been in place for one year, the special education coordinator who had initiated the inclusion program retired. This marked the beginning of a period of administrative instability for the school in general, and for the inclusion program in particular. The superintendent under whose auspices the inclusion program had begun resigned two years later. Over the six-year period starting with Stephen's initial inclusion in second grade, and ending with his placement in special education in what would have been his seventh grade year, the school had four different superintendents. Each of these men had a somewhat different position on inclusion; during this same period there were five different special education coordinators.[10] This instability in two of the three administrative positions most involved with the inclusion program temporarily increased the power of the third position involved, the principal. This principal had generally seemed to enjoy somewhat less power than most principals; the superintendent was housed in his (relatively small) building and seemed to be more involved in building administration than superintendents might be normally. Any initial reservations on the part of the principal about inclusion would easily have been overwhelmed by the joint influence of the superintendent and the original special education coordinator. At their departure, however, a new level of power came into reach for him.

Efforts to expand the inclusion program, particularly from the elementary into the junior high level, were considered unrealistic by the principal, whose own teaching experience had been at the secondary level. His assertion was that secondary staff would never accept inclusion at that level. However, some secondary staff did join a committee formed to facilitate the expansion of inclusion into the secondary level.

A superintendent whose philosophy of education did not encompass inclusion of students with severe intellectual disabilities was put in place in Stephen's fifth grade year. An individual with no background or experience in special education was placed in the special education coordinator's position. The following year, Stephen was transferred to a self-contained special education class for students with moderate mental retardation. This class is located in a secondary school outside of his home district.

The Special Education Classroom

Stephen's special education classroom is a large, airy room organized into two general areas. The front of the room is academically oriented, with two computers and rows of student desks facing a chalkboard and bulletin boards. Although Stephen and his classmates are adolescents, room decorations are typical of what one might see in early elementary level classrooms, with cartoon-style illustrations centering around readiness skills (e.g., the alphabet, numbers 1–10). The back of the room is equipped with a restroom and appliances such as a stove, refrigerator, clothes washer, and dryer. Also in the back of the room are the teacher's desk and a "time-out" area; i.e., a chair behind a screen that is used to seclude students for behavior management purposes.

"Typical" Special Education Students

Stephen's special education classroom teacher was asked to describe a typical student in his class:

> As far as functional level I would say, [the typical student] has difficulty with basic sight words, I would say, from all of the students that I have in my room right now, [the typical student may be able to read] words like "it," "to," [or] "out," but anything past 3–letter words they have trouble with.
>
> [The typical student] can tell time, maybe to the half-hour, but nothing past that. Has difficulty with articulation, with verbally forming sentences, difficulty writing simple sentences—I don't have anybody that can really write cursive right now. I'd say first grade level, most of them. And we have to work on behavior with everyone, constantly at this point. . . .
>
> With reading, it's got to be literal, you can't—it's even hard to kid around, because they don't really understand. They take everything literal. And steps have to be very—if you ask them to do something it has to be one or two steps, it can't be complicated. So it's very hard for them to understand unless it's a direct, literal statement. (11/25/97, pp. 7–8)

Stephen's abilities contrast with the description of the typical student in a number of ways, some of which have been outlined pre-

viously. In some cases his skills are below that of the "typical student"; e.g., he is unable to read even the simple sight words
described above.

In other cases his skills are more advanced. Stephen's complex
cognitive abilities are apparent in his communication style, e.g., in
his use of analogy, simile, and metaphor,[11] and in his sense of
humor. For example, after repeated interruptions in the interview
room, Stephen laughed and described these with the simile, "in-out,
in-out—like cartoon." The shade flapping at the open window also
prompted Stephen's laughter, along with the metaphor, "ghost."
Stephen's sense of humor was also observable during field observations, where he was observed to laugh often in response to classroom events or comments.

Despite difficulties with word-finding described previously,
Stephen possesses a strong vocabulary, which surfaces from time to
time. For example, his description of the movie *Toy Story* illustrates
his use of mature vocabulary and idiomatic expression; i.e., "crime,"
and "clean" (in reference to film content): "[*Toy Story*] more good
[than] other movies. Other stories have crime in them. *Toy Story*
good—doesn't have that in it. Just clean stuff in it." (10/9/97, p. 13)
In another excerpt, Stephen interpreted my request that he role-
play his mother as being "in [her] shoes":

> *Interviewer:* If you were your mom, what would you say?
>
> *Stephen:* Me, my mom?
>
> *Interviewer:* If you were going to act like your mom.
>
> *Stephen:* In my mom's shoes.
>
> *Interviewer:* Yeah, if you were in your mom's shoes, what
> would you say? (10/9/97, p. 14)

"Special" Expectations

According to Stephen, the special education program provides
little in the way of the age-appropriate conceptual learning that
was his strong point in the general education classroom:

> *Interviewer:* Do you have—social studies class?
>
> *Stephen:* Uh-uh. Not here.
>
> *Interviewer:* No? Do you have math class?
>
> *Stephen:* Mm-mm [indicating that he does not].

Interviewer: What else—do you have science class?

Stephen: Uh-uh. IIaven't started that yet.

Interviewer: Do you have—reading? English?

Stephen: . . . Just reading. . . . Reading circle. (10/9/97, pp. 4–5)

This description is consistent with that provided by Stephen's teacher and with field observations with one exception. His teacher described daily math instruction:

> By 9:00 we have math—we work on money skills, time skills, measurement, basic functional—basic math skills, like adding—single digit, and subtracting. (11/25/97, p. 5)

Stephen also showed me worksheets in his desk for adding single digits.

Life Skills Instruction

Many special education classes for students with significant disabilities adopt a functional, life skills philosophy. Self-help skills, independent living skills, leisure skills, community skills, and job skills are emphasized; instruction in these areas has been recognized as essential for students with significant disabilities (e.g., see Brown et al., 1981). Aspects of this philosophy were articulated both by the teacher and by one of the classroom aides. The teacher and Stephen provided concrete illustrations of its application in their interviews. For example, Stephen described instruction in domestic skills:

> *Interviewer:* What else are you working on?
>
> *Stephen:* Cleaning. Cooking. . . . Pizza. Square pizza.
>
> *Interviewer:* . . . What else are you learning?
>
> *Stephen:* Cooking cake. (10/9/97, p. 6)

However, even exemplary independent living skills opportunities were sometimes plagued by low expectations. Although Stephen and his classmates were involved in some functional activities, these were also likely to be performed by staff, with little or no student involvement. For example, during one observation, pies were being baked for a dinner with high school-aged students with disabilities. Staff took over one of the most important parts of the activity— determining when the pies were done and taking them out of the oven. Although a student was brought over to help once the pies were out, she had been left sitting at her desk during the critical process of determining when they needed to be taken out, and getting them out of the oven safely. In another example, a nondisabled peer came to the door to purchase popcorn that had been made to sell as a fundraiser for the class. However, Stephen and his classmates were left out of this interaction, one of the few opportunities available to them for meaningful interaction with nondisabled peers. Instead, the sale was handled entirely by the aide. And, although the teacher and the aide stated that it was Stephen's job to wash dishes and wipe off tables, the only person observed to be involved in these activities (in both instances when they took place during classroom observations) was the classroom aide.

Stephen's teacher is well-respected in the local educational community. The instruction in functional daily living skills provided in his classroom is an important aspect of any program for a student with significant disabilities. Stephen probably gets more of this in the special education classroom than he would in many inclusive programs. Depending on resources and philosophy, this aspect of the education of a student with disabilities may be neglected in some inclusive programs.

Other exemplary aspects of the special education class include that the tone in the classroom and behavioral expectations were largely age-appropriate. For example, students were not spoken to in "baby talk," were not playing with toys, or rewarded with stickers, as they are in some special education classrooms, even those for older students. The teacher is also recognized for his attempts to provide community-based instruction. This is another important aspect of any program for a student with significant disabilities, and one which is often lacking from both inclusive and self-contained special education programs. Without it, students with significant disabilities are unlikely to learn skills essential to successful participation in integrated community environments.

Low Expectations

THE READINESS APPROACH. As noted in the previous description of special education students in Stephen's class, staff perceptions of their functioning levels is low, approximately first grade level. This is reflected in the "readiness" nature of many activities. Instruction in alphabet letters and their corresponding sounds occurred frequently. The reading group activity that was observed featured an early elementary level story with cartoon-style illustrations. Although high interest/low reading level books are published, they were not evident in the special education class. And early elementary level stories are read to students even when the intent is not development of reading skills:

> We have group reading—just ask literal fact questions—and reward them with chips. I just want them to tune into listening. And try to make the questions very, very s[imple]—I give a lot of hints—it's mainly for listening. (11/25/97, pp. 6–7)

THE CONTINUUM. The readiness approach is part of a larger philosophy, that of a continuum of services, that is suffused throughout most service delivery systems for individuals with disabilities, including educational, residential, and vocational services. Services are ranked by their "restrictiveness," i.e., by the degree to which they infringe upon individual rights (Biklen, 1982). In education, the regular classroom is the "least restrictive environment." The following services are listed in order of increasing restrictiveness: (a) part-time pull-out services such as those provided in resource rooms, (b) special education classes with some mainstreaming into general education classrooms, (c) special education classes without mainstreaming, (d) separate special education day schools, (f) home instruction, and (e) instruction in residential settings other than the home. Placement of students in the least restrictive environment in which their needs can be met, with gradual movement through the levels of the continuum toward independence, is the professed ideal of the continuum of services philosophy.

The continuum of services philosophy is reflected in the description of job skills instruction provided by Stephen's special education classroom teacher; students who are "ready" work out in the school building, giving them access to individuals without disabilities, but students who are not deemed ready work in the segregated classroom:

> We set up jobs in the school—like sweeping, they work in the cafeteria, different jobs around the school . . . in the win-

ter they shovel off the sidewalks. . . . If I don't feel they're
ready to work in the school, then they work in the classroom. It could be sweeping, mopping, dishes—but they're
assigned a job and then they do that everyday. Then after
that, once they get proficient at that, then we find a job in
the school. (11/25/97, p. 2)

An assumption underlying the continuum philosophy is that segregated environments prepare people for integrated environments,
and that proficiency in segregated environments indicates readiness for integrated environments, enabling eventual movement
through the continuum toward independence. Similarly, failure at
more restrictive levels is assumed to predict failure at less restrictive levels. This is a problematic assumption (Taylor, 1988; Wieck
and Strully, 1992). First, there may be little coherence between
expectations in different environments; performance in one environment does not predict performance in the next. Second, individuals rarely move through the continuum to independence, or even
to less restrictive levels. More often, as in Stephen's case, any movement is to more restrictive levels; most often there is no movement
at all. The system that professes to move individuals progressively
toward independence in fact seems to function to maintain the status quo. As adult services are often based on those provided in
school, the pattern of segregation continues on into adulthood.

The third problematic assumption of the continuum is that
movement is based on skill level. Students would presumably learn
skills in the special education class that they need in integrated
environments, e.g., to participate in jobs along side nondisabled
peers. However, placement in the continuum is likely to be heavily
based upon on the degree and type of behavior management problems that staff experience with a particular student, as illustrated
in the special education classroom teacher's comments below about
readiness for jobs in the school at large. While social skills might be
conceived of as those that facilitate development of meaningful
relationships, "social skills" in this case seems to refer to an
absence of "behavior" (i.e., swearing or pushing):

Interviewer: What do you look for to know that they're
ready to have a job in the school [rather than in the special
education classroom]?

Teacher: Behavior. Because they're going to be dealing with
other students, or staff, in the halls, if they're sweeping, or

in the cafeteria. Motor skills—fine motor skills—gross motor skills. Just, social skills—if they walk by somebody in the hall and don't swear at them, or don't push them against the wall—then we know—things like that. Mainly behavior skills, social skills, and motor skills. (11/25/97, p. 2)

While instruction in social reciprocity skills can facilitate the development of relationships with nondisabled peers (e.g., Stainback, Stainback, and Strathe, 1983; Strain, Odom, and McConnell, 1984), the expectation at this school seems to be that students with significant disabilities disregard their nondisabled peers.

Learned Passivity

Some of the tasks in the special education class seemed extremely passive, as well as meaningless to some students. For example, each day starts out with a tracing/copying exercise, described by the teacher as follows:

We have a board, every morning it changes, they have to read it and copy it. Not all of them can copy it. If they can't copy it . . . we'll write it down and then they trace over it. (11/25/97, p. 4–5)

Stephen is one of the students that traces over it. Stephen is a nonreader; he cannot read what he is tracing. Based on the special education classroom teacher's previous description of the reading level of his students, it seems likely that few of Stephen's classmates would be able to read it either. The passage is several sentences long and, for these unaccomplished writers, seems to occupy a significant portion of the day. While tracing target vocabulary words can be part of a viable multisensory approach to reading (VAKT, or Visual-Auditory-Kinesthetic-Tactile; e.g., see Walker, 1996), the auditory component of the strategy, in which the student hears and says the word he or she is tracing, is critical. As this activity was structured as an independent "folder work" activity, the auditory component of the strategy was omitted. Stephen also traces answers that are written in for him on phonics and math pages. A few of the worksheets he showed me did not have the answers written in. On these he had written in his own answers, all of them wrong.

Several verbal activities seemed to follow the same pattern. The student would be asked for a response that he was unable to supply. A staff person would supply the answer, which would then be repeated by the student:

> *Weather and Calendar Activity*: The teacher announces that it is time for students to say their name, the weather, and the date. He calls on Stephen. Stephen comes up, but says none of the information requested correctly except his name. The teacher tells him what to say. Stephen repeats it and is rewarded with a token. (11/20/97; pp. 1–2)

> *Bingo Activity*: Stephen is the "caller"—he swings a small ball on a string toward a larger ball that falls onto a horizontal, roulette-style wheel with Bingo numbers and letters. Then he is to call out the number and letter. Since he is not able to identify letters or numbers, however, he can only repeat after the teacher. (11/20/97; p. 1)

> *"Reading" Groups*: The teacher splits the students into three groups—all seem to have pre-primer or primer level readers. Stephen's group has a story with one sentence and large illustrations on each page. For example: I can crawl, said the crab. The aide reads aloud and points to each word in the book, which he holds the entire time. Stephen seems baffled about these words, and just repeats after the aide. Each page is repeated several times. (11/20/97; pp. 2–3)

Success in these examples seems to refer to not making mistakes; the goal seems to be getting "the right answers" even if you can't do the work.

Segregation

A common perception exists that segregated placements shelter students with disabilities from taunting by nondisabled students. Yet that was not evident in this case study. As noted previously, Stephen was well-known to and accepted by nondisabled students in his home school; I saw little evidence of taunting there. Taunting seemed much more salient to the teacher of the special education classroom than to staff in the inclusion program. For example, when asked to describe his classroom rules, the special education classroom teacher briefly mentioned "raising your hand . . . to talk" and "asking permission before they do things in the room." Another rule, being "courteous and nice to everyone," was the first rule stated, constituted the bulk of his response to the "rules" question, and speaks to taunting that students placed in the special education classroom are expected to tolerate:

> Just be courteous and nice to everyone, is one rule. Everyone you see, no matter what's happened. If someone harasses students in the hall, you ignore them. If it continues, like 2–3 days in a row, then you tell someone, and of course if they're hit, you tell someone. But if someone calls you a name, you walk away. [Interviewer: The nondisabled kids?] Yes. It doesn't happen that often, but I have a couple of students that are impulsive, and if they get called a name, they push back or they call a name, and then I get told that my students are calling names. [Laughs ruefully.] So I tell them, the best thing for you to do, right now, is to ignore it. And if it continues, then I'll watch, and then we'll take care it. But right now, the best thing to do is ignore it. They'll come in and they'll say, "So-and-so stuck his finger up at me, or called me this." And I say, "Well, did you ignore it?" And they'll say, "Yes I did." [I say] "Good," and I'll reward them for ignoring the behavior. Because, before, in the past, I guess they got real upset, they would push the student, call them names back, and then the teacher would hear my student calling the other kid names, and then we'd go through the whole process. You can even get to the point where parents have to come in, [it] gets blown up way out of control, so [the rule is]—ignore it. (11/25/97; pp. 9–10)

Students in the special education class are bused in from neighboring districts; nondisabled students have not had the experience of growing up in the same community and learning in the same classrooms with them. Perhaps when nondisabled students have the opportunity to get to know a person with a disability on a personal level over an extended period of time they may be somewhat less inclined to engage in taunting.

There is little opportunity for nondisabled students to get to know students with disabilities who are placed in the special education class. Most of the day for Stephen and his classmates is spent in their classroom. Most are mainstreamed only for "home and careers" (formerly known as home economics) or "technology" (formerly known as wood or metal shop), art, and gym (every other day). They are scheduled to go into the community twice each week. One outing is for grocery shopping; the other is for bowling and is contingent on compliant behavior during the week.

Both Stephen and his teacher discussed the class's weekly bowling outing. However, bowling, particularly during weekday mornings or afternoons, is such a typical outing for groups of individuals with disabilities that it is virtually stereotypical, and offers little or no opportunity to form relationships with individuals other than paid staff and other individuals with disabilities from the same group.

Because Stephen is excused from gym and has adaptive physical education instead, his main opportunities for integration with nondisabled peers are during art and home and careers. I observed him during this class. Because of his adaptive physical education schedule, Stephen was in class for only about ten minutes. During that short time, much of the little opportunity there was for interaction with the teacher or students in the mainstreamed setting was intercepted (unintentionally) by the aide who accompanied Stephen to the class:

> At the teacher's request during a child care lesson, students are telling "terrible two's" stories about themselves. The aide quietly asks Stephen if he has talked to his mother about a story—he says that he has not. He laughs at the stories of the other students.
>
> The teacher asks Stephen if he has a terrible two's story. The aide says he does not. Stephen makes sounds of frustration and tells the aide that he wants to answer. The aide encourages him to raise his hand. The teacher calls on him, but does not understand what he is saying. The aide tells her that he is saying he was good at that age.
>
> Later, a student leans over to look at Stephen's rubric, which is sitting in front of the aide. The student says to the aide: How'd he do? Aide: He did perfect (tone of satisfaction).
>
> On the way out a few minutes later, the aide hands the rubric to the teacher and tells her his score.

Thus, Stephen had four opportunities to interact with people in the mainstreamed setting, and three of them were intercepted by the (well-meaning) aide. This is not surprising or atypical. People are likely to direct their interaction to the aide due to her very presence. For interaction with Stephen to happen would likely require active resistance by the aide to people directing their interaction to her. This is true of both inclusive and segregated settings; however, the problem is exacerbated in segregated settings due to the small number of opportunities for interaction with nondisabled individuals.

An Expectations Paradox

What does all this mean for Stephen? He does not fit the mold of the typical student in his special education class. In some areas, his skills seem to be much higher, e.g., his conceptual ability, and his capacity for abstract imagery and humor. From this perspective, the activities available to Stephen seem intellectually stultifying. But then, students with significant disabilities are not expected to be intellectual. One might say that Stephen's program is not individualized for him, though individualization is the hallmark of special education. But can it be? Is it realistic to expect a classroom made up entirely of students with significant disabilities to provide activities that are intellectually stimulating? Perhaps not. Perhaps this can only happen through a general education program.

In other areas Stephen has much lower abilities. His difficulty with labeling tasks, especially labeling of letters in this readiness environment, is quite pronounced in comparison to other students in his class. Most of his classmates are more able-bodied than he is, e.g., he is the only one who receives adaptive physical education or uses a wheelchair. His speech is more difficult to understand, and his syntax is poor (e.g., saying "me" instead of "I"). All of these attributes seem to contribute to a perception of Stephen in his special education class as among the lowest functioning students in the class. He is cast into a passive role in many activities that are beyond him, but his capacity for higher cognitive learning lies dormant.

Why has this happened? Various components of a functionalist educational system work together to produce this outcome, including homogeneous, "batch processing" of students in graded general education classes, the continuum philosophy and readiness approach in special education. Contributing to this problem may be that, given the expectation for individualized curriculum for students with disabilities, a special education teacher with a new student has little to go on. The teacher cannot make the general assumptions about what the student has already been exposed to that are implicit in the regular education curriculum. For example, the special education teacher may not know that Stephen has struggled for years without success to learn basic sight words. He may feel that the readiness approach is just what Stephen's education has been lacking.

This expectations paradox also seems related to the fact that Stephen does not fit into the "typical student" mold even for his special education class. Some of the students did seem to be somewhat better suited for some of the activities than Stephen did. But do the other students fit the typical student mold for this class? In this environment, how would one recognize higher capacities if they exist? If Stephen's classmates had had the benefit of Stephen's educational experience, might they show greater capacities than they do? Conversely, if Stephen had been educated for the past five years in this environment, would he have the capacities that he does?

Conclusion

I have attempted to acquaint the reader with Stephen and his educational experience, and to explore the micropolitical aspects of his placement in a self-contained special education class where it is argued that educational expectations are not only low, but are unjustifiably low. Low expectations, learned passivity, and segregation seem to predominate, and to severely limit Stephen's opportunity to learn.

It might be easy to place the onus for Stephen's lack of opportunity to learn upon the teacher. That is not my intent, nor is it my understanding of the situation. As noted previously, Stephen's teacher is respected in the educational community and has instituted many research-based practices that are important for students with disabilities, practices which are lacking in many other classrooms. Limitations on Stephen's opportunity to learn in this environment should not be attributed to poor teaching; rather they seem systemic. Individual agency is a necessary but insufficient condition for educational change. It seems next to impossible to provide equal opportunties to learn in a segregated system. Segregated educational placements seem to me inherently unequal, whether they are based on race, disability, or other factors.

Segregated classrooms are, of course, part of a larger educational system and society, one in which segregation has become the norm for people with significant disabilities. Although integration of people with significant disabilities is increasing, change has been slow and uneven. While acceptance of inclusion is growing, segregation is still perpetuated in the system. Conscious resistance, supported if not initiated by those in power, seems necessary for continued progress.

Power operates on multiple levels, including federal, state, and local. There was no change in state or federal policy during this time. In Stephen's case, administrative turnover in his district resulted in changes in the aims and philosophy of special education decision-making. Changes in his situation were influenced by the different backgrounds, beliefs, and strengths of various players involved at the local level, particularly those in powerful administrative roles. When those in power who were willing and able to support educational change on his behalf left the district, his inclusive placement became vulnerable to reversion to previously existing arrangements.

It must be said that the impact of Stephen's placement in a segregated special education classroom remains to be seen. It may be that more valued outcomes will result for Stephen through his special education class placement than if he had remained in an inclusive setting. However, the data on outcomes of segregated placements overall are not encouraging, and there seems to be little about Stephen's case at this point that would lead one to expect things to turn out differently for him.

Notes

1. This is not to imply that relationships with other people with disabilities are undesirable in and of themselves; rather that most of us would not want our opportunities to form relationships to be limited to a small group of people whose shortcomings have been intentionally matched to our own.

2. The Education for All Handicapped Children Act has been replaced by the Individuals with Disabilities Education Act of 1990 (or IDEA).

3. The Fifth and Fourteenth Amendments provide for due process and equal protection under the law.

4. Section 504 was the first federal civil rights legislation for people with disabilities.

5. Significant intellectual disabilities would include educational labels such as mental retardation, severe learning disabilities, pervasive developmental disorder, etc.

6. This experience includes administrative responsibilities in public and private educational settings and teaching responsibilities ranging from consulting teacher for inclusion (in a regular classroom), to resource room teaching, to teaching in a self-contained special education classroom. I was the teacher of and special education coordinator for the student whose story is told in this chapter, as well as the researcher of the case study. I have attempted to identify (in a reader-friendly manner) from which perspective I am speaking through my use of tense and voice: third person, past tense when I am speaking from my former role as teacher and coordinator, and first person, present tense when I am speaking in my current role as the researcher.

7. All proper nouns are pseudonyms.

8. I was Stephen's consulting special education teacher during his fourth and fifth grade years.

9. That is, support staff also benefited from collaboration with the general education classroom teacher.

10. Four of the five were women; I was the third in this succession.

11. According to Toepfer (1998), "students require formal operational (abstract) thinking capacity to understand metaphor and imagery" (p. 11).

References

Baumgart, D., Brown, L., Pumpian, I., Nisbet, J., Ford, A., Sweet, M., Messina, R., and Schroeder, J. (1982). Principle of partial participation and individualized adaptations in educational programs for severely handicapped students. *Journal of the Association for the Severely Handicapped, 7*, Summer, 17–27.

Biklen, D. (1982). The least restrictive environment: Its application to education. In G. Melton (ed.), *Child and youth services.* New York: Haworth. Cited by Taylor, 1988.

Biklen, D., Lehr, S., Searl, S., and Taylor, S. (1987). *Purposeful integration . . . inherently equal.* Syracuse, NY: Center on Human Policy, Syracuse University.

Bogdan, R., ed. (1982). *In the mainstream: Case studies of integrated education for children with disabilities.* Eric Document Reproduction Service No. ED 271 896.

Bogdan, R. and Biklen, S. (1982). Foundations of qualitative research in education: An introduction. *Qualitative research for education.* Boston: Allyn and Bacon.

Brown, L., Branston, M.B., Hamre-Nietupski, S., Pumpian, I., Certo, N., and Gruenewald, L. (1981). A strategy for developing chronological age-appropriate and functional curricular content for severely handicapped adolescents and young adults. *Journal of Special Education, 13*(1), 81–90.

Cole, D.A. and Meyer, L.H. (1991). Social integration and severe disabilities: A longitudinal analysis of child outcomes. *Journal of Special Education, 25*(3), 340–351.

Education for All Handicapped Children Act of 1975. U.S. Public Law (142). 94th Cng., Pub.L. No. 94-142. §1401, 20 U.S.C.A.

Erwin, I.W. and Clapp, S.L.C. (1967). *Friends of themselves.* Boston: Christopher Publishing House.

Golomb, K. and Hammeken, P. (1996). Grappling with inclusion confusion? *Learning, January/February*, 48–51.

Good, T. (1981). Teacher expectations and student perceptions: A decade of research. *Educational Leadership, 38*, 415–422.

Hoyle, E. (1988). Micropolitics of educational organizations. In Westoby, A. (ed.), *Culture and power in educational organizations.* Milton Keynes, England: Open University Press.

Individuals with Disabilities Education Act, 20 U.S.C. § 1400 *et seq.*

Inskeep, A.D. (1926). *Teaching dull and retarded children.* New York: Macmillan.

Lawrence-Brown, D. (1998). *Inclusion: A new idea? An interview study of one-room school teachers.* Manuscript submitted for publication.

Lincoln, Y. and Denzin, N. (1994). The fifth moment. In Denzin, N. and Lincoln, Y. (eds.), *The handbook of qualitative research.* Thousand Oaks, CA: Sage.

Lipsky, D.K. and Gartner, A. (1995). The evaluation of inclusive education programs. *National Center on Restructuring and Inclusion Bulletin, 2*(2), 1–6.

Lutz, F.W. (1988). Witches and witchfinding in educational organizations. In Westoby, A. (ed.), *Culture and power in educational organizations.* Milton Keynes, England: Open University Press.

McDonnell, A. and Hardman, M. (1989). The desegregation of America's special schools: Strategies for change. *Journal of the Association for Persons with Severe Handicaps, 14*(1), 68–74.

McLaughlin, M., Warren, S., and Schofield, P. (1996). Creating inclusive schools: What does the research say? *Impact, 9*(2), 4–5.

Morrow, J. (1996). What's so special about special education? *Education Week,* May 8.

National study of inclusive education. (1994). New York: National Center on Educational Restructuring and Inclusion. (Eric Document Reproduction Service No. ED375606)

New York State Education Department. (1993). *A parent's guide to special education for children ages 5–21.* Albany, NY: Author.

Peshkin, A. (1988). In search of subjectivity—one's own. *Educational Researcher, 17*(7), 17–20.

Rehabilitation Act of 1973, Pub. L. No. 93–112, Title V, Section 504, 29 U.S.C. § 706.

Rist, R.C. (1970). Student social class and teacher expectations: The self-fulfilling prophecy in ghetto education. *Harvard Educational Review, 40*(3), 411–451.

Robinson, N. and Robinson, H. (1976). *The mentally retarded child.* New York: McGraw-Hill.

Rogers, J. (1993). The inclusion revolution. *Phi Delta Kappa Research Bulletin, 11,* 1–7.

Sapon-Shevin, M. (1992). Celebrating diversity: Curriculum that honors and builds on differences. In S. Stainback and W. Stainback (eds.), *Curriculum considerations in inclusive classrooms: Facilitating learning for all students.* Baltimore: Brookes.

Safford, P. and Safford, E. (1996). *A history of childhood and disabilities.* New York: Teachers College Press.

Seidman, I.E. (1991). *Interviewing as qualitative research: A guide for researchers in education and the social sciences.* New York: Teachers College Press.

Skrtic, T.M. (1995). *Disability and democracy.* New York: Teachers College Press.

Sleeter, C. (1986). Learning disabilities: The social construction of a special education category. *Exceptional Children, 53*(1), 46–54.

Smith, M.L. (1982). *How educators decide who is learning disabled: Challenge to psychology and public policy in the schools.* Springfield, IL: Charles C. Thomas.

Soltow, L. and Stevens, E. (1981). *The rise of literacy and the common school in the United States: A socioeconomic analysis to 1870.* Chicago: University of Chicago Press.

Spradley, J.P. (1980). *Participant observation.* New York: Holt.

Squibb, P. (1981). A theoretical structuralist approach to special education. In Barton, L. and Tomlinson, S. (eds.), *Special education: Policy, practices, and social issues*. London: Harper and Row.

Stainback, W., Stainback, S., and Strathe, M. (1983). Generalization of positive social behavior by severely handicapped students: A review and analysis of research. *Education and Training of the Mentally Retarded, December*, 293–299

Stanley, W.B. (1986). Critical research. In Cornbleth, C. (ed.), *An invitation to research in social education*. Washington, DC: National Council for the Social Studies.

Staub, D. and Peck, C.A. (1994). What are the outcomes for nondisabled students? *Educational Leadership 52*(4), 36–40.

Strain, P., Odom, S., and McConnell, S. (1984). Promoting social reciprocity of exceptional children: Identification, target behavior selection, and intervention. *Remedial and Special Education, 5*(1), 21–28.

Strully, J. and Strully, C. (1985). Friendship and our children. *Journal of the Association for Persons with Severe Handicaps, 10*, 225–227.

Taylor, S. (1988). Caught in the continuum: A critical analysis of the principle of the least restrictive environment. *Journal of the Association for Persons with Severe handicaps, 13*(1), 41–53.

Toepfer, C. (1998). *Rationale for middle level education*. Unpublished manuscript, University at Buffalo.

Tyack, D. and Cuban, L. (1995). *Tinkering with Utopia*. Cambridge, MA: Harvard University Press.

Walker, B. (1996). *Diagnostic teaching of reading: Techniques for instruction and assessment, 3rd ed.* Englewood Cliffs, NJ: Prentice-Hall.

Wallin, J.E.W. (1914). *The mental health of the school child: The psychoeducational clinic in relation to child welfare*. New Haven, CT: Yale University Press. In Winzer 1993.

Wallin, J.E.W. (1924). *The education of handicapped children*. Boston: Houghton-Mifflin. In Winzer, 1993.

Wieck, C. and Strully, J. (1992). What's wrong with the continuum? A metaphorical analysis. In L. Meyer, C. Pick, and L. Brown (eds.), *Critical issues in the lives of people with severe disabilities*. Baltimore: Brookes Publ.

White House Conference on Child Health and Protection. (1931). *Education and training, Section 3*. New York: Century.

Winzer, M. (1993). *The history of special education: From isolation to integration.* Washington, D.C.: Gallaudet University Press.

Wlodkowski, R.J. and Ginsburg, M.B. (1995). *Diversity and motivation: Culturally responsive teaching.* San Francisco: Jossey-Bass.

Yell, M. and Shriner, J. (1996). Inclusive education: Legal and policy implications. *Preventing School Failure, 40*(3), 101–108.

York-Barr, J., Schultz, T., Doyle, M.B., Kronberg, R. and Crossett, S. (1996). Inclusive schooling in St. Cloud: Perspectives on the process and people. *Remedial and Special Education, 17*(2), 92–105.

6

ễ❧

"They Don't Want to Hear It":
Ways of Talking and Habits of the Heart
in Multicultural Literature Classrooms*

Suzanne M. Miller
and
Gina DeBlase Trzyna

I am a man of substance, of flesh and bone, fiber and liquids—and I might even be said to possess a mind. I am invisible, understand, simply because people refuse to see me. . . . It is sometimes advantageous to be unseen, although it is most often rather wearing on the nerves. Then too, you're constantly being bumped against by those of poor vision. Or again, you often doubt if you really exist.

—Ralph Ellison, *Invisible Man*, p. 3.

Without the possibility of action, all knowledge comes to one labeled "file and forget," and I can neither file nor forget. . . . There's a possibility that even an invisible man has a socially responsible role to play.

—Ralph Ellison, *Invisible Man*, p. 439.

* This work was sponsored, in part, by the National Council of Teachers of English Research Foundation Grant-in-Aid and the Professional Development Network Fallingwater Project of the Graduate School of Education, University at Buffalo. The opinions expressed here do not necessarily reflect the position or policy of these sponsoring organizations.

The English classroom has frequently been promoted as the best hope for fostering multiculturalism in a dialogue where students learn "to understand the complexity of the world and the many perspectives involved" (Nieto, 1991, p. 219). In particular, reading literature is construed as a sense-making activity which can contribute to the sharp and critical mind by stimulating attention to dilemmas, alternative human possibilities, and the many-sidedness of the human situation (Bruner, 1986; Langer, 1990, 1995; Miller, 1993; Rosenblatt, 1978). In this view, literature study can theoretically provide opportunities for meeting many goals of pluralistic education where voices interact and where students reflect, think critically, increase cultural awareness, decrease ethnocentrism, and create a global perspective (e.g., Sleeter and Grant, 1994).[1]

Based on this promise of multicultural literature, many have argued for diversifying the literature curriculum to include previously unheard voices (e.g., Applebee, 1993; Miller and McCaskill, 1993; Rogers and Soter, 1997). In the last few years some changes have occurred. For example, Applebee's (1993) studies of the literature curriculum in the United States suggest that recent literature anthologies have included more works by non-white men and women. But at the same time, he reports, only 19% of the book-length works which teachers *used* were written by women and 2% by non-white authors. A number of recent ethnographic studies in secondary schools suggest that English teachers' reasons for using multicultural literatures vary due to local contextual and personal belief issues (e.g., Adams, 1995; Athanases, 1993; Bigler and Collins, 1995; Kutno, 1996; Miller, 1996a, 1996b; Rogers, 1997; Zigo, 1996). Taken together, these studies suggest that introducing multicultural texts (i.e., texts representing culturally marginalized perspectives) into the curriculum is only one aspect of a more complex pedagogical challenge. Bringing multiple perspectives into the classroom requires engaging students in dialogues about their responses to such texts and about sociopolitical issues raised by texts. Often, though, school contexts simultaneously constrain diverse perspectives while posing as politically neutral. If we are to allow social and political issues "so close to the surface of students' lives" to "enter the official stream of talk" (Hynds, 1997, p. 259) then, perhaps, we need to make plain "the power dynamics inside and outside of our classroom that make democratic dialogue impossible" (Ellsworth, 1989, p. 313).

We were curious about what we could learn concerning the

sociopolitical dynamics of teaching multicultural literature in sociopolitical contexts from ethnographic studies. In this chapter, we first present the results of our cross-study analysis to demonstrate teachers' differing views of empowering students and how those views influenced their multicultural text approaches and students' learning. Then, we elaborate a specific incident revealing the politics of curriculum practice in one class we studied; in part, this is the story of Derrick, a black student struggling to act in socially responsible ways within a school and curriculum which he feels has rendered his blackness, to use Ellison's metaphor, "invisible."

Three Views of Empowering Students

Through a cross-study comparative analysis—in which we recursively read, annotated, developed themes (LeCompte, Millroy, and Preissle, 1992)—we traced patterned linkages between teachers' views of empowerment and culture and the ways of talking and thinking developed over time across ethnographic cases. The studies of teaching multicultural literature, presented in Table 1, were recent well-documented ethnographies of classrooms where teachers had articulated diversifying the literary canon as a goal. Each researcher followed rigorous methodological procedures, such as those outlined by Athanases and Heath (1995), including regular long-term participant observation (from six months to two years) and use of multiple data types and perspectives to triangulate findings. In each case, researchers interviewed the teacher and students and, in most cases, collected artifacts related to literature learning, including student writing. The studies were conducted in different instructional settings (high school, middle school, integrated English-History classes) and in different geographic locations. They were grounded in a range of theoretical frameworks, such as anthropology, ethnography of communication, critical literacy, and sociolinguistic theory. Yet themes recurred across these studies, suggesting that a larger understanding of teaching multicultural literature in secondary school might emerge by cross-case analysis. A major recurring theme of "empowerment" emerged across the ethnographies, but teachers differed in their view of how to empower students. These views were influenced by patterns of beliefs about the purpose of multicultural education and texts which influenced the talk and activity and student learning.

Table 1
Selected Studies on Multicultural Literature Classrooms

Studies	Teacher(s)	Classes/School	Ethnographic Framework(s)
Adams, 1995	Ms. LaFitte	8th gr./Working Class Deep South	critical interpretivist
Athanases, 1993	Reiko Carolyn	10th gr./urban San Francisco	ethnography of communication
Bigler & Collins, 1995	Mrs. L.	8th gr./small city Upstate New York	anthropology, critical literacy
Kutno, 1996	Meg Jake	10th gr./suburban 12th gr./suburban NYC metropolitan	sociocultural, multicultural theories
Miller, 1996a	Rachel Lauren Brandy	11th gr./suburban 12th gr./suburban 11th–12th gr./urban Western New York	sociocultural and critical literacy
Miller, 1996b	Sharon Ron	11th gr./suburban heterogeneous Upstate New York	sociocultural and critical literacy
Rogers, 1997	Chris	11th gr./urban Mid-Western U.S.	sociolinguistic, interpretivist
Zigo, 1996	Jenny	9th gr./suburban	sociocultural

In their classes, the thirteen teachers from the ethnographic cases enacted multicultural empowerment by focusing mainly on one of these approaches:

- providing cultural information
- providing access to academic literacy for marginalized students
- fostering student dialogue and reflection on multiple cultural perspectives

Themes within and across these teacher approaches reveal that teachers' beliefs and actions were influenced by their interpretations of the nature of literary texts, of relevant disciplinary knowledge, and of the role of cultural difference in the school. Using a sociocultural framework for the analysis, we have foregrounded talk as a central tool for learning (Vygotsky, 1978, 1987; Wertsch, 1991) and a major constituent of values and beliefs. In general, the analysis reveals that teachers' ways of talking about texts led to very different kinds of student engagement and learning. In the following section we use findings from the studies to illustrate these differing patterns of talking and thinking about multicultural literature.

Empowerment as Providing Cultural Information

Three of the teachers saw multicultural empowerment as *possessing* cultural information. They added multicultural literary texts to their curriculum, and treated them as containing information to be transmitted. Teachers acting from this belief system directed attention back to the text features and information when students raised current issues of racism and prejudice. From this frame of reference, topics for discussion were often constrained. For example, Ms. LaFitte (Adams, 1995) said that having her 8th graders read *Roll of Thunder, Hear My Cry* was "an excellent tool to get students to talk about racism" (p. 29). However, whole-class talk centered on questions that the teacher reproduced from a teacher's manual, and followed a recitation pattern of interaction with the teacher asking for short factual answers and evaluating correctness of students' responses about the book. Quizzes and a unit test further emphasized reading as mainly learning information. The novel explores racism in the South in the 1930s through the eyes of a 10-year-old black female, but Ms. LaFitte distanced that time and place from their own southern setting with comments like, "The dialect of the Deep South is hard to understand."

The emphasis on the factual knowledge about this distanced culture also supplanted any discussion of students' personal responses or experiences. Although the interviewed students, both black and white, seemed quite perceptive about the "hidden racism" in the school, the teacher felt there was no problem: "Racism is not a problem here, so we don't need to start something that so far we've managed to avoid," she said. In this excerpt from whole-class discussion (Adams, 1995), Terrence's feelings about the racist behaviors in the book did not seem to be welcome, either:

LaFitte: If you were Black and read the book, you might get angry.

Black female: It don't bother me.

Terrence: It bothered me when they burnt that Black man.

According to the researcher, the teacher quickly ended discussion, saying, "The author did not write this book to make you take negative action" (p. 34). Although talking about the Holocaust in Europe was "safe," the researcher concluded, "The persecution of the Logan family in *Roll of Thunder, Hear My Cry* and/or oppression of Blacks in the South today were not perceived as safe topics and, thus, were to be avoided." Cultural knowledge about racism stayed within the boundaries of the long ago and far away in this class and did not enter into discussion as current emotions or stories. In an interview Terrence, a student of African American descent, said,

> I guess Ms. LaFitte don't want any racial stuff, cause, you know, some people might get upset and fight cause of that, stupid stuff like that . . . I risk getting in trouble to say what I think is right.

Often, though, when parts of the book made Terrence angry, "I just be quiet so I don't get in trouble." In this report Adams (1995) has called this tendency to distance multicultural issues from immediate settings and personal experiences the "Not in my back yard syndrome," a generalized concern for these issues of racism *elsewhere*.

According to Bigler and Collins (1995), Mrs. L. similarly focused on information to be found in multicultural texts to avoid discussion in her classroom. Her questioning style was to solicit one-word or one-sentence factual answers, thus limiting opportunities to voice opinions or responses. She had felt some departmental pressure to include multicultural literature in her curriculum, and when the department arranged a visit by Latina author Nicholasa Mohr, Mrs. L. read Mohr's story "Once Upon a Time" to the class:

> *Mrs. L:* [reading] Nicholasa Mohr was born in Manhattan, where she grew up in El ____? [Pauses.] The word begins with B. [Points to the two Puerto Rican students in the classroom.] You Hispanic students have some insight here? [No response from two students. Long pause.] *Barrio.* She grew up in *El Barrio.*

The researchers felt students' lack of engagement and interpreted the scene as one of many instances of the teacher communicating to students "her own discomfort with ethnic difference," particularly with what she called this "Puerto Rican literature." Mrs. L. believed that texts had fixed cultural knowledge and "universal themes" which might, like any text, empower students with greater information. Minutes after the above excerpt she "disparaged the vernacular used by the main characters" when she stopped reading to say: "These kids haven't had Mrs. L.'s grammar class yet." She was a good traditional teacher, Bigler and Collins (1995) conclude, but felt uncomfortable moving beyond what she saw as factual aspects of texts and mainstream language, toward more "dangerous discourses" about race and ethnicity.

The ethnographers describing these classrooms reasoned that the dominant metaphors guiding these teachers were those of transmitting information, of "banking education" (Freire, 1970) in which the teacher dispenses knowledge to passive student recipients. They argue that teachers who have passed through an educational system dominated by such authoritative knowledge, often take this stance to their teaching of multicultural literature, too. Without opportunities to re-envision knowledge as socially constructed, these teachers actively excluded student aesthetic responses, personal experiences, and community knowledge as out of place. In these circumstance, students had little opportunity to make sense from their frames of reference. They were being socialized into a passive "culture of silence" (Freire, 1970) even in the teaching of multicultural literatures.

Empowerment as Access to Academic Literacy

In the second approach to multicultural empowerment, teachers provided *access* to mainstream literacy for diverse students, particularly those from cultural groups seen as marginalized in the past. Rather than using aesthetic response (Rosenblatt, 1978) and the empathy of "lived-through experience" to develop awareness of multicultural perspectives (Greene, 1992), these teachers tended to construct awareness of perspectives and cultural differences of "others" analytically, through guided close reading of text. In these classrooms, culture was treated as a more-or-less fixed entity to be logically derived from reading. Opportunity for student response to and thinking about literature in discussion varied across the classes in this group, but much more teacher-student dialogue occurred in journal writing than in speaking. Generally, these teachers focused their attention to the written word, more than to the spoken word, and to the linear analysis, rather than the narrative experience (Bruner, 1986, 1996). They grounded their views in an American belief in hard work, individualism, and the power of academic literacy to equalize social injustice.

The teachers in this group were most concerned about the processes of analyzing text—skills they felt students needed to learn, both for individual enrichment and to negotiate standards expected of good students and literate people. The teachers told stories about students they had seen who easily "fall between the cracks," never gaining access to academic literacy. Jenny (Zigo, 1996), an experienced teacher in a suburban school, relied extensively on demonstrating and explaining her own approaches to assignments, teaching students approaches such as "finding a narrow focus" and "showing, not telling" in writing and "supporting the theme" and "understanding characterization" in reading. She emphasized students' learning the kind of academic literacy she associated with success in American high schools, an approach toward literature Jenny referred to as learning "strategies of deep reading." For example, students were often asked to re-read to find and quote textual evidence. The scaffolded process for this kind of reading became for students *the only way* to read and write, and most learned to follow this mainstream academic approach to all texts.

Although some of these teachers were avid readers who occasionally shared their own responses, little class time was given over to students' sharing responses or discussing possible meanings. Summary and analysis tended to supplant building personally meaningful interpretations (Langer, 1995) and aesthetic response and reflection (Newell and Durst, 1993; Rosenblatt, 1978; Vygotsky, 1971). For instance, in a discussion of the novel *Shabanu*, Jenny helped students with the process of constructing an unfamiliar cultural perspective, to understand why Shabanu's family needs outweighed her feelings about a marriage partner. Jenny approached this topic as a deductive analytic process of finding evidence from the text for the singular teacher-provided interpretation: the harsh desert climate had shaped their community norms. In Jenny's class, all public meaning-construction was guided in this way. From the perspectives of the teachers in this group, such talk was aimed at empowering students with logical-deductive tools for academic literacy, mainly to develop abilities to write about literature in formal academic formats.

In addition, while teachers in this group sometimes used open-ended questions, they nonetheless in their talk steered student responses to literary texts towards opinions held by the mainstream culture. For example, Jenny (Zigo, 1996) scaffolded her ninth-grade students' search for evidence in *To Kill a Mockingbird* to support the idea that Tom Robinson, the African-American accused of rape, was courageous. One white student, Brittany, questioned this view, arguably the mainstream perspective. Brittany asked whether the author hadn't made Tom a stereotypically passive Negro. The teacher acknowledged this as a "good question," but cut off discussion, saying there was no time to explore it at that moment, that they would come back to it the next day after they finished supporting the Tom Robinson-as-courageous idea. Discussion of Brittany's question never occurred, however, and few similarly challenging questions were raised for the remainder of the unit. This teacher explicitly focused on scaffolding the academic literacy learning of students with special attention to those with different needs (a girl who was deaf), with different language fluency (boys and girls who spoke English as a second language), and with different home socialization (boys and girls from working class backgrounds). Although she read multicultural literature avidly and included it from time to time as whole-class reading, Jenny selected books for their potential to push students' academic literacy learning (e.g., analysis of how the author constructed text to create a theme) by tracing department or course themes (e.g., "responsibility"), and not for their possibilities to engage students in dialogues about their responses to such texts or about sociopolitical issues raised by texts.

In this group of teachers, multicultural texts were sometimes selected because they *contained* the theme of empowerment through education and academic literacy. Brandy Davis (Miller, 1996a; also Trzyna, 1997), an African-American teacher in a largely African-American urban classroom, used multicultural literature to provide stories of how people could be empowered by literacy and schooling. For instance, she selected *Manchild in the Promised Land* for her 11th grade class in order to introduce Claude Brown, a Black gang member who became a lawyer and writer, as a positive role model. She wanted to show "some alternative paths in life" she felt were often missing, particularly for African-American males in their urban communities. Brandy focused in classroom talk on her analysis of Claude Brown's changing attitudes toward his street life in 1950s Harlem, which she constructed through a series of questions about changes in his responses and actions over time. Brandy did not see classroom conversations as the means for raising and pursuing questions about society and racism, and when students' strong emotions about the text arose, Brandy did not have strategies for dealing with them. We will return to Brandy's class-room later to examine more closely how her singular literacy-as-empowerment approach to enacting multicultural curriculum influenced her teaching and her students' experience in the class and was influenced by the politics of the school.

Fostering Student Dialogue and Reflection

In the third view of empowering students, eight teachers saw multicultural empowerment as fostering student *dialogue and reflection* on the multiple, sometimes conflicting languages for understanding texts and social issues. These teachers treated culture as a complex relationship between individuals and social groups in which meanings and values are shaped and transformed through social relations (Hoffman, 1996). In these classes, differences in students' cultures and their ways of thinking were seen as natural resources for open-forum discussion aimed at reflecting on multiple viewpoints on texts and the world (Bridges, 1979). Such discussions were seen as essential components of empowerment where participants' social and cultural knowledge of other texts, media, and lived experience became part of the conversation and meaning-making. In varying degrees, classes formed democratic communities—valuing difference and talking/acting together. These teachers did not ignore learning cultural knowledge from texts or learning academic literacy in analytic essays—the two approaches favored by the first two groups of teachers; however, responding to and understanding texts through discussion was con-strued by teachers in these classes as the primary means of empow-erment. Seven of these teachers were identified through a lengthy progressive focusing process specifically aimed at seeking out teachers who were using multicultural literature discussion as a central activity (Athanases, 1993; Kutno, 1996; Miller, 1996a, 1996b). In these different contexts teachers engaged students in talk and activity which emphasized open-forum discussion and other activities for learning to make personal and social connec-tions, to engage in social and critical inquiry, and to develop social "habits of the heart" (Bellah et al., 1996).

Within this group of teachers who emphasized discussion of

multicultural texts, teachers particularly emphasized making personal and social connections through discussion of stories as instruments of empathy. Suburban teachers like Lauren (Miller, 1996a) and Meg (Kutno, 1996) used *The Learning Tree* and *The Joy Luck Club* to provide insight into U.S. cultural groups not present in their mostly white schools. They both provided opportunities for students to share their initial feelings and thoughts about their reading of texts. Often Lauren asked students to answer questions such as how they felt about the mother or if they had ever had experiences like the daughter's. Meg, similarly, asked students to engage with the text and orally share their written responses after reading *The Fifth Son*; she used those responses as the basis to initiate discussion of the texts. These teachers invited students to consider humanizing possibilities by both understanding their own experiences and "looking through diverse others' eyes" (Greene, 1992).

Open-forum discussion of student stories, experiential responses, and questions were central to each class with this group of teachers. Links between the individual and the group grew through conversations about responses, stories, and experiences and was evident in many interview comments. In one team-taught integrated Literature-History class (Miller, 1996b), for instance, the English teacher Sharon said the class discussion was the glue that held the group together. Ron, the social studies teacher, said, "It's like food for them." One of their students, Kim, told me, "The class wouldn't be the same if any one of the people wasn't there . . . like when Jason was gone everybody knew it. . . . It's such a big web almost." By the end of the year, Kris saw herself as part of a "network of people who spread multiple possibilities." In light of Kris's work over the school year, detailed in her case study (Trzyna and Miller, 1997), her words suggest a new vision of herself as an active member of a democratic community. The metaphors of "network" or "web" emphasize a context of mutual teaching and learning, blurring the boundaries of who learns, who teaches, and what constitutes appropriate knowledge in school.

The teachers in this group were at different places in learning how to empower students by fostering dialogue and reflection. Some of the teachers also specifically scaffolded social and critical inquiry of multicultural texts, the contexts in which they were written, and the related worlds in which students lived. These teachers explicitly invited issues of race and diversity into discussions; students learned to raise and explore these and other issues openly. In the Athanases (1993) study, Reiko's 10th grade urban class, in particular, challenged students to explore issues of race and diversity with the support of their teacher. For example, in small and large-group discussions students talked about segregation and about the taboo in *Black Boy* of mentioning the mixed-race ancestry of Richard Wright's mother. Reiko took up the challenge of introducing race into the discussion of a more canonical work, *Othello*, the story of a valorous Moor living in Venice who marries Desdemona, a white woman: "I want to bring something up. . . . Do you think Othello's being a non-European contributed to any of the outcome?" A number of students answered "Yes," and Reiko followed up: "In what way? And a related question, to what extent was Othello's and Desdemona's love undermined by society? . . . Anybody want to talk about that?" The students wanted to talk about that and an extended discussion ensued in which the African American students were actively involved. Tanisha told a personal story about the experiences of her bi-racial parents as a way to elaborate and connect to the text while pursuing issues of race in the play. Later Reiko asked for some speculative thinking: If Othello were the only black man in Omaha, did students think that the fact that he was black would undermine his confidence? In this conversation students made links from a more distant time and place to one familiar to students and used hypothetical thinking to place themselves in the action of the literature. Later, in an analytic paper, Reiko's students formulated an opinion about the text and supported their own constructed thesis: thus, academic literacy was a goal in this classroom, but not the only goal. During discussions students shared experiences and the teacher moved them to talk about issues of culture, race, and ethnicity in ways which are distinctly different from the aversion to and distancing of these topics which were tendencies among the teachers who taught from the first two theories of empowerment.

Taken together, these three different approaches to "empowering" students through multicultural literatures represent different politics and present very different opportunities for learning. We return now to one of the classrooms to examine an incident in Brandy's 11th grade English class where the teacher's curricular and pedagogical objectives were enacted from the second perspective of providing access to mainstream academic literacy for marginalized students. This incident provides a pivotal point from which to examine what views of empowerment can mean for students and for multicultural curriculum practice.

Conflicts of Race and Power in the Literature Classroom

In this section we examine an incident in which the students and an 11th grade English teacher, Brandy Davis, struggled when issues of race and power arose in their class. These issues were brought to the forefront when Derrick, an African American student in Brandy's class (Miller, 1996a; Trzyna, 1997), expressed passionate and deeply personal feelings of anger and frustration at the social injustices which Claude Brown felt and with which Derrick identified in his reading of *Manchild in the Promised Land.*

This text is an autobiographical coming-of-age story set in inner city Harlem during the 1950s. Claude is a young, African American man who quits school and becomes more and more involved with a life of crime, gangs, and drugs and eventually spends time in prison. Fortunately, through the mentoring of a teacher, Claude is able to find his way out of this harmful life path. He eventually finishes school, graduates from law school, and becomes both a lawyer and writer.

To begin, we position the reading of the text *Manchild in the Promised Land* in the context of the school and the learning environment of this particular urban class. Derrick and his classmates attended a largely Latino/a and African American public school with a college preparation program in western New York (18% white students), with 60% of students below the poverty level. These were not the best and the brightest in the school district, Brandy explained. She saw Renaissance High School reputationally as second tier behind a handful of more prestigious ones. Her students had not been accepted into the top academic magnet schools in the testing and application system used to assign high school placements. To some extent, these students had chosen to be successful, but Brandy saw them as also lured by the call of gangs and drugs in their neighborhoods.

In interviews we conducted with Brandy, she gave compelling reasons for teaching multicultural literature. Among them were these three: 1) to enable students to become independent thinkers; 2) to help students understand how literature relates to life; and 3) to have students develop an opinion about the literature they read. This stance toward literacy seems akin to a reader-response (Rosenblatt, 1978) perspective on teaching literature in her reference to relating literature to life. Brandy's stated intent was to guide students through an empathetic connection to the characters and events in the text. However, she never moved too far from her own analytic reading of the text. Although she said she intended for students to make strong experiential connections to Claude Brown and the series of incidents in which he changed his life through literacy, her pedagogy and question-posing allowed for only a thematic analysis of the story.

One other aspect of the learning environment important in the class was Brandy's underlying sense of caring that framed the relations she constructed with her students. Brandy's vision of caring was exemplified in a myriad of almost daily events such as the candy bars she would tape to the quizzes she returned and her reference to the students being a "family" and the class as a place where they did not have to be embarrassed by mistakes. This caring was often felt and reciprocated by her students who told us that their teacher "is not just into getting her lesson across. She's about teaching. Teaching is more personal. It seems like she cares."

These two notions of teaching—belief in the potential of literacy to engage students in positive life changes and this ethic of care—formed the center of Brandy's teaching and provide insight into the established social dynamic at the time the class was reading *Manchild in the Promised Land*. When asked about her reasons for teaching *Manchild*, Brandy expressed concern for the future of her students, particularly the African American males:

> I have a lot of young men in my class who have kind of turned off. They think that [life in the inner city] is the only thing for them. But [Claude Brown] turned his life around and became a success story.

She wanted the young men in her class to connect Claude Brown's experiences to their own and to understand that

> He's the same as you. He was stealing. He was in the hood. He was in gang activity. He even went to juvenile homes. I mean, he had it bad. But he looked at himself, looked at the situation, and decided there's more. I can do more. I can be more. I don't have to accept this. This doesn't have to be the end of it for me. I really kind of want them to get that message.

Brandy's motivation for teaching *Manchild* stated here as "to get that message," guided her stance toward this text. By helping her students to make connections between their own lives and the life of Claude Brown, she would use the literature text as a vehicle for advancing the traditional American dream of the individual pulling him or herself up by the bootstraps, surmounting social obstacles, and making "a success story" of one's life. Brandy hoped to interrupt the lived experiences of her students by presenting them with alternatives. She did not perceive the goals of teaching multicultural literature as that of interrogating the sociocultural politics of experience which might stand in the way of these alternatives, though. Brandy, in her teaching of *Manchild,* explicitly made the decision to avoid issues of power and racism. In a class of students comprised predominantly of students of color, this decision effectively preempted the validity of an aesthetic or critical response to literature arising from one's own "lived through experience" (Greene, 1992). Later, we'll explore her reasons for this decision and suggest its implications for teaching multicultural literature.

THE "INCIDENT." During the late Fall, students were required to present oral reports on *Manchild in the Promised Land*, working in collaboration with a partner to devise a plan for talking about their particular chapter. The reports tended toward plot summary, and Brandy would generally ask clarifying questions in an effort to assist students to think more about themes she saw in the story. Often, too, she would connect class discussion to current local events. For example, in one case, students were talking about how the characters in *Manchild* were more concerned about their reputations on the street as fighters than they were about the risk of getting hurt or killed. Brandy recalled a news story about a young man recently found dead in his car, shot in the head, and asked the class "Was it worth it"? A male student replied that you can't go around in the hood being afraid because then people are more likely to cause you trouble. Brandy agreed that you can't go around being afraid. However, she reframed this lack of fear as a result of not running with gangs and asserted that it is possible to live in the hood and not get caught up in a "violent lifestyle."

As this small exchange illustrates, Brandy used the students' oral reports to engage the class in talk about their understanding of the text. She led students to consider the book as a story with a "message" and to think about alternatives to violence as a way of life. But she did not interrogate the larger sociocultural/sociopolitical context which contributes to the characters in *Manchild* opting for a life on the streets. Her focus was solely on the capacity of the individual to surmount these obstacles and rise above life situations. As we'll now see, the way in which Derrick takes up meaning in *Manchild* was not in keeping with Brandy's purpose.

Derrick and his partner reported on the chapter in which Claude Brown becomes increasingly aware of the growing power of the Black Muslims in Harlem. More and more of Claude's friends are converting to the Muslim faith as an expression of their resistance to the oppression inflicted on them by a white society. His friends speak about the need for the black man to rise up and revolt against the white man. Throughout the chapter, there is much talk about the anger that black men feel towards white society and their readiness to die for the sake of the revolution. They also speak of how the white man has robbed them of their identity. One of Claude's friends tells him:

> Man you know what's wrong with people out there? They don't realize who they are. They don't realize what they are. We're not Negro, and we're not colored. These are words that somebody else gave us, that the white devils gave us . . . to help rob us of our own identity. We're black men and we've even been taught to be ashamed of it, when, actually we should all be proud of it.

At this point in the book, Claude is at a crossroads in his life. He's trying to understand where he fits, where he belongs in a white world. And although he does not accept what he believes to be the extreme views of his Muslim friends, he feels the same frustration as they feel. And so does Derrick. These three themes—loss of identity, revolution, and the effect of societal forces outside of one's immediate control—came together for him in a configuration which prompted him to enter into the text in a racial and gendered way. This became clear when Derrick delivered his oral report as well as later in his subsequent interviews.

Derrick began his part of the report by explaining the sequence of events in the chapter, but within a very few minutes, he was no longer able to contain the intensity of his emotional connection to Claude Brown's story. When Derrick referred to the Muslim revolution and the willingness of black men to die for freedom, he exclaimed in a voice overcome with passion and anger, "Black people are killing other black people! . . . That's not impressing me! If you want to impress me, black people should kill the white man!"

The response of the class was immediate and emotional. Miranda, an African American girl, shouted out, "That ain't right!"

Several white girls began to cry and, as one of the girls later told the school principal, "Some of us were scared . . . there's going to be a black revolution!" Brandy immediately ended the oral report and told Derrick to "sit down." The remainder of the class period degenerated as students angrily argued among themselves. After the class, several of the white girls apparently went to the principal. They said that they believed Brandy was racist because, in their opinion, she did nothing to punish Derrick for his statement.

The next day when class began, Derrick was initially absent from the room. Brandy began the class by telling students that they needed to talk about what had happened the day before. She expressed her opinion that those students who had gone to the principal should have come to speak to her first and those who thought she was racist really didn't know her at all. As Brandy continued, it became clear that her objectives were to get students to forget about what Derrick had said and to put it behind them. "You have a right to be offended," she told them, "but if he's going to apologize, why can't we get over this? Twenty people who see a single incident will see it twenty different ways. We'll never come to a resolution about this, which is why I don't want to talk about it." As she spoke, students became more and more animated and emotional. One white male student commented that if it had been a white student who had made the remark, the black students would never have "stood for it."

At this time, Derrick and the school principal, a white middle-aged man, entered the room. Derrick sat at his desk while the principal spent several minutes addressing the class. Throughout his lecture, the students remained attentive and quiet. He made several points which are significant in understanding the school's stance toward race and diversity and the ways in which this stance emerged in this classroom. He began by telling the students that they were all his kids. He told them that he had served in Vietnam, where he had been wounded three times, and even in its darkest moments, America is his country and he supports it. When he was in a bunker, he told them, he didn't care if the person next to him was black. He just wanted to know that the man was his friend and would help him. The principal went on to ask the students if they had ever bothered to look around the school auditorium during assembly and notice the diversity of students. He told them that there were many different faces, black, white, and Asian and the school derived its strength from this diversity. Whether we came to this country because of slavery or because of political or religious persecution, he said, every one of us has made a contribution to make America what it is today: Different isn't good or bad, it's just different. He finished by telling the students, "You are the future of this country," and concluded that the way they chose to relate with each other would determine that future.

When the principal was done speaking, Derrick walked to the front of the room and read to the class a letter of apology. The writing of this letter, as well as its contents, was entirely Derrick's idea. No one demanded that he write the letter or even suggested that he apologize. In part, his letter read:

> I would like to apologize for the comment that I made yesterday about killing the white man. . . . When you are in the predicament of being oppressed for so long and your own people are fighting amongst themselves and you come from the type of environment such as a Claude Brown, the inner frustration builds up. When I was speaking of the white man, I mean the man that raped my mother. I mean the man that laid off my father. The man that had my sister strung out on crack. And the man that beat my brother to death. . . . I am not apologizing because people are angry at me, for this is what I feel. But I apologize for not fully addressing myself. . . . The one thing that no one else can ever put shackles on is the mind and what you believe. I spoke my mind and that's what was a mistake and I realize my mistake. . . . I am not a racist. . . . But like Claude Brown, I'm going through a refining process. In the future, I will try not to make a generalization like that because I thought about if the situation was reversed.

When he was done reading, no one spoke to Derrick or acknowledged his apology. Within a few seconds of his finishing, the bell rang to end the class period. In a subsequent interview, Derrick said that he wrote this letter as soon as he got home that afternoon as a way of explaining and clarifying what he had been trying to express in his oral report.

Kochman's (1981) description of African American styles of communication suggests that in general African Americans tend to use more emotionally intense argumentation with forceful outputs, such as raising the voice, as contrasted with European Americans' preference for discussion and subdued voices. In contrast to his outburst in class, Derrick's apology seems carefully considered and constructed. Assuming that Derrick has not had extensive experiences with written apologies, we think it is possible to interpret his initiative at writing this one as an attempt to use a dominant cultural approach to conflict resolution to maintain relationships with the students and the teacher in his class, perhaps with the school. His protection of the sensibilities of the class while asserting his right to his feelings of frustration was rhetorically difficult. We sense his choice of "mentors" in this task, consciously or not we do not know, was Martin Luther King, Jr. Derrick's apology revoices (Bakhtin, 1986) King's words (1963) in "Letter from a Birmingham Jail" as he explains why he and the Southern Christian Leadership Conference did not wait to stage non-violent demonstrations to protest racial discrimination in the city:

> But when you have seen vicious mobs lynch your mothers and fathers at will and drown your sisters and brothers at whim; when you have seen hate-filled policemen curse, kick, brutalize and even kill your black brothers and sisters with impunity; when you see the vast majority of your twenty million Negro brothers smothering in an air-tight cage of poverty in the midst of an affluent society . . . then you will understand why we find it difficult to wait. (p. 9)

This enlarging of the "family" to include many Negro mothers and fathers, sisters and brothers, was the same strategy with the same cadence which Derrick employed. In this same letter, Martin Luther King, Jr. also responded to Elijah Muhammad's Muslim movement, which Claude Brown and then Derrick struggled with. King saw it as a force of "bitterness and hatred" which is "nourished by the contemporary frustration over the continued existence of racial discrimination" (p. 21). If racism had been a permitted topic of open conversation in the class or in the school, Brandy might have provided the historical context for the chapter Derrick reported on, a historical dialogue among diverse voices on this issue, including the voice of Malcolm X—who embraced and then criticized the black separatist Muslim movement. Such an approach would have made racism and those most affected by it visible in the classroom as participants in an ongoing discussion. A major problem of silencing voices and erasing perspectives was one Martin Luther King stated in 1963 about the dilemma of black Americans who were "bogged down in the tragic attempt to live in monologue rather than dialogue" (p. 7). Derrick and Brandy and the other students in their class seemed to be "bogged down" in this same attempt to force a singular interpretation on complex texts and social issues.

Derrick yearns for such a dialogue, it seems, and much of Derrick's thinking, expressed in what he said and what he wrote, is grounded in his struggle for voice, for visibility—for identity as a young, African American man. In interviews with him, Derrick expressed frustration over his belief that he had been trying to tell "other people" the "true story" of black people but that no one wants to listen to him:

> Even the black students in the class don't like me saying stuff about black people. . . . It makes me feel like the only person in the class. . . . If we're having a discussion, somebody is suppose to say, "I hear you Derrick. I hear what you're saying." . . . [Instead] they all are jumping on me . . . and I feel like the whole world's on me.

Looking for some confirmation, some recognition and acknowledgment—"I hear what you're saying"—if not endorsement, Derrick felt he received none, and this claim was in part borne out by others. In interviews with other students, both black and white, as well as the teacher in this class, they all expressed strong opinions about the need to *not* speak of issues of race. Beth, a white female in the class, explained her rationale, revoicing the principal's concerns:

> We can't go anywhere unless we unite as a people. A people completely. And Derrick's always trying to separate the black people.

Javier, a male of Latino descent, explained what he saw as the general school context:

> Because there's a lot of different races here [at the high school], the class discussions try not to surround around that because . . . it's a really touchy subject.

Although Javier claims that race was "a really touchy subject" in the school, Amanda, an African American female in the class, completely dismissed race as an issue:

> I try to stay away from [Derrick] when he starts talking
> about black this and black that. We're *one* because we all
> here together and we gonna also have to survive together.
> He's not going to survive if he keeps thinking the way he
> thinks. . . . [Racism] is not even an issue to us.

Amanda first points to the necessity of unity of Americans "to survive together," much like the principal's Vietnam bunker imagery;
but then she singles out Derrick as "not going to survive" as an individual. Perhaps racism "is not even an issue" among those who perceive lethal danger for Derrick due to "the way he thinks." As Spina
and Tai (1998) argue, the "invisibility of race" is constructed
socially through the discourse of schooling and becomes internal-
ized by those who choose to be successful academically; they
develop a personal identity without race. Perhaps these students,
too, have found that to be successful students in this school, they
must attempt "to render their skin color—their Blackness—meaningless" (p. 40).

The most elaborated reflection on the need to silence talk of
racism came in an interview with Brandy Davis, the teacher of
African American descent:

> In a school like this sometimes you get [racism] dredged up.
> Then what do you do with it once you get it *open*? Once we
> start talking about this, how do we change? Are we going to
> change our feelings? Are we going to change where we live?
> It's not going to change anything. *So let's just not talk about
> it*. Not because I think it doesn't need talking about. But
> then, once you get it out there, it should effect some change
> and a lot of times it doesn't. *[School] is not the place to chal-
> lenge it. It should be, but it isn't* [our emphasis].

In "Talking about Race, Learning about Racism," Beverly Tatum
(1992) analyzes this unwillingness to hear about racism as a type
of withdrawal from feelings of anger and guilt. In a society such as
ours, she claims, which is strongly predicated on the notion of meritocracy, individualism, and a just society, an intellectual discussion
around racism is likely to reveal what we are most reluctant to
acknowledge. Namely, that racism is not as much within the
purview of the individual as it is a systemic problem that individuals—black or white—have little control over. This distancing from
race and racism, then, became a coping strategy for Brandy to close

down talk about systemic issues she believed could not be challenged in her school.

Derrick's remark highlighted not so much the larger sociopolitical issue of racism in an academic or intellectual debate, but the lived experience of racism in the life of Claude Brown and Derrick and, perhaps, of other members of this 11th grade English class. The perceptual metaphor which Ralph Ellison uses to portray a black man's experience of racism seems relevant here: "I am invisible, understand, simply because people refuse to see me." Because Derrick made racism visible by interrupting the tacit rules of silence to which the school and the students had subscribed, Brandy and the students felt the classroom as a safe space for learning was jeopardized. The collectivity they had felt woven into the social fiber of the classroom seemed to them to be suddenly torn.

All of this is by way of reminding that, although Brandy saw *Manchild* as a place of connection between the African American males in her class and Claude Brown, she did not acknowledge the political overtones of a text that is, at its core, about racism and the unequal distribution of power in our society. When Derrick, in his reading of the text, took up this agenda in the context of a classroom that was depoliticized, no one was prepared to respond to, let alone validate, the way in which he emotionally reacted, perhaps his desperate attempt to open the sociopolitical aspects of the text to critical dialogue. The result, in part, is that both the teacher and the students felt forced to retreat further into an exclusively thematic analysis of Claude Brown's story of positive change. For several months following this incident, the work of the class was centered around closing in the space that Derrick had opened. Brandy talked to Derrick outside of class and told him to "keep quiet" for awhile, mentoring him about the way he should present himself. Much later she referred to his efforts to stay in this "muzzled mode."

"A SOCIALLY RESPONSIBLE ROLE." Yet, part of the irony in the tension created between Derrick's construction of the text and that of his fellow students and the teacher's construction is that it is quite plausible that his reading can also be construed as a socially responsible act of caring. Although he might not have chosen the most appropriate way of conveying his message, as he readily admitted in his apology, Derrick's intent was not one of harm he said, and we believe him. Rather, he desires to bring to conscious awareness those social inequities which he said was leading to frustrations and to African Americans killing each other.

Fordham's (1996) ethnographic work in a predominantly black high school in Washington, DC, is pertinent here. In her portrait of the complexities of understanding blacks' "dilemmas of race, identity, and success" in a community with a history of resistance to school values, Fordham suggests that coping strategies for successful students include transforming black identity into the "purely symbolic" in an effort to achieve academic and thereby economic success. Competing forces include "the dominant society's minimal academic expectations for Black students and their classmates' internal policing for group solidarity," for cultural identity as antagonistic to academic success (pp. 235–236). In contrast, "group solidarity" among blacks and whites in Renaissance High required assimilation of blackness as invisible because it was seen as irrelevant to the quest for academic and economic success. Awareness of race and racism was construed as antagonistic to a unified culture. The vision of the American Dream was constructed in the school as equally within everyone's grasp, if blackness were invisible.

The effects of being black or being white in the school or society were not acceptable topics for conversation except in the form which Brandy offered—lessons for American economic success. This fact had troubled Derrick more and more over his high school years. As he learned more about African-American history outside of school from a "mentor" in his neighborhood, he wanted to bring this community knowledge into the classroom. Whenever he did, however, most responded negatively. Brandy told us that the American History teacher had had trouble with Derrick, for example. "There have been several situations in classes. . . . He and Mr. Grey had some disagreements. And if you know Mr. Grey, he's the type who is not going to back down. It's better that [Derrick] back down." When we asked Derrick if race and racism were topics he had talked about in classes, he said: "In [U. S.] history we talked about that a lot this year and I was mostly the head of that. We got into some really heated discussions about it. The teacher got a temper about it and stuff." Derrick explained one example:

> We got into an argument about where the first man came from and stuff like that because I told the teacher that in third grade or something like that I was taught that man first originated in Greece. And everybody knows that's not

true. And I was just telling him that. And he took it the wrong way. He took it like I'm saying that *he's* telling *me* that.

The social studies teacher felt Derrick was stirring up trouble, Brandy later explained, but after that Derrick and the teacher had "learned to get along, to co-exist peacefully." Derrick's classmates remembered these incidents and were scornful of his efforts—Why didn't he just keep quiet? Why did he keep bringing up that "black stuff"?

Thus, tension materialized when Derrick gave voice to what others had silenced. This pervasive silencing amplified the deep frustration that he felt. Derrick was beginning to historicize racism. He deeply felt the personal effects of racism in his own life and he possessed a strong conviction to speak the truth as he had experienced it. Derrick was becoming critically aware of what was left out of school and its complicit code of silence. He remained strong in his conviction to tell other people what he knew even though, as he told us, "They're not trying to hear it all the time."

But it is not Derrick's words alone which ricocheted dangerously through the space for learning in this classroom. As strongly worded as his language was, its impact has to be seen in light of the politics that shaped this classroom and the school lives of the students and the teacher. This issue is, perhaps, best exemplified in the language of the principal's comments to the class. With his focus on ideological unity and his felt need to define a common society, he framed for the students and the teacher "a cant, a correct vocabulary, a proper way to think and be aware" (Hoffman, 1996, p. 547). Any other way of talking and thinking about race and difference was unacceptable. To do otherwise would require critical reflection[2] on texts and society and what counts as knowledge in the school. In the case of a text that is as much about race and racism as it is about individual success, this might mean examining issues of power and control, a path construed by the school as potentially dangerous. By making blackness and black experience visible, Derrick violated school norms, which had become the norms of the students and the teacher. Ralph Ellison (1947), perhaps, captures Derrick's dilemma: "Without the possibility of action, all knowledge comes to one labeled 'file and forget,' and I can neither file nor forget. . . . There's a possibility that even an invisible man has a socially responsible role to play" (*The Invisible Man*, p. 439).

When we look more closely at the school and curriculum politics around the teaching of multicultural literatures, we see other layers of irony. In this school, as Brandy has pointed out, there is no space for talk around issues of race, racism, and hierarchical social relations because, she feels, there exists no effective means, in the context of the classroom and the school, for this kind of talk to lead to transformative understanding. From such a perspective, the discourse around multicultural literatures excludes a critical self-awareness because, according to Hoffman (1996), such an exclusion safeguards the cultural need to define a common society. In so doing, the perception is that a "safe" space for learning and constructing meaning are preserved. Yet reading texts such as *Manchild in the Promised Land*, which like all novelistic discourse is dialogic (Bakhtin, 1986) or constructed from multiple voices, we create the potential for multiple meanings. In constricted school contexts where multiple meanings are perceived as "dangerous" meanings, teachers and students do not have the support or the strategies they need (taken up in the next section) with which to successfully negotiate multiple and conflicting meanings which emerge from students' social identities and cultural experiences. The outcome is a story like Derrick's. This story is a dramatic example of where reader response falls short with multicultural texts when the dialogue among differences is not an expected and accepted part of the critical negotiation of meaning. It points to what is sometimes missing from literature study in the school and what a pervasive norm of "no discussion" can mean for multicultural education.

Multicultural literature requires questioning and dialogue. Derrick filled in the gaps of *Manchild in the Promised Land*—gaps present in all stories (Bruner, 1986; Iser, 1978)—with his own experiences. He felt the gaps between the discourse allowed in school and the realities of Claude Brown's and his own communities. Derrick's story raises many questions about the status of knowledge and the contexts for schooling, including these: What role might school play in examining these gaps, these problems, as a source of potential hope in and through a dialogue to generate understanding? What would happen if Derrick and his classmates had had the chance to contextualize this autobiography in its historical context with its diverse voices? What if Derrick's raising of alternative black perspectives was construed as "socially responsible" action in the school? What if Brandy had chosen to "teach the conflicts" in the text? (Graff, 1992). What role can school play for Derrick, "as he wonders how blackness colors his life"? (Weaver, 1994, pp. 229–230).

A Case for the Conversational Curriculum

To begin to answer these questions, we return to the third approach to teaching multicultural literature, to consider this case of Derrick and Brandy's class in the context of other classroom possibilities. In doing so, we want to keep in mind how Derrick might have fared in such contexts where differences in cultures and ways of thinking were not seen as deviance, but as natural resources for a dialogue aimed at critical reflection on multiple viewpoints on texts and the world. In the discussion-based classes where teachers actively taught students to question what counts as knowing, the teachers tried to hear what students were saying, and conflicting perspectives were an expected part of the conversation.

Another vision of the American Dream in one such course, an interdisciplinary 11th grade American History and Literature course called "American Dreams, Lost and Found," was created by Sharon and Ron (Miller, 1996b). Their largely white suburban high school in upstate New York with 1500 students was located in a community at the state median on measures of wealth. Their heterogeneous classes tended to attract a more diverse group of students, though; for example, one focal class comprised of (all self-identified)—sixteen European Americans, four African Americans, and four Jewish Americans. The course integrated literature and history from multicultural perspectives within each of four generative themes: immigrant/Native American experiences; justice and oppression; labor; and education. The teachers did not use a U.S. history textbook, they explained to students, because the textbook perspective on American history was a singular one, lacking an interplay of points of view. They turned, instead, to primary sources, like the Constitution, the texts of pivotal Supreme Court cases, and diaries and other first-hand accounts; to literature written from multiple cultural perspectives (e.g., of African Americans, Native Americans, Italian and Slovakian immigrants, Appalachian poor); and to works, including film and documentaries, representing other voices marginalized in textbooks, (particularly women, Vietnam War veterans, laborers). The stories of people's lives in specific times and places were thus made available to students through literature texts and fiction films *and* through autobiography, biography, documentary, and reports. The emphasis in this interdisciplinary class on generating a multiplicity of perspectives and reforming curriculum to reflect the histories and cultures of eth-

nic groups and women is central in descriptions of transformative knowledge for multicultural education (e.g., Banks, 1993,
1995).

For the justice and oppression theme, students read Ann
Petrie's novel *The Street*, watched the documentary *Eyes on the
Prize*, and researched and reported on relevant people, groups,
events. A major continuing project in the class was to question
the notion of a singular "American Dream"; students wrote about
their initial impressions of the "American Dream" and reconsid-
ered it in a final synthesizing paper after looking at American
experience/history all year from multiple perspectives. One student, Kris, described the literature-history integration in this
way: "We talk about the little struggles of people, rather than
only the big struggles of countries." Knowledge of the popular
and local cultures became an explicit topic for consideration,
when Sharon and Ron asked students about the sources of
stereotypes, discrepancies, misconceptions uncovered in their
reading, writing, talking, researching, and reflecting. One hand-
lettered poster on their classroom wall contained what one student told us was Sharon and Ron's motto: "There is no path. We
make the paths as we go."

The diverse materials fueled Sharon and Ron's problem-pos-
ing pedagogy (Freire, 1970), their means of teaching students to
question and construct understanding from the multiple ways of
seeing and knowing. The following brief excerpt from that class
occurred during a discussion of history textbooks, as students used
a critical questioning strategy the teachers had taught students to
use: "Who is speaking? What is the speaker's agenda? What voices
are left out?" Students here had been disagreeing about what
knowledge should be in textbooks:

1. Kris: This is for Andre. Just wondering, if you were in a
   concentration camp and someone was writing about that
   in a history book, wouldn't you want the story of the people in there to be in the book?"
2. Andre: What is a fact? It should just tell what happened.
3. Mark: Facts can also be quotes from people . . .
5. Pam: If a text just had facts it would be thin.
6. Marcos: We could make a book with all facts, but what
   would be the point of reading that book?
7. Lori: It's like, you know there was a Russian Revolution,
   but you don't know what it was about.

Kris (#1), who had written in her journal that reading Native American stories in the class has "set a fire" inside her, asks the class to look through the eyes of someone in a concentration camp to understand the importance of people's stories being represented in history. Despite her passion for this topic, she addresses Andre respectfully, with an explicit appeal to look through others' eyes to understand the human consequences in these public events. Andre (#2) names a problem that has been implicit in the talk about the nature of "facts"—what are they?—and Mark (#3) contends that what people have to say, their stories, would count as "facts," a redefinition to include subjectivities in the factual. Marcos (#5) and Lori (#6) take up her "just facts" idea and collaborate briefly on the idea that history needs to include people's stories in order to understand "the point" or "to know what it was about." They are arguing that we need multiple perspectives to understand human experience. In Sharon and Ron's class, where entering into critically reflective discussions about multicultural literatures had been central, students began to question singular views of historical "facts" which replaced multiple stories of experience—or in Kris's words, "the story of the people."

We wonder what might have happened had Derrick been a part of this class? Or if Brandy had been teaching in this school where support for dialogue about differences had been developed. Perhaps Derrick could have brought his deep interest in African American history and experiences of racism in his life to the many projects of writing, discussing and inquiring. A detailed case study of Rose (Zigo and Miller, 1996), a student in Sharon and Ron's class, provides in its conclusion one possibility for a year-long journey:

> Rose has moved from passively distancing herself from other Blacks, to acknowledging the impact of racism on her own life, and actively seeking out opportunities to explore history, culture, and literature to understand better Black peoples, her Jamaican roots and African American kin. . . . Through the reading of multicultural texts, responding in the safety of her journal, and eventually through taking a more active role in the ongoing dialogues encouraged within the classroom discourse space, Rose has engaged in a more powerful literacy. (pp. 35–36)

In her study of an urban high school where critical discussion was discouraged, Michelle Fine (1987) found destructive silences instead of such a critical literacy—learning "to read, write, create, critique, and transform" (p. 172). Analyses of the influence of teacher beliefs on multiculturalism (Rios, 1996) suggest that the powerful press for silencing talk about race, class, and gender in schools seems to be rooted in cultural stereotypes, unreflective judgments equating difference with deficiency, and the acquiescence of educators who don't want to "rock the boat," a recurring metaphor. Yet other urban school studies (e.g., Athanases, 1993) describe teachers in a university collaboration who—like Sharon and Ron—routinely invited student perspectives and experiences and critical questioning of texts and society to enter into class conversations. Clearly, Brandy did not use multicultural literature for such purposes. Such conversation was undermined by her conflicting disciplinary vision of an authoritative meaning in text and by the politics of her urban school, as represented by the principal's vision of celebrating diversity while quieting talk about racism. If Brandy herself had ever had experiences of struggling with texts, tracing their implications out into the world for social and cultural inquiry, she might have begun the conversation with student connections to the text and the history of Claude Brown's situation— those things that Derrick brought to class in anger. Cutting the text and students off from personal and historical connections was what Brandy had learned to do—in her professional preparation and in this school. The urban and suburban teachers who transformed their curriculum and practice did so in complex transactions, rethinking in their classrooms most often with collegial support for boat-rocking within the cultures of school and society.

In all of the studies reviewed, teacher beliefs constructed within the norms and values of the school and society mediated and constrained the problems and possibilities for students' reflection, literacy learning, and democratic community. The first two versions of empowerment described have merit: cultural knowledge *is* important, and so is gaining access to academic literacy. The teachers who taught from these belief systems perceived they were doing what was best for their students. However, these theories of empowerment as enacted in the studies limited the possibilities for aesthetic response and critical reflection, sometimes cutting students off from their own responses, questions, and thinking. When literature was treated as the source of specific instructive themes or messages, that singular vision constrained what could be said and who could say it. Complex aspects of narratives invite multiplicity (Bruner, 1986, 1996; Rosenblatt, 1978); multicultural literature invites seeing through "minority position perspectives" (Sleeter, 1995). Constraining the possibilities for multicultural narratives, consciously or not, required tight control of the topic and the ways of talking. Brittany's question in Jenny's class, Terrence's response in Ms. LaFitte's class, and Derrick's emotion in Brandy's class all met similar fates.

Empirical work based in sociocultural Vygotskian theories (e.g., Brown, Collins and Duguid,1989; Lave, 1988; Vygotsky, 1978, 1987; Wertsch, 1991) illustrate how talk and activity can structure our ways of thinking and our motivation to engage. From this sociocultural perspective, learners interiorized more than what is directly taught through talk and activity. They also learned stances, attitudes, beliefs, ways of thinking about themselves and the world. Interpreting the study findings from this framework, "No literature discussion" in classes meant students were being enculturated into reading practices which tended to devalue personal and social knowledge and perspectives, thus devaluing multicultural perspectives and the critical questioning which they can prompt. There was little sense in those classes that "the learning outcomes are open" in a way that "democratizes knowledge" (Bridges, 1979, p. 68–69). Students were not so much engaged as potential sources of insight, as much as the teacher engaged them as benefactors of insights, typically of pre-formulated and authoritative school knowledge.

Missing Links between Self and Society

The patterns in these ethnographic stories of the teachers and their students suggest an underlying American ideology of individualism shaping the first two theories of empowerment (Hoffman, 1996). They reflect schools' pervasive focus on individual self-efficacy and self-esteem with high expectations and a "sloganized American dream" (Hamilton, 1996, p. 203). Maintaining the "culture and language of individualism," Bellah and his colleagues (1996) argue, has brought modern American society to a civic crisis in which we "harden our hearts and look out only for ourselves," a disengagement from the larger society which threatens social coherence.

This analytic review across studies with one elaborated case supports the argument that critically empowering students in a multicultural democracy requires more than individualist views of culture, learning, and literacy (Miller, 1993, 1997). To strengthen the endangered capacities—"sense of connection, shared fate, mutual responsibility, community"—we need a pedagogy and curricular contexts which teach us to talk and think and act together (Bellah et al., 1996). The principles and practices of democracy learned through dialogue among differences, promise to construct a cultural capacity for social connection and responsibility (Bellah et al., 1996), what Greene (1992) calls "an expanding community." The teachers taking the dialogic approach to empowerment provided "a working vision of how [such] a society can operate" (Bruner, 1996, p. 79).

In their notion of "reciprocal history" Cornbleth and Waugh (1995) conceptualize a social studies curriculum which focuses on "the interactions and interconnections among diverse individuals and groups over time and in their social-environmental context . . . examined from multiple perspectives or vantage points" (p. 197). We suggest that such a "transformative multiculturalism" would usefully include literature as an occasion for social and cultural inquiry into perspectives. Discussion about differences may not lead to agreement, but could avoid misunderstanding and non-understanding, "thus to better inform action" (Cornbleth and Waugh, 1995, p. 198). In a congruent transdisciplinary vision of the "curriculum as conversation," Applebee (1996) proposes that acting to know the world requires entering into an ongoing dialogue for inventing our understanding in genuine inquiry, linking us and our ideas with others. Classes in urban and suburban schools using a dialogic approach to multicultural texts shaped critically reflective literacy practice and a sense of social connection. If we are to tap the contributions literature and dialogue can make for multicultural education, we might begin by envisioning an expanding classroom community in supportive school contexts where Derrick and all young people can learn both critical habits of mind and social "habits of the heart" (Bellah et al., 1996).

Notes

1. Portions of this chapter have been published in *The Language and Literacy Spectrum*, Volume 8, 1998, and are reproduced with permission.

2. One reader suggests that more than critical reflection is required: "Couldn't a 'touchy' subject be handled poorly and cause more harm than good, as the educators at this school seem to be concerned might happen? This is not to deny benefits of critical reflection—but it seems more com-

plicated than that." We agree that the situation is complex, could be handled poorly, and requires attention beyond the level of classroom processes as well. There are, however, examples of teachers who have created positive contexts for critical reflection on literature and society within classrooms situated in oppressive institutions, providing students with tools for rethinking power relations and the possibilities for social action (e.g., Athanases, 1993; Miller, 1996; Rogers and Soter, 1997). Our point here is that issues of pedagogy—what actually is enacted in classrooms—must be considered as a central issue in curriculum politics.

References

Adams, N.G. (1995). What does it mean? Exploring the myths of multicultural education. *Urban Education, 30*(1), 27–39.

Applebee, A.N. (1993). *Literature in the secondary school: Studies of curriculum and instruction in the United States.* Urbana, IL: National Council of Teachers of English.

Applebee, A.N. (1996). *Curriculum as conversation: Transforming traditions of teaching and learning.* Chicago: University of Chicago Press.

Athanases, S.Z. (1993). Discourse about literature and diversity: A study of two urban tenth-grade classes. *Dissertation Abstracts International,* 54, 05. (University Microfilms No. 93–26, 420)

Athanases, S.Z. and Heath, S.B. (1995). Ethnography in the study of the teaching and learning of English. *Research in the Teaching of English, 29*(3), 263–287.

Bakhtin, M. (1986). *Speech genres and other late essays.* In C. Emerson and M. Holquist (eds.). Austin: University of Texas Press.

Banks, J.A. (1993). The canon debate, knowledge construction, and multicultural education. *Educational Researcher, 22*(5), 4–14.

Banks, J.A. (1995). The historical reconstruction of knowledge about race: Implications for transformative teaching. *Educational Researcher, 24*(2), 15–25.

Bellah, R., Madsen, R., Sullivan, W., Swindler, A., and Tipton, S. (1996). *Habits of the heart: Individualism and commitment in American life.* 2nd ed. New York: Harper and Row.

Bigler, E. and Collins, J. (1995). *Dangerous discourses: The politics of multicultural literature in community and classroom.* Albany: National Research Center on Literature Teaching and Learning, State University of New York.

Bridges, D. (1979). *Education, democracy and discussion.* Winsor, England: NFER.

Brown, C. (1965). *Manchild in the Promised Land.* New York: New American Library.

Brown, J.S., Collins, A. and Duguid, P. (1989). Situated cognition and the culture of learning. *Educational Researcher, 18*(1), 32–42.

Bruner, J. (1986). *Actual minds, possible worlds.* Cambridge, MA: Harvard University Press.

Bruner, J. (1996). *The culture of education.* Cambridge, MA: Harvard University Press.

Cornbleth, C. and Waugh, D. (1995). *The great speckled bird: Multicultural politics and education policymaking.* Mahwah, NJ: Erlbaum (previously published by St. Martin's Press).

Ellison, R. (1947). *The invisible man.* New York: Random House.

Ellsworth, E. (1989). Why doesn't this feel empowering? Working through repressive myths of critical pedagogy. *Harvard Educational Review, 59*(3), 297–394.

Fine, M. (1987). Silencing in public schools. *Language Arts, 64* (2), 157–174.

Fordham, S. (1996). *Blacked out: Dilemmas of race, identity, and success at Capital High.* Chicago: University of Chicago Press.

Freire, P. (1970). *Pedagogy of the oppressed.* New York: New Seabury Press.

Graff, G. (1992). *Beyond the culture wars: How teaching the conflicts can revitalize American education.* New York: W. W. Norton.

Greene, M. (1992). The passions of pluralism: Multiculturalism and the expanding community. *Educational Researcher, 22*(1), 13–18.

Hamilton, M. (1996). Tacit messages: Teachers' cultural models of the classroom. In F. A. Rios (ed.) *Teacher thinking in cultural contexts.* Albany: State University of New York Press.

Hoffman, D.M. (1996). Culture and self in multicultural education: Reflections on discourse, text, and practice. *American Educational Research Journal, 33*(3), 545–569.

Hynds, S. (1997). *On the brink: Negotiating literature and life with adolescents.* New York: Teachers College Press.

Iser, W. (1978). *The act of reading.* Baltimore: Johns Hopkins University Press.

King, M. L., Jr. (1963). *Letter from the Birmingham Jail.* New York: Harper Collins.

Kochman, T. (1981). *Black and white: Styles in conflict.* Chicago: University of Chicago Press.

Kutno, S. (1996). *Policy, practice and learning in two English classrooms: Interpretations of culture, diversity and literacy.* Paper presented at the annual meeting of the National Council of Teachers of English. Chicago.

Langer, J.A. (1990). The process of understanding: Reading for literary and informative purposes. *Research in the Teaching of English, 24*(3), 229–260.

Langer, J.A. (1995). *Envisioning literature: Literary understanding and literature instruction.* New York: Teachers College Press.

Lave, J. (1988). *Cognition in practice: Mind, mathematics and culture in everyday life.* Cambridge: Cambridge University Press.

LeCompte, M.D., Millroy, M.L., and Preissle, J. (eds.) (1992). *The handbook of qualitative research in education.* San Diego, CA: Academic Press.

Lee, H. (1960). *To kill a mockingbird.* Philadelphia, PA: Lippincott.

Marshall, J.D., Smagorinsky, P., and Smith, M.W. (1995). *The language of interpretation: Patterns of discourse in discussions of literature.* NCTE Research Report No. 27. Urbana, IL: National Council of Teachers of English.

Miller, S.M. (1993). Why a dialogic pedagogy? Making space for possible worlds. In S.M. Miller and B. McCaskill (eds.) *Multicultural literature and literacies: Making space for difference.* Albany: State University of New York Press.

Miller, S.M. (1996a). *Negotiating diversity in conflicted space: English teachers constructing multicultural education in the sociopolitical contexts of schools.* Final report to the NCTE Research Foundation.

Miller, S.M. (1996b). *Making the paths: Constructing multicultural texts and critical-narrative discourse in literature-history classes.* Albany, NY: Center for English Learning and Achievement. This report is available on-line at http://www.albany.edu/cela.

Miller, S.M. (1997). Language, democracy and teachers' conceptions of "discussion": What we know from literacy research. *Theory and Research in Social Education, 25*(2), 196–209.

Miller, S.M. and McCaskill, B. (eds.) (1993). *Multicultural literature and literacies: Making space for difference.* Albany: State University of New York Press.

Mohr, N. (1975). Once Upon a Time. In *El Bronx remembered*. New York: Harper Row.

Montecinos and Tidwell (1996). In F. A. Rios (ed.) *Teacher thinking in cultural contexts*. Albany: State University of New York Press.

Newell, G.E. and Durst, R.K. (1993). *Exploring texts: The role of discussion and writing in the teaching and learning of literature*. Norwood, MA: Christopher-Gordon Publisher.

Nieto, S. (1991). *Affirming diversity: The sociopolitical context of multicultural education*. White Plains, NY: Longman.

Parks, G. (1963). *The learning tree*. London: Corgi Books.

Petry, A. (1992). *The street*. Houghton Mifflin.

Rios, F.A. (Ed.) (1996). *Teacher thinking in cultural contexts*. Albany: State University of New York Press.

Rockefeller, T.K.Oh, T., Massiah, L. (1990). *Eyes on the prize: America at the racial crossroads*. Blackside Inc: PBS Video Series.

Rogers, T. (1997). No imagined peaceful place: A story of community, texts, and cultural conversations in one urban high school English classroom. In T. Rogers and A.O. Soter (eds.), *Reading across cultures: Teaching literature in a diverse society*. New York: Teachers College Press.

Rogers, T. and Soter, A.O. (1997). *Reading across cultures: Teaching literature in a diverse society*. New York: Teachers College Press.

Rosenblatt, L.M. (1978). *The reader, the text, the poem*. Carbondale, IL: Southern Illinois University Press.

Sleeter, C. (1995). Reflections on my use of multicultural and critical pedagogy. In C. Sleeter (ed.), *Multicultural education, critical pedagogy, and the politics of difference*. Albany: State University of New York Press.

Sleeter, C.E. and Grant, C.A. (1994). *Making choices for multicultural education: Five approaches to race, class and gender*. New York: Macmillan Publishing Company.

Spina, S.U. and Tai, R.H. (1998). The politics of racial identity: A pedagogy of invisibility. *Educational Researcher* 27(1), 36–40, 48.

Staples, S.F. (1991). *Shabanu: Daughter of the wind*. New York: Random House.

Taylor, M. (1976). *Roll of thunder, Hear my cry*. New York: Dial Press.

Tan, A. (1989). *The joy luck club*. New York: Putnam.

Tatum, B.D. (1992). Talking about race, learning about racism: The application of racial identity development theory in the classroom. *Harvard Educational Review, 62*(6), 1–24.

Trzyna, G.D. (1997). *"They don't want to hear it": Struggle and conflict in the multicultural literature classroom.* Paper presented in November at the annual meeting of the National Council of Teachers of English in Detroit.

Trzyna, G.D. and Miller, S.M. (1997). *A case study of learning: Personal narrative, critical reflection, and Kris's ways of knowing.* Research Monograph Series. Albany, NY: Center on English Learning and Achievement.

Vygotsky, L.S. (1971). *The psychology of art.* Cambridge, MA: M.I.T. Press.

Vygotsky, L.S. (1978). Mind in society. In M. Cole, V. John-Steiner, S. Scribner, and E. Sauberman (Eds.). Cambridge, MA: Harvard University Press.

Vygotsky, L.S. (1987). Thinking and speech. In N. Minick (ed. and trans.) *The collected works of L. S. Vygotsky: Vol. 1, Problems of general psychology.* New York: Plenum.

Weaver, M.S. (1994). Improvisation for piano (After *Mood Indigo*). In M. M. Gillan and J. Gillan (eds.) *Unsettling America: An anthology of contemporary multicultural poetry* (pp. 229–230). New York: Penguin Books.

Wertsch, J.V. (1991). *Voices of the mind.* Cambridge, MA: Harvard University Press.

Wiesel, E. (1985). *The fifth son: A novel.* New York: Summit Books.

Wright, R. (1969). *Black boy: A record of childhood and youth.* New York: Harper and Row.

Zigo, D. (1996). *"All our students are literate": Empowering discourses for less proficient students in a heterogeneous English class.* Paper presented at the annual meeting of the National Council of Teachers of English. Chicago.

Zigo, D. and Miller, S.M. (1996). *Cases of change in a literature-history integration: A Jamaican girl and a Jewish boy.* Final Report submitted to the National Research Center for Literature Teaching and Learning. Albany, NY: NRCLTL (Grant Number G008720278).

7

આ

Curriculum as a Site of Memory:
The Struggle for History in South Africa*

Nadine Dolby

> Pastness is a central element in the socialization of individuals, in the maintenance of group solidarity, in the establishment of or challenge to social legitimation.
>
> —Immanuel Wallerstein (1991, p. 78)

Immanuel Wallerstein's comment on the significance of the control of "pastness" reminds us that history is a critical field of struggle in society, and that no particular historical narrative of a nation at any one time is guaranteed in advance, but instead is a product of contemporary political, economic, and social conditions. The discourse of history changes in numerous circumstances: after a revolution; when a military dictator takes over; when an economic and/or political system collapses; when a previously marginalized group within a society moves to, or towards, the center. Both monumental shifts and a continuous flow of small changes which affect the present guarantee that history is always an open, fluid discourse, which represents at any given moment, "the relation between a present and its past" (Berger, 1972, p. 11).

*The research reported here was supported by a Fulbright award.

In South Africa, history was at the center of a prolonged and bitter conflict during the apartheid years. Afrikaner nationalist historians, claiming scientific "truth" and "objectivity" had control over the history curriculum in schools (Grundlingh, 1990). However their dominance did not go unchallenged: liberal, Marxist, people's, social, Africanist, and revisionist historians all questioned the ideological investments and political project of a history which was used to "provide an intellectual defence for the political domination and control by a white minority government over the black majority" (Kros and Vadi, 1993, p. 92). With the legal and political end of apartheid, the debate over various approaches to the history curriculum are now embedded within the discussions and programs of numerous committees and commissions, all working towards producing a curriculum which more fairly and accurately represents the history of all South Africans.

However as this work proceeds, multiple "sites of memory" (Simon, 1994) simultaneously flourish within South African society. In this paper I examine how one public, government-sponsored site of memory, the Truth and Reconciliation Commission, interacts with a second site of memory, a history classroom in a predominantly white, prestigious girls' high school in Durban, South Africa, which I call Glenmore Girls' High.[1] Through an examination of the interpenetrating dynamics of these sites and their observed impact on the students' interpretation of history, I hope to draw attention to the importance of understanding curriculum within a wide social, political, and cultural context, not solely the narrower confines of the classroom and the school.

Undoubtedly other sites of memory, which I do not discuss specifically, also affect students' interpretation and mediation of the past, including the personal experiences and views of their family and friends, and the official and unofficial views of civil institutions, such as the church. As this study proceeds from an interpretive framework, my intent is less to isolate causal factors or exhaustively map students' positionalities than to provide a cultural analysis of the intersection of two discursive spaces. That is, I explore how a group of students, with a generally shared racial and class background, interpret the history of apartheid in the context of the specific historical conjunction that was South Africa in 1996. What is of interest here is how students interact with the predominant national narratives of "truth" and "reconciliation" which permeated many, if not all, aspects of South African society when this study was undertaken.

human rights in our country, so that the suffering and injustices of the past never occur again."

In early 1996 the Committee on Human Rights Violations began public hearings throughout the country, taking statements from victims or family members of individuals who were killed, tortured, detained, or in other ways suffered gross violations of their human rights. The Committee on Amnesty did not begin public hearings until November 1996. However, speculation, coupled with public discussions of the issue of amnesty, who must apply, and the naming of perpetrators insured that even without actual hearings, perpetrators and amnesty entered the national discourse. Finally, the Committee on Reparation and Rehabilitation is involved with making policy recommendations to the President based on the findings of the other two committees, and thus its work will only come under intense public scrutiny toward the end of the TRC's existence.

Consistent with its mandate, the TRC focuses attention on the cathartic and healing process of truth-telling, both for the individuals involved and more broadly for the South African nation. This healing process, which the TRC literature asserts is vital for the national process of unity and reconciliation, works to illuminate historical truths. As a nation gathers around these stories, it can begin the process of accepting and forgiving its past, and then moving on to a more unified future. Asmal, Asmal and Roberts comment, ". . . we must faithfully record the pain of the past so that a unified nation can call upon that past as a galvanizing force in the large tasks of reconstruction" (1996, p. 6).

As a pedagogic site, the TRC functions to highlight particular truths about apartheid but simultaneously de-emphasizes other truths. For example, in requiring both members of the former government and the banned opposition parties to participate in its hearings, the TRC may suggest an equivalence between the severity of their human rights violations. Commenting on this issue, Asmal, Asmal and Roberts write,

> . . . if reconciliation is to remain solidly grounded, there must be a further recognition: that the old apartheid system was not just practically unsustainable, a 'mistake.' It was, rather, deliberately evil. . . . There was no moral similarity between the goals, instincts, basic values, or even the tactics, of those who fought to end apartheid, when measured against the values and conduct of those who struggled to uphold it. (1996, p. 6–7)

Additionally, and of particular concern to this essay, the TRC gives heightened visibility to the suffering of black victims and the confessions of white perpetrators. In this way the commission structures a historical narrative which emphasizes blacks as victims, whites as perpetrators, and de-emphasizes other dynamics of the apartheid period, such as those of struggle and agency.

While the hearings of the TRC continued through 1998 this paper is solely concerned with its construction and impact during the first few months of its public hearings during 1996, the period which coincides with my research at Glenmore. It is important to remember therefore that my analysis is focused on the TRC's influence and public voice at that specific historical moment—my interpretation of the TRC and its impact on the students at Glenmore Girls' High could have been extremely different if I had conducted this research at a later point.

Glenmore Girls' High[3]

The second new site of memory is a high school history class at Glenmore Girls' High School (GGHS), a formerly white, now multiracial school, located in a predominantly white area of Durban in close proximity to the University of Natal-Durban. At the time of this research the school of 1200 was approximately 70% white and 30% black, the black number including many coloured and Indian girls.[4] However, for purposes of this paper, I will consider the impact of the TRC's historical narrative only on the white students for two reasons: 1) given the small number of black students in the class, it is difficult to provide any generalizable statements about their reactions and 2) furthermore, any analysis of the positions of the black students must also take into account the specificity of their racial identity and differing racial positions within apartheid categorizations (African, Indian, or coloured)—the complexities of which are well beyond the limits of this essay. The white students, given in general a shared gender, race, and class background, are more easily discussed and analyzed as a group, which does not preclude differences among them.

The students who participated in this study were in a project class at the school, which is designed for academically successful and advanced students. Students in project classes are given greater independence in academic work and are specifically targeted for the development of critical thinking skills. During the second academic term of 1996, Mrs. West,[5] the class' history teacher, agreed at my request to teach a unit on the history of apartheid.[6] This, in itself, was a significant intervention, in that the history of apartheid is not taught systematically or regularly in South African schools at this time. Instruction is scattered and sporadic and most often depends on an interested and committed teacher and supportive administration. The national history matriculation exam in 1996 included a question on the history of apartheid but it was one choice among several, thus allowing teachers and students to avoid the topic.

Data collection included observation of approximately ten lessons on the history of apartheid from 1948 to 1960, up to and including the events of the Sharpville massacre. Subsequently 20 of the 25 students in the class were interviewed in groups of 4 to 8 students, and I had two conversations with Mrs. West. The racial composition of the project class was approximately equivalent to that of the school as a whole.

In the remainder of this paper I examine how these students negotiate between these two sites of memory: the TRC and Mrs. West's history classroom. I examine instances of divergence in how the historical narrative of apartheid is framed in each site and argue that the pedagogic site of the classroom is not the dominant one. While Mrs. West's presentation and interpretation of South African history certainly influences her students' view of history, her historical narrative is unable to pierce the story told by the TRC, which operates at a national level to consolidate the "truths" of apartheid.

History in Mrs. West's Classroom

Mrs. West's unit on the history of apartheid covered the time period from 1948, when the Nationalist party took control of the government, to 1960, the year of the Sharpville massacre and the subsequent banning of the African National Congress and the Pan African Congress.[7] Her approach to teaching stresses active student participation and the development of critical thinking skills. For example, her lesson on the Freedom Charter includes an exercise during which students write their own Freedom Charters and then compare them to the one that the Congress Alliance wrote in 1955. In addition she continually asks students to step into the positions of different actors: Africans protesting at Sharpville, the policemen who fired, the politicians who drafted the laws which structured apartheid, the ordinary black people whose lives were changed forever by the force of those laws. Finally she often asks students to critically compare different views of historical events. For example, when teaching about Sharpville she read two contrasting passages which described the event: one taken from a people's history textbook from the 1980s, the other from an Afrikaner nationalist textbook from the 1970s. Broadly conceived her method and philosophy of teaching could be characterized as critical pedagogy (Giroux, 1997), as she actively engaged students in questioning accepted truths and interpretations of history and was committed to presenting a historical narrative that stressed the agency and power of people to be a force for change.

For the majority of the white girls in Mrs. West's class the lessons on apartheid brought many surprises. Previous to the unit they had little factual knowledge about the history of apartheid and were often astonished to find out that change had been so recent. One girl, Jolene, comments,

> I didn't realize it was so recent it was that way. Some of the laws, I looked at my birth certificate at one time, and it said registered as white, and I couldn't believe that that was on my birth certificate. I thought, it didn't really matter to me. I was quite shocked to see it.

Mrs. West's class also provided an opportunity for students to learn more details about the history of the African National Congress and President Mandela. For some students, these lessons prompted a re-evaluation of what they previously thought. Leanne reflects on her changed attitude regarding the African National Congress:

> I didn't know much about the ANC, I thought they were just a terrorist organization. I had no idea they were a peaceful organization, they tried as much as they could to be peaceful and eventually did resort to some violence. I just thought they were a bunch of murderers who went around to kill people and then their leader went to jail and all of a sudden became our president. I had no idea what the ANC was really about.

Mandy relates in a similar vein,

> Before I was not very pro Mandela, but afterwards I came
> to see it was okay. Because before I didn't see how we could
> have someone who was in jail [as president], but Mrs. West
> taught us all the points.

And a few girls, like Susan, reported that their views changed dramatically because of Mrs. West's class. She comments,

> I've sort of grown up in a family, we've been a bit racist at
> times and so I've grown up with those same thoughts and
> idea. But like, when we studied apartheid I realized that
> was a very biased view and I actually decided to change my
> view because I'd been prejudiced before.

In the above comments there are perhaps few surprises. It would be expected that privileged, white students would know little about the structure and impact of apartheid, and it is of course possible that some students, like Mandy and Susan, might change their perspective.[8]

But as my interviews with the students progressed, other, more significant patterns began to emerge. Though Mrs. West had structured a historical narrative which stressed themes of the role of agency and political struggle in the movement for change, the students' comments, for the most part, refused her interpretation and emphasis. Instead, many of them overlaid her historical presentation with the predominant themes emerging from the Truth and Reconciliation hearings, thus replacing her concentration on agency and struggle with an emphasis on morality and confession. In the following section I will pair discussion and reflection on the TRC with Mrs. West's students' comments on the history of apartheid, noting how their discursive construction of history often replicates that of the TRC. By doing so I am not trying to suggest that the students thought only or exclusively through discursive patterns circulating in the larger society. Instead, I am trying to draw attention to the phenomenon that Mrs. West's history and the history promoted by the TRC hearings stressed different facets of the realities under apartheid, and that the students generally seemed more inclined to be comfortable with and accept the TRC's foci as opposed to Mrs. West's.

Black Victims: The Discourse of Morality

While Mrs. West's historical narrative focuses on blacks as victims *who took action* against their suffering through political struggle, the historical narrative of the TRC tends to construct blacks very differently. This construction leads to two predominant discourses in the classroom: that of seeing blacks only as passive victims and the consequent emotions of white guilt.

As the fall of 1996 progressed, TRC hearings became a daily feature on the nightly, state-run newscast and were prominently covered in both daily and weekly newspapers. Overwhelmingly, the footage was of black victims of apartheid telling stories of horror: mothers weeping over the deaths of their children, older men telling of lives which were destroyed because of torture and abuse they endured twenty years or more ago. The victims, their harrowing stories and devastated lives, impinged strongly, if momentarily, on national consciousness. While certainly the suffering of blacks under apartheid is a critical part of the historical memory under construction at the TRC, because these stories which portray blacks solely as victims are not countered by other stories which might emphasize other responses to apartheid, a discourse of morality and pity begins to structure a nation's response to its past.

For the white students in Mrs. West's class there is a general acceptance of the moral violations of apartheid. The TRC is seen as an opportunity for correcting gross human rights violations and, simultaneously, informing an ignorant public. One student, Diane, reflecting the position of many of the white girls in Mrs. West's class, comments,

> The Truth Commission thing, all the stuff that comes out, we never knew anything about how they were being abused and tortured . . . we didn't realize it was that bad, that things like that were happening.

The white girls expressed shock at the inhumane treatment of blacks under apartheid and pity, as another white girl, Sarah, relates, "One woman was crying and crying and crying and crying because her daughter was killed, and that person does deserve to get something."

The moral condemnation of the human rights violations of the apartheid government is understandable—the acts coming to light through the TRC are heinous ones. But the sustained focus on what were, for the most part, traumatic individual experiences under the apartheid system, shifts the focus away from the systemic imposition and enforcement of laws which structured and controlled every aspect of the lives of both ordinary people and the politically aware and involved.

Perhaps more importantly for my purposes here, moral condemnation of the past in the current atmosphere is a relatively easy task. For the girls in Mrs. West's class it is expected and accepted that they will emotionally respond to the stories presented at the TRC, and simultaneously to claim that they as individuals would never support such human rights abuses. What however, becomes more difficult for them is to engage with Mrs. West's version of history, which continually asks them what they would do if they were alive during the 1950s and 1960s. Except for one or two white girls in the class, all concede repeatedly that they would have done nothing to stop the imposition of the laws, nor would they have joined any protests. So, though Mrs. West continually stresses that apartheid would not have ended without collective political action, the white students for the most part cannot understand this connection. One exception to this general trend is Anna, who comments on Mrs. West's unit on apartheid:

> It just changed people's ideas. You see the situation in a different light. You look through different people's eyes: a black person's, an Indian person's, a coloured's, a white's. You see everyone's situation, you just don't see white.

While Anna is able to view history through inhabiting multiple positions, the majority of the white students do not.

In response to the overwhelming stories of black suffering, the white girls consider and weigh how much guilt they should feel for the actions of previous generations. At times the students express that they feel forced to feel guilt. One girl, Beverly, relates how her grandmother reacts to the books and materials on apartheid she brought home during the unit:

> She kept on stopping me and saying she doesn't think that's right. She thinks it's biased, and she said she thinks they are trying to change the books to like make it, because blacks are allowed in our schools, to like make us feel sorry for them. She's not prejudiced in any way but she was saying she thinks the books are a bit biased.

Nadine: What do you think?

Beverly: I think they could be.

Nadine: Could you give me some examples?

Michelle: I mean, quite a lot of the Sharpville pieces we got . . . most of them were like they were peaceful, and suddenly during that peaceful gathering, shots rang out and lots of people were dead. You know, they really put it forward that we should feel guilt because these policemen just shot peaceful people and children were killed, and they told how children tried to protect themselves with plastic bags and stuff, and really hammered it in that we were bad.

Guilt is an omnipresent emotion as the students struggle to figure out how to make sense of their collective past. But as the quotes above indicate, the guilt then quickly turns to feelings of resentment and charges that the material Mrs. West used was biased. Some girls feel that this bias is understandable and that it is natural that things would be more "pro-black," as they define it, for the next few years. But others, like Samantha, feel that the lessons have lacked in perspective and balance:

What I think was really overboard was in our notes where it said they learned English at school but only enough to obey their white master, and I thought that was pushing it a bit far.

Often students try to tie the past to the present by making the assertion that blacks, as well as whites, can be racist. One student, Linda, argues in reference to the reading material used in class:

Also what I found is that they only said about the whites being racist about the blacks. But just for one example in this school there are a lot of blacks who go around making fun of the whites [in Zulu]. They make such bad comments, like I speak Zulu fluently and some of the comments they make about my friends are actually so scary, they are so rude.

White students' initial reaction to learning about apartheid both through the TRC and in their classroom reflects their attempts to understand previous generations' actions and to situate themselves in their new reality. First, they reject the human rights violations of apartheid. As black victims relate their stories through the mechanism of the TRC, students easily join into and accept the almost universally accepted position that these actions were wrong. While to readers in the United States and elsewhere, the condemnation of apartheid might seem commonplace, it is important to remember that widespread disavowal of apartheid by South African whites is not a phenomenon with a long history. Despite their disassocation with apartheid and disapproval of its action, many of the students are hesitant to feel guilt—believing that "the past should stay in the past" and pointing that based on their experiences, blacks, too can be racist, and interpretations biased. As evidence, they point to Mrs. West's notes and their perception of the actions of their black classmates.

A second powerful discursive construction of the past which impacts students is that of confession and forgiveness. While Mrs. West never directly addresses this theme, it is a prevalent discourse undergirding the TRC hearings.

White Confession

For the TRC, reconciliation is achieved through truth and truth, in the case of perpetrators, involves confession. Thus began, in 1996, a societal emphasis on confession, usually though not exclusively white confession. This is not to suggest that everyone saw the need or value in confessing. Some, like PW Botha, denied that their actions required confession. However for those who do confess it appears that ramifications will be few or non-existent. Confession becomes a simple act of speaking, of truth-telling which leads not to punishment, but to reconciliation. As *The New York Times* reported on December 11, 1996,

> In a move that signals that the most heinous crimes of apartheid will be forgiven rather than punished, South Africa's Truth and Reconciliation Commission granted amnesty today to a white police officer who was already serving a life sentence for his role in the slaying of 11 people. (Daley, 1996)

This pairing of confession with reconciliation is a unique and defining aspect of the negotiated South African state. Confession is safe, when, as in this instance, it is located within national priorities of reconciliation.

Furthermore, confession is an individual act; people confess at the TRC as individuals, while systemic responsibility is obscured or deflected. This trend is clearly demonstrated in, for example, the National Party's submission to the TRC, in which they refused to take responsibility for the apartheid system and PW Botha's later refusal to apologize for his government's actions, instead claiming that "Presently a perception exists that your commission is engaged in a witchhunt against the Afrikaner and the security forces of the previous government" (PW Won't Say, 1996, p. 12). Though more recently the TRC has held hearings which focused on the systemic abuses by the education system and the press, the TRC's sustained focus on individual victims and perpetrators during the period of this research obscured the planned and deliberate nature of apartheid.

Finally, in confession all attention is focused on the perpetrator and concern is expressed for his fate. As Sandile Dikeni comments,

> The Europeans love it [confession]. It pushes the moral high-ground back to white people, forces me to accept that they're not entirely bad. They feel sorry, man! We'll kill you if you don't forgive. They'll hug you to death and you don't have an option. And I hate it! (Gevisser, 1996, p. 16)

The white students in Mrs. West's class have compassion for those who confess and are inclined to forgive. During an interview with a group of white students, they asked me what punishments would be administered by the TRC, and I explained the concept of amnesty, adding that it appeared that many individuals who confessed would get amnesty. The following exchange followed my comment:

> *Jolene:* I think that's good, that's very nice. The person who did, say, order the Sharpville shootings, they can confess and maybe they'll feel better. But I don't think they should be condemned for something that happened so long ago. Okay, it killed a lot of people, but why kill another person.
>
> *Debbie:* People who are confessing, I don't think they are going to have the best life after that, people are going to know who they are and there are going to be a lot of bad feelings towards them.

Helen: They might start over, they'll feel better about themselves and they'll start a new life.

In this exchange the victims of the Sharpville massacre are absent, as are ideas of justice and Asmal, Asmal, and Roberts' (1996) concern with the interpretation of apartheid as systemic oppression. Instead the girls' concern is for the perpetrators, their lives, and their futures. While the nation as a whole may debate the wisdom of retribution and the role of forgiveness, the discourse of reconciliation obscures public condemnation of these acts leading to a situation where students can feel pity and concern for both victims and perpetrators.

Often, students express pity for perpetrators based on the assumption that previous generations were less enlightened than the current one. During several class discussions, there are comments such as "People didn't know better," which suggest that South African society passed through a stage of infancy and thus whites who murdered and tortured cannot be held fully responsible for their actions. There is, in general, an acceptance that in the past whites were unaware. Helen comments:

> I think that the majority of the whites had no idea it was that bad for the blacks, they just lived in their white area and didn't see what the black homelands were like. I think they weren't aware.

Shirley, however, makes the important point that perhaps whites were not simply ignorant but that they did not want to know:

> I think a lot of people didn't know about it but they actually really didn't want to find out about it. Because they were fine, they lived happily, they had all the luxuries and they didn't actually want to find out why black people were poor and how bad it was. Because it wasn't affecting them.

But now, through the maturation of South Africa society, they have come to new realizations. One white girl, Beverly, comments:

> I think quite a few people that were so racist during the apartheid era have come to recognize that they were wrong, and surely they know it's wrong.

The public narrative of white confession has strongly influenced the white students' interpretations of the past. Confession, and its resulting emphasis on the humanness of the perpetrator, creates misplaced pity for perpetrators as is demonstrated in the white students' comments about those who killed people at Sharpville. This type of emotional reaction, which is structured through the form and emphasis of the TRC, can lead quite easily to the impression that apartheid was a mistake, instead of, as Asmal, Asmal, and Roberts (1996) argue above, deliberate evil.

In making these comments I am not suggesting that adolescents should be able to critique the discursive construction of history which is created at the TRC. Few students would be able to do that. What is of concern is recognizing that Mrs. West's history lessons, designed to convey to students the vibrancy and power of collective change, cannot speak to the students' understandings of history, which are framed through the national discourse of reconciliation. In other words, I want to stress that the possibilities they can imagine are circumscribed by the representations of historical truth coming from the TRC.

Resituating Curriculum

Curriculum is, among other things, undoubtedly a political project as the new sociology of curriculum and critical curriculum theory have demonstrated over the past twenty years (e.g., Pinar et al., 1995). Teachers such as Mrs. West who "teach against the grain" (Simon, 1992) try to recapture the history of collective struggle so to be able to provide their students with different narratives of the past, and in the process, point them towards the possibility of envisioning and creating new scripts for the future.

Mrs. West's interpretation and approach to teaching about South Africa's past is designed to emphasize that apartheid was a system with political, economic, cultural, and social aspects. Examining and critiquing apartheid's institutional manifestations (e.g., laws) and the actions of the state (e.g., the shootings at Sharpville) are key aspects of Mrs. West's pedagogical approach. Revealing the machine which was apartheid, its structures, and the ramifications of its actions should serve to focus students' attention on the collective nature both of the crime and of the resistance. Mrs. West seeks to provoke not guilt but a sense of shared responsibility for the past, but more critically, for the present and future. Ideally, such an approach should engage students in a critique of both past and present injustices and inequality, and empower them to act collectively for change.

But Mrs. West's curriculum, as enacted in her classroom with her students, interacts with numerous other sites of memory, including the one of predominant interest in this paper, the TRC. For the white students, who have little or no previous knowledge about apartheid, Mrs. West's narrative has only minimal impact. Many students expressed that they had learned something valuable which they had not known before. But beyond the absorption of new facts, Mrs. West's narrative was not so much resisted, as ignored. They did not dispute her story that change happened through the concerted efforts of many ordinary people, but instead found little relevance for it within the contemporary rubric of reconciliation.

South African history, of course, did not dictate that Mrs. West's students ignore her narrative or embrace reconciliation. One can imagine scenarios in which white, middle-class students are angry and bitter, feel defensive, or re-embrace white supremacy. Within the private confines of their homes, students may express some, or all, of those sentiments. But in the public space of the classroom, the national discourse of reconciliation structures their interaction with the past.

The TRC's goals are future-oriented—it promises civil, national, and collective peace through putting closure on the past in the spirit of reconcilation. While the TRC may not have set out to craft a particular construction of South African history, by virtue of its powerful location in society it is in a position to do exactly that. Its legitimacy as a body operating under the direction of the state guarantees that its focus on individual perpetrators and victims has implications for citizens', and specifically here, students', interpretations of the past. By this I do not mean to condemn the actions or decisions of the TRC, but to recognize that as a site of memory it should be analyzed in light both of the historical context under which it was established and the dynamics it creates for the future.

For the last 30 years, curriculum theorists have been concerned with questions of how knowledge is organized, engaged with, critiqued, and resisted. But as scholars such as Simon (1994), Giroux (1994), and others suggest, schools are not the only or the predominant pedagogical site. Efforts to create engaged, critical teachers like Mrs. West, while important, are not adequate by themselves. Such teachers alone cannot transform schools into oppositional sites which produce questioning, critical, involved citizens of a particular nation-state or more broadly the world. Other sites of memory, such as the TRC, exert a powerful influence on creating students' "mattering maps" (Goldstein, 1983).

Through examining one instance of the ways in which two sites of memory interact and conflict, I emphasize that the discourses of any classroom can be interpreted through its interaction with outside forces that shape students' lives and perceptions. In the case of Mrs. West's classroom, the influence of the TRC and its particular construction of history has implications both for how her students understand apartheid, and how they might position themselves as actors in the still unfolding narrative of the new South Africa.

Notes

1. The majority of formerly white schools in Durban are single sex. At the time of this research, there were only two co-ed formerly white high schools in the metropolitan area, both of which were dominated by lower middle-class and working class students, and thus seen as having poor academic standards.

2. The TRC is concerned only with human rights violations which occurred within the context of political conflict in South Africa. A victim of violence must prove that s/he was targeted because of specific political beliefs and/or affiliation. Similarly, to be eligible for amnesty, a perpetrator must also show evidence of political motivation for his/her actions.

3. All names are pseudonyms.

4. Under apartheid, individuals were designated, in general, as members of one of four population groups: African, Indian, coloured, or white. The term "black" then emerged as a category which encompassed Africans, Indians, and coloureds, and signified their common oppression under apartheid. I will use "black" in that way in this essay. However, as necessary and relevant, I will use the above-mentioned specific racial categories. My use of these categories in no way serves as an endorsement of biologically deterministic conceptions of race. Instead, it signifies my understanding of the historical and contemporary import of constructed racial categories within the South African reality. Additionally, in common usage in South Africa, "black" is equated with "African." Thus, in direct quotes from students, black should be understood in that way.

5. Mrs. West, like over 95% of the teaching staff at GGHS, is white. This staffing pattern is typical of formerly white schools, which have in general been resistant to hire black teachers because, as they argue, of concerns about the quality of their training, and the maintenance of stan-

dards. The most common exception to this unwritten policy is that formerly white schools will employ African teachers to teach Zulu.

6. When I met with Mrs. West early in the academic year, she indicated that she had taught a unit on apartheid in previous years and was considering teaching it again in 1996. My request to conduct this research in her classroom was certainly a factor in her decision to include the unit.

7. Space constraints do not allow for me to explain the content of Mrs. West's lessons on apartheid. See Harker (1994) for a succinct overview of apartheid policies, implications, and a chronology.

8. It should not, however, be assumed that black students have substantially more knowledge than whites. Many, if not most, black students are equally uninformed.

References

Asmal, K., Asmal, L., and Roberts, R. (1996). *Reconciliation through truth: A reckoning of apartheid's criminal governance*. Cape Town: David Phillips.

Berger, J. (1972). *Ways of seeing*. London: British Broadcasting Corporation and Penguin Books.

Daley, S. (1996). South Africa frees apartheid killer, hinting at broad amnesty. *The New York Times*, 11 December, A15.

Gevisser, M. (1996, July 26). A voice of truth and dissent. *Mail and Guardian 12*(30), p. 16.

Giroux, H. (1994). *Disturbing pleasures: Learning popular culture*. New York: Routledge.

Giroux, H. (1997). *Pedagogy and the politics of hope: Theory, culture, and schooling*. Boulder, CO: Westview Press.

Goldstein, R. (1983). *The mind-body problem*. New York: Laurel Press.

Grundlingh, A. (1990). Politics, principles and problems of a profession: Afrikaner historians and their discipline, c. 1920–1965. *Perspectives in Education 12*(1), 1–19.

Harker, J. (Ed.). (1994). *The legacy of apartheid*. London: Guardian Newspapers Limited.

Kros, C. and Vadi, I. (1993). Towards a new history curriculum: Reform or reconceptualisation? In N. Taylor (ed.), *Inventing knowledge: Contests in curriculum construction*. Cape Town: Maskew Miller Longman.

Pinar, W., Reynold, W., Slattery, P., and Taubman, P. (1995). *Understanding curriculum: An introduction to the study of historical and contemporary curriculum discourses*. New York: Peter Lang.

PW Won't Say He's Sorry. (1996). *Daily News* (Durban, South Africa), 22 November, 12.

Simon, R. (1992). *Teaching against the grain: Texts for a pedagogy of possibility*. New York: Bergin and Garvey.

Simon, R. (1994). Forms of insurgency in the production of popular memories: The Columbus quincentenary and the pedagogy of counter-commemoration. In H. Giroux and P. McLaren (eds.), *Between borders: Pedagogy and the politics of cultural studies*. New York: Routledge.

Truth and Reconciliation Commission (1996). *Truth: The road to reconciliation*. (Available from Truth and Reconciliation Commission, 9th floor, Old Mutual Bldg, 106 Adderley Street, Cape Town, 8001, South Africa)

Wallerstein, I. (1991). The construction of peoplehood: Racism, nationalism, ethnicity. In E. Balibar and I. Wallerstein (Eds.), *Race, nation, class: Ambiguous identities*. London: Verso.

8

ẽ↩

Understanding Shifts in British Educational Discourses of Social Justice

---

Gaby Weiner

This essay focuses on recent educational developments in the United Kingdom, and in particular on seeking to understand what implications New Right and New Labour education policies have had for social justice and educational in/equality. It draws on the work of Young (1990) to reflect on British discourses of social justice within education; in particular those of social reconstruction of the 1940s, and of school effectiveness and 'zero tolerance' of failure, of the 1990s. It argues that despite the stated intention of new Labour governments in both the 1940s and 1990s to enhance social justice, both educational administrations were profoundly conservative in education. It argues, in particular, that recent education discourses promoted by New Labour—of 'the failing school,' 'school in/effectiveness,' 'inadequate teachers,' 'league performance tables,' 'male underachievement,' and 'inner city blight'—are inherently unfair and therefore inappropriate for the redistribution of educational rewards or increased social justice.

Preamble

The concept of social justice includes all aspects of institutional rules and relations insofar as they are subject to potential collective decision. The concepts of domination and oppression rather than the concept of distribution, should be the starting point for a conception of social justice. (Young, 1990, p. 16)

A review of social justice and equality debates in the United Kingdom and how they have gained currency, shifted, and reformed over the last two decades, seems timely for a number of reasons. Such changes have resonated with Young's 1990 re-framing of the concept of social justice away from Rawlsian conceptions of distributive justice (Rawls, 1971), and also mark two important specific shifts. First, a shift of a personal nature. I have recently moved to take up a post in Sweden and have therefore left, at least temporarily, the immediate educational policy context of the United Kingdom. Second, after 18 years of Conservative government, with its main aim of rolling back the welfare state and its hostility to social equality goals, Britain elected a Labour government (on 1 May 1997) with a stated commitment to increasing social justice.

However, almost as soon as the celebrations died down, it was apparent that the New Labour party was very different from the old Labour party, and appeared to have more in common with the New Right than might have been anticipated. The Labour manifesto commitments, upon which the 1997 general election was fought, were modest not only because of what was widely recognised as the increased conservatism of the British electorate after Thatcherism. The leaders of New Labour, themselves seemed more tolerant of the Conservative government legacy of low-tax, individualism, and deregulation, if rather more critical of the widening gap between the rich and the poor in Britain and of its unequal social outcomes. Simultaneously, as a lecture by Andrew Turnbull, a senior civil servant at South Bank University at the beginning of 1998 pointed out, the centralised government political machinery which was developed to win a general election, found the Labour leadership more comfortable with leading from the front than with the democratic, sometimes unwieldy decision-making processes of old Labour. Moreover, New Labour's commitment to modernisation, a main plank of its election and immediate post election strategy, appeared largely restricted to culture and the media. Government policy remained deeply conservative for both the economy and education.

Thus, despite an initial rhetorical flurry of statements concerning the wish to extend educational equality, there seemed little which separated the education policy of the new (Labour) administration from the old (Conservative) one. Indeed, not only was there a disturbing continuity of previous conservative education policies, but the attacks on teachers, researchers, academics and teacher trainers intensified, as 'old' Labour critics of New Right and New Labour policy were sidelined or cast as anti-modernisers, and as the emasculated Conservative Party could find little with which to disagree.

But at the beginning, early policy initiatives looked highly promising: for example, the withdrawal of the nursery voucher scheme, increased emphasis on the education of children with special needs, and evident awareness and concern about working class and/or black and/or male academic underachievement. However these did not constitute the main plank of New Labour's educational agenda, as any glance through the educational and daily press would confirm. The main agenda appeared rather more dominated by concerns to increase student performance (as measured by examinations and tests) in what were termed 'core' subject areas (literacy, numeracy, science, and information technology) and identification of the most successful strategies to 'raise standards', nationally and locally.

There was little interest shown, for example, in how such changes might affect children and what wider set of values and curricula would be needed to prepare young people for citizenship in the twenty-first century. Rather there was prominent emphasis on promotion of futurist information technology skills and access to the internet, and somewhat contradictorily, on improving literacy and numeracy (that is, reading and arithmetic) which appeared to hark backwards to nineteenth-century 'old' conservatism and traditionalism.

The implications of this quite complex agenda and how we can understand the shifts in perceptions of social justice constitute the main task of this chapter. It draws on Foucault's (1972) conception of archaeology in which he contrasts his archaeological approach with the history of ideas, "an uncertain object, with badly drawn frontiers, methods borrowed from here and there, and an approach lacking rigour and stability" (p. 136). Yet, for Foucault, the history of ideas is able 'to cross boundaries of existing disciplines, to deal with them from the outside, and to reinterpret them' (p. 137). Archaeology, on the other hand, tries to define and expose discourses themselves, not 'the thoughts, representations, images, themes, preoccupations that are concealed or revealed in discourses' (p. 138). Thus Foucault's archaeology has several principles. Its main aim is to define discourses in their specificity and 'to show in what way the set of rules that they put into operation is irreducible to any other' (p. 139). It does not set out to illuminate a moment or recapture that 'elusive nucleus in which the author and the *oevre* exchange identities'. Rather archaeology is a rewriting of what has already been written as 'a systematic description of a discourse-subject' (p. 140).

Such an approach allows for flexibility and malleability, and avoids implications of chronology, linearity, or progress. And such an approach appears to accommodate my attempt, in this paper, to identify discourses of social justice. Two 'snapshots' are provided, of specific periods when British social justice discourses in education have held particular meanings: the 1940s, immediately following World War II; and the 1990s, the decade preceding the millennium. Significantly both periods shared a similar setting of a landslide Labour government elected in, after a long period out of office.

The aim, thus, is to explore how the conceptions of social justice concerning education (long the provenance of the Labour Party) held in the two periods resonate, not only with Rawlsian notions of distributive justice which focus mainly on the possession of material goods and social position, but with Iris Young's five faces of injustice: exploitation, marginalisation, powerlessness, cultural imperialism, and violence. Rawls (1971) argued that in a fair society, distributive justice occurs when individuals acquire claims to share in social benefits regardless of moral behaviour or level of prosperity.

> The sum of transfers and benefits from essential public goods should be arranged so as to enhance the expectations of the least favoured consistent with the required savings and the maintenance of equal liberties . . . a central feature of this conception of distributive social justice is that it contains a large element of pure procedural justice. (Rawls, 1971, p. 304)

However, Young argues that Rawlsian concepts of distributive justice do not go far enough and do not acknowledge more recently developed understandings about injustice.

> Other aspects of justice include decision-making procedures, the social division of labor, and culture. Oppression and domination, I argue, should be the primary terms for conceptualizing injustice. (Young, 1990, p. 9)

Thus, the injustice of *exploitation*, according to Young (1990), consists 'in the social processes that bring about the transfer of energies from one group to another to produce unequal distributions' (p. 53). In the context of United Kingdom education, this could be applied to the largely female teaching workforce which has become increasingly vulnerable to the demands of predominantly male managers, headteachers (principals), and senior inspectors (Maguire and Weiner, 1994). *Marginalization* refers to when 'a whole category of people is expelled from useful participation in social life' (p. 53) and is evident, for example, in the increasing number of school exclusions in the 1990s in the United Kingdom, particularly of black male secondary school students (Gillborn and Gipps, 1996). *Powerlessness* comes from the lack of 'authority, status and sense of self that professionals tend to have' (p. 57), and may be seen in the lack of involvement in, and choice over, their children's schooling of working-class parents compared with middle-class parents (Ball, 1997). *Cultural imperialism* 'involves the universalization of a dominant group's experience and culture, and its establishment as the norm' (p. 59) and is exemplified by the United Kingdom national curriculum which depicts a white male bourgeois view of the world (Burton and Weiner, 1990). *Violence* is here less concerned with the acts of systematic violence against oppressed groups, than with 'the social contexts surrounding them which makes them possible and even acceptable' (p. 61), for instance, as indicated by the levels of bullying and harassment being reported in United Kingdom schools currently (Whitney and Smith, 1993).

According to Young, evidence of the presence of any of the categories indicates injustice, though in different ways and with different ramifications. Thus 'the presence of any of these five categories is sufficient for calling a group oppressed. But different oppressions exhibit different combinations of these forms, as do individuals in the groups' (Young, 1990, p. 64).

This reorientation of concepts of social justice seems particularly applicable for education, as indicated above and as we shall see later. First, however, the next two sections provide a brief outline of the two periods under discussion.

1940s: Educational Discourses of Social Reconstruction and Elitism

The hereditary curse upon English education is its organisation upon lines of social class. (Tawney, 1931, p. 142)

But economic efficiency and social justice tend to be uncomfortable
bedfellows and the particular conception of 'equality of opportunity' which came to dominate English education in the immediate
pre-war and post-war periods owes more to the concern over
wastage of talent than to Tawney's concern for a common culture.
In this conception [of equality of opportunity] . . . class differences
per se were not objected to; class differences between those with
equal ability were what had to be eliminated. (Halsey, Ridge and
Heath, 1980, p. 5)

The main target of excavation for this period is its emphasis
on, and the survival of, selective schooling, despite the existence of
what has been viewed as the most "radical" of the post-war Labour
administrations.

As World War II drew to a close in Britain, there was a huge
national wish to rebuild a better society for future generations. The
wartime coalition government, "united in sacrifice and endeavour"
(Murphy, 1971, p. 110) articulated the need for improved schools
and greater social justice in education provision. This was to be
achieved, for example, by extending the school leaving age (to 15),
providing free secondary school for all, mounting a huge building
programme to replace war-damaged and/or sub-standard school
buildings, creating a teacher training programme to deal with the
massive teacher shortage, and removing religious divisions in education.

However attention has been drawn to the grudging nature of
many of these policies, and also to the fact that they had fundamentally conservative outcomes. For example, in a reappraisal of
Rab Butler, the Conservative architect of the 1944 Education Act
which bore his name and which was later operationalised by the
incoming Labour administration, Ponting criticises the failure to
create parity of esteem between different school types and con-
cludes:

This was culpable neglect and a sordid squandering of a
golden opportunity by a man who knew little and seems to
have cared less about the lives of his less-privileged fellow
citizens or the economic future of his country. Nearly half a
century later we are still lamenting the sorry state of
British education and training. (Ponting, 1990, p. 86)

Ponting refers here to the outcomes of a coalition government
report (the Norwood Report, 1943) leading to the 1944 Education

Act, which recommended the implementation of a system of secondary school selection on a national scale that is a tripartite (or three-way) system of grammar, technical and secondary modern schools, which had begun in the 1930s. Pupils were allocated to their school on the basis of so-called intelligence or IQ tests at the age of 11 which were supposed to be predictive of future academic potential. The belief in the veracity of IQ testing remained, despite various Inspectors' reports between 1922 and 1939 which had drawn attention to the lower test results of poorer children (Floud, Halsey and Martin, 1957). Selection was included in the 1944 Education Act, and on the landslide election of the Labour government in 1945 the decision was taken to retain selection rather than replace it with a common or comprehensive school system, as had been instituted in other European countries (Benn and Chitty, 1996).

The historical legacy of this decision, as Ponting (1990) points out above, was disastrous for many, and has continued to be so. Thus, as Halsey et al. (1980) describe, selective schooling created a ladder into state-funded higher education, which further favoured the educationally advantaged:

> . . . the 1944 Act continued the growth of selective secondary schooling and, particularly in the 1960s, there was an expansion of higher education on a selective basis. The costs of the different forms of education have been such that success in the selective process did not diminish but, if anything, widened the distance between those who got most and those who got least out of the public purse towards the cost of their schooling. (Education of All Handicapped Children Act of 1975, Pub. L. No. 94–142. § 1401, 20 U.S.C.A.)

Similarly, Ainley (1993) points out that the education policy of the post-war Labour administration of 1945–51 ensured that the British class system remained largely intact. Rather than the development of a unified system of state schooling, the tripartite secondary system (grammar, central/technical, secondary-modern) mirrored the three traditional divisions of male labour (brain, non-manual, manual). In practice, state secondary schooling became bipartite as most of the planned central/technical schools failed to materialise. Tripartism was produced, nevertheless, through the combination of private and public schooling viz.

private (called 'public' or independent) schools for the gentry, grammar schools for the middling classes and secondary moderns for working class children.

Other aspects of social justice in education which are more familiar to us today were largely invisible at the time. "Race" and ethnicity issues in education were characterised as colonial rather than "home" concerns, disability remained medicalised in that the responsibility for the education of "abnormal" children lay with the Ministry of Health, and gender differences in education were viewed largely as "natural." Thus, the main response to women of government in the immediate post-war period was to direct them back into the home in order to leave the labour market open for the returning heroes, a response also reflected in the tolerance of so-called natural differences in girls' and boys' schooling (Dean, 1991). For example, girls tended to progress faster than boys in the earlier school years (between the ages of 5 and 11)—and in fact, IQ tests at the age of 11 had a higher pass mark for girls than boys to prevent girls outnumbering boys in the grammar schools. However girls fell back from the age of 13 onwards and were notably under-represented both in entry for public examinations and in numbers who matriculated.

The main conception of social justice or equality of opportunity in education held during this period, then, was of social and economic reconstruction which left elite forms of schooling intact. However in other spheres of government, more egalitarian policies prevailed, for example, the right of the male worker and his family to a range of welfare benefits. These included free education up to the age of 15, and further if he (sic) showed academic potential; a family wage so that he could afford to support a wife and children at home; free access to health-care; and a secure, pensionable retirement.

1990s: Educational Discourses of Regulation and Competition

When we take a half-century leap to the last decade of the twentieth century, we see a different discourse of education emanating from a new Labour administration. If reconstruction and elitism mark the 1940s, terms such as excellence, competition, and marketisation have stood as metaphors for the 1990s as the quotes below, taken from the education press, show.

"English come bottom of the class in maths" (*Independent*, 11.6.1997)

"Benchmark tables will puncture complacency" (*Times Educational Supplement*, 30.1.1998)

"Success starts to heal the scar of bad publicity" (*Times Educational Supplement*, 30.1.1998)

"Star Schools in Basics Crusade: Chief inspector invites 50 top primaries [elementary schools] to be at the cutting edge of training" (*Times Educational Supplement*, 13.2.1998)

The aim of this section is to excavate educational discourses of social justice of 1990s' Britain, focusing particularly on the School Effectiveness Movement (SEM), a pivotal educational force in 1990s British schooling. SEM was originally proposed by researchers (e.g., Rutter et al., 1979; Mortimore et al., 1988) but increasingly became incorporated into Conservative government policy-making in the late 1980s and 1990s. School effectiveness studies emphasise the relationship between teaching and school ethos, and differential outcomes of schooling as measured by examination and other forms of assessment. In attempting to counter a perceived lowering of standards overall, particular prominence was given to these ideas as they seemed to offer simple solutions to what had previously been seen as complex problems. These in turn produced new educational discourses and vocabularies (e.g., performance/process indicators, value-added) which placed the responsibility directly on schools, rather than local or central government, for enhancing and improving the quality of education for the children in their care (Reynolds, 1994; Gray and Wilcox, 1995). SEM proved enticing because of its claim that schools could free pupils and their performance from local and/or socio-economic influences and origins. Thus the level of "standard" achieved was perceived as primarily the responsibility of the "excellent," "good," "satisfactory," "mediocre," "bad," or "failing" teacher or school (Slee, Weiner, and Tomlinson, 1998).

Significantly, and this is particularly poignant given my own and others' earlier work on girls' educational underachievement, the gains made by girls arising, say, from the work of feminists in the 1970s and 1980s, were met with indifference and marginalisation by predominantly white male politicians, bureaucrats, and researchers. Thus, in failing to come to terms with girls' greater participation into education, policy-makers seemed bent on restoring the social justice agenda of the 1950s. Accordingly, girls and young women (now re-inscribed as high achievers) were rendered invisible, as white male youth, once again, became the main object of school reform and concern (Weiner, Arnot, and David, 1997). A similar denial of previous social justice gains was evident in what Gillborn (1995, 1997) calls the "deracialisation" of education policy-making under Thatcherism. Deracialised policy discourses appear inclusive; yet by denying difference, they exclude specific minority groups. Gillborn identifies two further dimensions of deracialisation:

> First, there is a tendency to subsume "race" amid other categories. This robs "race" of any special status and denies its claim to attention. Second, the consistent failure/refusal to conceive of racism as anything but a small scale problem of individual ignorance and "prejudice." (Gillborn, 1995, p. 33)

However, in recent years, there have been proportionally (and increasingly so) higher numbers of black students excluded from (or being thrown out of) school, often for poor behaviour, by schools under pressure to produce academic high achievers (Gillborn and Gipps, 1996). This has raised questions about students' entitlement to an education and thus forced "race" questions onto the Labour agenda once more.

Urban schooling has also become a target of criticism and concern, as the publication of the national results of the Standard Assessment Tasks (SATs) and league tables of test and examination results showed that many urban schools performed relatively poorly compared with other parts of the country. Thus, for example, a 1993 government report on urban schooling couched its findings in largely negative terms: as "disadvantaged urban areas . . . poorly served by the education system" (OFSTED, 1993). Similarly a 1995 United Kingdom government report *Performance in City Schools* defined city schools as those in areas where a large proportion of population has low socio-economic status, where housing and health are poor, where educational qualifications among adults are low and where there are a large number of minority ethnic groups (House of Commons Education Committee, 1995).

Thus, inner city schools were produced within SEM discourses as largely inadequate and likely to fail because "success" and "failure" were measured on the basis of raw assessment scores rather than on the quality of teaching, management, or expectation. Also, the demarcation between so-called "good" and "bad" schools which was refined by inspectors according to school effectiveness criteria, resulted in a devaluation and/or lack of acknowledgement of the *extra* level of skills and training needed by staff teaching in poorer urban contexts. The increased demands made by a heavy bureaucratic and regulatory system ironically removed attention from the very issues it sought to address—reflection on, and improvement to, teaching and learning. Finally, there seemed to be an implicit criticism of many practices and outcomes that constituted the lived experience and values of those studying and teaching in poorer urban areas who, whatever they did, *could never be good enough*—that is, they could never reach the top of any league table.

SEM, thus, needs to be viewed against the backdrop of rhetorical support by New Labour for enhanced social justice as outlined above, yet alongside the numerous other reforms instigated by the New Right and, latterly, by New Labour. Each "reform" has seemed to increase the power of politicians and bureaucrats, reduce the role and autonomy of professionals, and heighten anxiety and workload among schoolteachers and teacher educators. Thus, it seems, politicians and bureaucrats have found it in their interest to use the various outcomes of the reforms together with the research on specific "school effects" to export responsibility for educational success or failure *away* from central government and bureaucracy and *towards* individual schools, teachers, and children. Ignored has been widespread evidence, both in the United Kingdom and abroad, showing economic and social factors as far more influential than that of the individual school or teacher (for example, Gray et al., 1995; Gibson and Asthana, 1998).

1990s educational discourses of regulation and competition, then, have had a complex relationship with social justice. While the main target of education policy was to improve standards for *all* students (with "zero-tolerance" of poor schools), those most benefitting seemed to be elite boys and girls attending suburban, independent, or selective schools, and working-class white boys, whose under-performance was of prime concern to policy-makers (Weiner, Arnot and David, 1997). Under-achieving working class girls, excluded black boys, sexist, racist, and homophobic behaviour and practices, and inadequate support for students with disabilities were all largely absent from the social justice agenda.

Young's Faces of Injustice

So what can we make of the excavation of the two decades, and their social justice discourses? It seems that the issues and stances taken up over social justice have considerable similarities although they are half a century apart. Both Labour administrations had, what may be termed, "radical" aspects of policy: for example, in the 1940s, the creation of the welfare state and in the 1990s, devolution and the creation of assemblies for Scotland and Wales, and genuine attempts to halt the impasse of violence and sectarianism in Northern Ireland. However both administrations appeared particularly un-radical in education policy, and apparently willing to take on the mantle of previous Conservative administrations' conceptions and frameworks. While, rhetorically committed to social justice, the policies pursued resulted, in the 1940s, in a divisive, class-based education system that has lasted to the present day, and in the 1990s, a de-professionalised, competitive system of schooling which continues to reward the privileged and to castigate the urban poor.

How can we explain this conservatism in policy from left-leaning administrations seemingly committed to destabilising the status quo and eliminating inequalities. Because of the complex and shifting nature of social class composition and of patterns of affluence and poverty, between the two periods, Young's (rather than Rawls') conceptualisation of social justice as five faces of injustice/oppression may be more useful in helping us to understand how this has happened. Table 2 tentatively applies Young's categorisation to the educational discourses of the 1940s and 1990s.

Others may disagree about how the table has been completed to accommodate Young's five categories. The point, however, in identifying educational discourses is not that they need to be judged on the basis of accuracy or correctness, but rather, on the basis of how they are able to shape the way we think (and have thought) about education, and in particular, about who benefits and who does not. New Labour appears exceedingly conscious of the work of discourse. For example, a notable feature of New Labour's strategy in government has been to influence and shape policy discourses through the appointment of "spin-doctors" whose job it is to "put the spin" on specific events and issues so as to present the government in the most favourable light. Employing Young's categories enables us to pierce the rhetoric, and detect an apparent reversion to the "norm" of traditional patterns of social and educational inequality—for girls, female teachers, black, working class, and/or urban students and

Table 2
Young's Faces of Injustice/Oppression: Two Education Eras

Faces of Injustice/ Oppression	1940s: Educational Discourses of Social Reconstruction and Elitism	1990s: Educational Discourses of Regulation and Competition
Who were/are the exploited?	• emergency trained teachers • women in home . . . etc.	• largely female teaching force . . . etc.
Who were/are the marginalized?	• 11 plus failures • girls/young women . . . etc.	• black and minority ethnic pupils, students and parents • girls and young women • excluded or unsupported students . . . etc.
Who were/are the powerless?	• non-professionals • parents • pupils . . . etc.	• teachers and teacher trainers • working class parents and pupils • teacher unions . . .etc.
Who were/are the imperialists?	• politicians • education civil servants • teacher unions . . . etc.	• education bureaucrats (e.g., Ofsted, TTA, SCAA)[1] • politicians • Quangos/Task Forces government appointees[2] • upper and middle class parents . . . etc.
Who were/are the violent?	?	• bullying management practices • racist groups and individuals . . . etc.

1. Ofsted: Office of Standards in Education
   OTA: Teacher Training Agency
   SCAA: Secondary Curriculum and Assessment Authority

2. Quango: Quasi Autonomous Non Governmental Organisations
   Task Force: New Labour government-appointed consultation panel on specific themes.

parents—with more groups than in the 1940s, excluded and alienated, for example, trade unions, teachers and teacher trainers. In contrast, those who have had their power enhanced in the 1990s include central government, politicians, bureaucrats (such as inspectors), middle- and upper-class parents and senior managers.

The question that arises is two-fold. First, how useful is Young's categorisation as a means of identifying social injustice in education? It certainly provides some illumination of why it has felt so oppressive to work or study in British education in the 1990s, why so many teachers left the profession, and why it has been necessary for high profile advertising campaigns to encourage young people to look upon teaching as a potential career.

Second, why did education escape the radical shake-up used for other aspects of state policy by the Labour administrations of the 1940s and 1990s? Why was Labour so forceful in opposition yet so weak on social justice issues in education when in government? A number of explanations present themselves: the hegemonic influence of long-standing and entrenched elite educational values on non-elite educated politicians; the difficulty of maintaining ideological commitments when faced with the practicalities of office (something Margaret Thatcher, however, seemed to find easy enough); treasury-driven policy-making and subsequent under-resourcing of education; "commonsense" conservative assumptions about what "the people" want from schooling and so on.

Inevitably, the specific and enduring nature of the British class system (with the Royal Family at the apex) continues to be reproduced and reconstructed in the British education system, and thus has had a particular impact on how national conceptions of "excellence" and "achievement" are framed.

While it is necessary to be cautious about drawing firm conclusions from a government, at the time of writing only in its second year of office, one would have expected a more courageous education strategy aimed at eliminating disadvantage from New Labour. Perhaps, however, what New Labour's educational conservatism illuminates is its complete failure to identify or develop a fresh social democrat or socialist alternative for education which is able to successfully challenge the current socially divided one.

References

Ainley, P. (1993). *Class and skill: Divisions of knowledge and labour*. London: Cassell.

Ball, S.J. (1997). On the cusp: Parents choosing between state and private schools in the UK: Action within an economy of symbolic goods. *Journal of Inclusive Education, 1*(1), 1–18.

Benn, C. and Chitty, C. (1996). *Thirty years on: Is comprehensive education alive and well or struggling to survive?* London: David Fulton.

Burton, L. and Weiner, G. (1990). Social justice and the national curriculum. *Research Papers in Education, 5*(3), 203–227.

Dean, D. (1991). Education for moral improvement, domesticity and social cohesion: Expectations and fears of the Labour Government. *Oxford Review of Education, 17*(3), pp. 269–285.

Floud, J.E., Halsey, A.H., and Martin, F.M. (1957). *Social class and educational opportunity*. London: Heinemann.

Foucault, M. (1972). *The archaeology of knowledge*. London: Tavistock.

Gibson, A. and Asthana, S. (1998). Schools, pupils and examination results: Contextualising school "performance." *British Educational Research Journal, 24*(3), 269–282.

Gillborn, D. (1995). *Racism and antiracism in real schools*. Buckingham: Open University Press.

Gillborn, D. (1997). Racism and reform: New ethnicities/old inequalities. *British Educational Research Journal, 23*(3), 345–360.

Gillborn, D. and Gipps, C. (1996). *Recent research on the achievements of ethnic minority pupils*. London: HMSO.

Gray, J. and Wilcox, B. (1995). *Good school, bad school*. Buckingham: Open University Press.

Gray, J., Reynolds, D., Fitzgibbon, C., and Jesson, D. (1995). *Merging traditions: The future of research on school effectiveness and school improvement*. London: Cassell.

Halsey, A.H., Heath, A.F., and Ridge, J.M. (1980). *Origins and destinations: Family, class, and education in modern Britain*. Oxford: Clarendon Press.

Maguire, M. and Weiner, G. (1994). The place of women in teacher education: Discourses of power. *Educational Review, 46*(2), 121–139.

Mortimore, P., Sammons, P., Stoll, L., Lewis, D., and Ecob, R. (1988). *School matters: The junior years*. London: Open Books.

Murphy, J. (1971). *Church, state and schools in Britain*. London: Routledge and Kegan Paul.

Office for Standards in Education (OFSTED) (1993). *Access and achievement in urban education*. London: HMSO.

Ponting, C. (1990). Rab Butler. *Independent Magazine*. 3 November, p. 86.

Rawls, J. (1971). *A theory of justice*. London: Oxford University Press.

Reynolds, D. (1994). School effectiveness and quality in education. In P. Ribbins and E. Burridge (eds.), *Improving education: Promoting quality in schools*. London: Cassell.

Rutter, M., Maughan, B., Mortimore, P., and Ouston, J. (1979). *Fifteen thousand hours*. London: Open Books.

Slee, R., Weiner, G., and Tomlinson, S. (eds.) (1998). *School effectiveness for whom? Challenges to the school effectiveness and the school improvement movement*. London: Falmer Press.

Tawney, R.H. (1931). *Equality*. London: Unwin.

Weiner, G., Arnot, M., and David, M. (1997). Is the future female? Female success, male disadvantage and changing gender patterns in education. In A.H. Halsey, H. Lauder, P. Brown, and A. Stuart-Wells (eds.), *Education, economy, culture and society*. Oxford: Oxford University Press.

Whitney I. and Smith P.K. (1993), A survey of the nature and extent of bullying in junior and secondary schools. *Educational Research*, 35(1), 3–25.

Young, I. (1990). *Justice and the politics of difference*. Princeton, NJ: Princeton University Press.

9

ళ

National Standards and
Curriculum as Cultural Containment?

Catherine Cornbleth

National (or nationwide in the United States) systems of mass education have been a key means of nation-building, especially of transmitting the national persona and providing socialization for national citizenship, thereby incorporating diverse populations (e.g., Tyack, 1974; Archer, 1984; Boli, Ramirez and Meyer, 1985; Olneck, 1989, 1990). In so doing, education systems have tended to maintain the cultural hegemony of dominant groups such as successful entrepreneurs and various experts. They also serve to prepare workers for the economy (i.e., support capitalist—or other— relations of production) and confer credentials that allocate individuals to different positions in society (i.e., rationalize social and economic inequalities). In these ways, mass schooling serves societal political, economic, and stratification functions as well as individual demands for enlightenment, practical skills, and/or status (e.g., Collins, 1977; Tyack and James, 1985; Tyack, 1995).

It is well established, for example, that public schooling in the U.S. has served and continues to serve purposes of Americanization and assimilation—of building a national citizenry— in large part by controlling curriculum knowledge through curriculum policymaking and by shaping the conditions of curriculum practice. (By curriculum knowledge, I mean the selection, organization, and treatment of knowledge in curriculum documents and curriculum practice including opportunities made available to students to critique and construct as well as to receive knowledge.)

Group and national identities, however, are rarely if ever static, fixed across time and circumstance. Instead, they are continually refashioned, in part by interactions with other groups and nations. Despite recent movement toward national standards and assessments in the U.S., it is not at all clear to what vision or version of the U.S. and its peoples students are to be assimilated or (re-)socialized.

Alongside the renewed nation-building and nationalizing efforts in the U.S. is a countermovement toward racial/ethnic/cultural (not necessarily political or economic) diversity. As the latter gains momentum, it spurs the former, especially among those who have benefited from established arrangements of power and privilege. Populations in the U.S. and elsewhere are becoming more diverse with individual and group movements across national boundaries, differential group birthrates, the mixing of various groups, and the increasing refusal of previously subordinated groups to continue participation in their own submersion. Instead, various groups are seeking public recognition, acceptance, and inclusion in public schooling and school curricula. School versions of U.S. history, for example, would do well to include more of the histories and cultures, the experiences and perspectives of the peoples who have made and now make up the U.S.—in the main text, not merely in sidebars and special features or supplemental materials. As increasing numbers of "us" look, sound, and act differently from an idealized, circa 1950s, white, European, middle class norm—or pre-1965 immigrants—mainstream as well as conservative calls for tangible common culture increase.

Efforts to renew the nation-building purposes of public schooling also have been given impetus by globalization. As economies and popular cultures, for example, become increasingly globalized, nation-states may be in danger of losing their separate identities and *raisons d'etre*. The perceived threats to nation-ness are both internal and external. It is not surprising, then, to witness movements toward national standards and/or curricula, usually in the name of quality and equity, in nation-states with previously decentralized (or fragmented) education systems and curricula such as Great Britain as well as movements to reinvigorate long-centralized and post-colonial ones such as Sweden and South Africa. Moreover, the nation remains a potent source of identity and loyalty for many citizens. The nation (like the local community or region in an earlier age) is a symbolic anchor in a rapidly changing and often hostile world. Disputes about the vision of the nation to be passed on to future generations via school curricula can be seen as competing efforts to reset that symbolic anchor.

How do the tensions between nation-building and racial/ethnic/cultural diversity play out in curriculum policymaking and classroom practice? What are the social and political as well as pedagogical implications? And, what can we learn cross-nationally from each other's experiences in these areas? While my focus is on the U.S. experience, the issues and my interests are far broader. I begin with some background to these issues and the U.S. context and then use classroom cases drawn from California and New York as illustration of policy-discourse-practice relationships.

Social Identities

The multicultural identities of interest here are both individual and national. Not only are increasing numbers of Americans claiming mixed racial/ethnic/cultural heritage, but the U.S. national population as a whole is becoming less European-based. By social identity, I refer to a person's configuration of self-designated significant group memberships and their meanings to that individual, their interconnections, and their salience in one or another setting. An urban high school senior, for example, who described herself as black, female, teen-ager, Christian, and a leader, distinguished two senses of being black.

> Black in one perspective is the color of your skin. . . . I never understood that when I was little. I'm not black, I'm brown. But, that was a way of identifying skin color. And then there's another perspective as far as the way you act. Being black is more a state of mind than it is skin color. Black, to me, not to say that the black race is superior or anything like that, signifies strength. (JW, 5/9/96, p. 3)

By national identity, I refer to the prevailing images and reputation of the nation portrayed in public media, school classrooms, and everyday discourse, especially the values, interests, or creed associated with the nation. Have, for example, consumerism and the mall replaced citizenship and the forum as preeminent symbols of America?[1]

Both individual and national identities are assumed to be in-the-making, that is, continually being maintained or modified.[2] They are fluid more than fixed constructs, contingent or context-dependent, and sometimes contested. Multicultural identities are necessarily multifaceted and possibly but not necessarily fragmented or contradictory.

Individual and collective identities, at least in the 1990s U.S., are shaped by history and social structure as well as biography (Mills, 1959) and biology. They are more complex and fluid than even a generation ago and certainly more so than the emerging American persona of Crevecoeur's or Tocqueville's gaze. As one example, for a female, high school basketball player of mixed-European, Catholic heritage, there are situations in which athletic team membership overrides other aspects of her identity, situations in which being female is most salient, and so forth. At the same time, there is evidence that group memberships interact. For example, being female shapes how one plays the athlete role, and being of European heritage and Catholic shapes how one sees oneself as a woman. The multiple group memberships are relational, not simply categorical.

It could be argued that personal identity itself is a relation—or set of relations or interrelations—not a property or set of properties. In this view, we see or define ourselves in relation to other individuals and various groups, specific life situations, and so forth.[3] And as these situations and relations change, so do I.

A corollary of this conception of multifaceted identity is that within-group similarity and coherence (whatever the category selected for sorting purposes) often is much less than assumed or than might have been the case in the past. Even university professors, for example, are a much more heterogeneous lot today than was the case when most current university faculty members were undergraduates. Among the implications of within-group diversity is that any group-based identity marker is apt to be an oversimplification and ought to be treated cautiously, tentatively. A further note is that even if members of a designated group all appear the "same," they would not necessarily be united or get along well. This is not to argue for individualism, for eschewing all group charac terizations and affiliations to celebrate some ideal-type, supposedly autonomous or unique individual. The individual is, after all, formed in social circumstances. This is to argue for treating group categorizations and characterizations as partial, multiple, situation-specific, and fluid (e.g., McCarthy, 1995).

These examples serve as cautions against assuming that either individual or group racial/ethnic/cultural identities are singular or fixed. The complex and changing experience and perception of being Asian-Canadian or African-American, for instance, should warn against a static, patchwork quilt or mosaic concept of race, ethnicity, or culture—or individual or collective identity—or school curriculum.

Identity Politics and Common Culture

Perhaps because of the United States' disparate beginnings and relatively brief history, national leaders have long sought a common national identity if not a common culture. Particularly in the past century, the notion of common culture has gained mass appeal, seemingly as a defense against changing circumstances and/or diversification associated with industrialization, urbanization, immigration, technological innovation, and globalization as well as external enemies of the moment. The recent movement toward national standards and assessments can be seen as part of a recurring search for certainty and stability through common practice if not consensus. When the student body becomes more diverse, as it has with the increased immigration of the past three decades, curricular efforts to constrain that diversity appear to increase as well, suggesting an inverse relationship between social and curricular diversity. At the beginning of the 20th century, these efforts were called Americanization or assimilation; now the language is one of common culture and national standards—of tangible commonality more than common ground.

Unfortunately, perhaps, the often-appealed-to common culture in the U.S. is a myth whose history dates to the nation's founding (Appleby, 1992). The myth of America's common culture gives the appearance of national social and cultural unity as long as it is not scrutinized too closely, and it serves to privilege those who subscribe to it and who are accepted by earlier adherents and self-appointed gatekeepers.

Myth is a widely held belief with tenuous connections to pertinent evidence or circumstance (Eliade, 1963). Although moderns tend to think of myth as false belief and to assume they have rid themselves of such vestiges of a pre-scientific age, all cultures have their guiding myths. Like the ancients, moderns see their beliefs as "truths"—as common sense, empirically established fact, or natural law (Toulmin, 1982). Whereas ancient myths were historical and particular, modern myths such as common culture tend to be abstract and transhistorical. Through repetition and reification, the abstraction then comes to be treated as "real" or natural (see, e.g., Barthes, 1957/1972).

For example, in textbook histories and other national self-presentations, the purported elements of common culture are substituted for the actual lived cultures of individuals and groups. The myth is taken for the histories, cultures, experiences, and perspectives of those who have made and constitute America (Cornbleth and Waugh, 1995). Then, ironically, whoever does not reflect or abide by the mythic common culture is treated as deviant or other.

Related to the abstract quality and sometimes scientific veneer of modern myth is the appearance of universalism. What is created in particular social and historical circumstances is decontextualized and made to seem universal. The notion of common culture constructed in the early national period of U.S. history in an effort to meld thirteen English colonies into the nation envisioned by the Constitution and its framers, for example, is held out as a common culture for all times. Myth "transforms history into nature," thus "giving an historical intention a natural justification, and making contingency appear eternal" (Barthes, 1957/1972, pp. 129, 142).

If there was to be a common culture or national identity that distinguished the new American nation from its Native American, European, and African sources, such a culture and identity would have to be created (see, e.g., Anderson, 1991). And, given the various peoples who constituted the U.S., it would have to be a civic culture and community, not an ethnic one. Thus, there is the U.S. democratic civic culture (Almond and Verba, 1963) characterized by political principles and institutions and by ideals yet to be realized. These include government by consent, due process and equality before the law, minority rights, and majority rule.

The U.S. civic culture is based historically, following Fuchs' (1990) analysis, on the principles that "ordinary men and women can be trusted to govern themselves through their elected representatives, who are accountable to the people" (p. 5), that all adult citizens are eligible to participate as equals in public life, and that citizens are "free to differ from each other in religion and in other aspects of their private lives" (p. 5). When public, civic culture is reified as a tangible, common culture, problems arise. What constitutes this rarely specified common culture? (McDonald's, TV, jeans, and sneakers?) Problems also arise when a putative common culture intrudes into the private sphere as a coercive morality. It appears that common culture is used as a rallying cry in defense of a dominant, or would-be dominant, culture and the political and economic status quo.

There is reason to expect that homogenizing efforts on the part of contemporary common culturalists are more likely to undermine U.S. national unity than to strengthen it (see Cornbleth, 1997a). In a compelling essay written some twenty-five years ago, historian John Higham (1974) well describes the "divergent unities" that have kept the U.S. "hanging together." In his analysis, widely shared beliefs or ideologies, both republican and religious, have provided social cohesion. Key aspects of these ideologies have been decentralization and diversity. Concurrently, overlapping group memberships offer community and personal connection, a sense of belonging that the abstract and emotionally distant nation cannot provide. Breaking down group affiliations—especially other people's group affiliations—be they geographic, racial-ethnic, professional, or social, would leave individuals more isolated and alienated, both from one another and from America.

So, in the 1990s, when many individuals are seeking community, or belonging, in affinity groups of varying contours including race-ethnicity, religion, and gender, educators and policymakers might well consider the possibility that they are, in fact, coming together, not splitting further apart. Such group memberships may be creating the networks of local ties that sustain the encompassing national institutions.

Curriculum Politics and Policies

What is taught in school is necessarily only a small portion of available knowledge. Apart from the differences between the knowledge and practice of academic disciplines and their transformation into school subjects, curriculum knowledge in general and social studies-history in particular represents what Williams (1961) calls a "selective tradition." He distinguishes "the lived culture of a particular time and place, only fully accessible to those living in that time and place" (p. 49) from the recorded culture of a period and contemporary selections from and recreations of the recorded culture, i.e., the selective tradition. He reminds us that representations of the history and culture of a society will change over time because they reflect contemporary values and special interests. These representations are "a continual selection and interpretation . . . a continual selection and re-selection of ancestors" (p. 52). For example, which authors and works of literature will students be asked to study? Which times, places, peoples, and cultures?

Schools as Arenas

As shown in chapter 1 of this volume, public schooling in the U.S. has long been an arena in which battles are fought over U.S. values and priorities as a nation and what vision of America and Americans society will attempt to pass on to the next generation. Curriculum policymaking is more complex and contentious now than even a decade or two ago given widening differences in social values and interests, increasing knowledge and specialization, and expanding state involvement (see, e.g., Cornbleth, 1990, ch. 7). This contentiousness is exacerbated by ongoing efforts to devise national standards and assessment mechanisms in the school subjects recognized by former President Bush and the National Governors Association in their 1989 summit statement of national education goals. These efforts were reiterated in Bush's America 2000 education strategy statement of April 1991, again in President Clinton's Goals 2000: Educate America proposal of April 1993, and more recently in vaguer statements about standards and exams. If curriculum knowledge is to be shaped at the national rather than the state or local level, the stakes are raised and control is likely to be even more strongly contested.

The public, compulsory nature of schooling along with its nation-building mission makes conflict over curriculum knowledge and its control inevitable in all but the most homogeneous, traditional societies. Not solely academic or professional matters, questions of curriculum knowledge are bound up with questions of interest and equity in the larger society. Curriculum contestation becomes problematic when the debate is limited to questions and/or participants and/or outcomes determined by the individuals and groups currently in power—when the playing field is tilted so that no contest is possible. To the extent that the debate is open, curriculum stands to be reinvigorated and the public interest reaffirmed.

Against this background of continuing but not necessarily inevitable tensions between diversity and nation-building, including competition for social and economic benefits, I move to examination of how the tensions have been playing out in U.S. curriculum policymaking and classroom practice.

Curriculum Policies that Mute Multiculturalism

Over the past dozen years, both national standard-setting activities and case studies of state-level curriculum policymaking in California and New York illustrate that increasing racial/ethnic/cultural diversity in the U.S. is being met once again with efforts to contain that diversity by curricular as well as other means. As the student body becomes less European-based, social studies curriculum guidelines seem to be becoming more so, despite the appearance of multicultural inclusion. Many of those involved in state curriculum policymaking and national standard-setting activity seem oblivious to the multicultural identities just described, either ignorant of the social demographics or wishing them away.

The 1987 social studies curriculum guidelines and 1990 state-approved school textbooks in California, for example, have been described aptly as "put[ting] everyone in the covered wagon" (Joyce E. King, quoted in Waugh and Hatfield, 1992, p. A-18). In other words, non-Europeans have been invited into the story of America on terms set by others. "The price of the ticket," to borrow from James Baldwin (1985), has been high. More specifically:

> California's version of American history was based on an immigrant perspective that in effect subjugated Native Americans, African-Americans, and former Mexican citizens in the Southwest to the status of ride-alongs, rather than primary participants and shapers of America's dynamic hybrid culture. (Cornbleth and Waugh, 1995, p. 12)

And the immigrant prototype has been European, most often 17th, 18th, or early 19th century western and northern European, largely ignoring Asian and more recent Central and South American immigrant experience.

There is no equivalent to the Euro-immigrant narrative of California's story of America in the New York social studies or national history standards documents. New York simply returns to a traditional view of U.S. political history with a few mentions of "individuals and groups who represent different ethnic, national, and religious groups" (NYSED, 1996, p. 5), usually unspecified except for "Native American Indians."⁴

The voluntary national history standards were developed by UCLA's (University of California at Los Angeles) National Center for History in the Schools, then co-directed by U.S. historian Gary Nash and elementary social studies educator Charlotte Crabtree, with funding from the NEH (National Endowment for the Humanities) when it was headed by Lynne Cheney and the Education Department when Diane Ravitch was assistant secretary. A few years later, in 1994, Cheney led the conservative critics of the resulting standards. Nash and his group bowed to the conservative opposition and revised the standards; they did not, however, give in entirely or give up and run. For example, the revised edition omits (from Era 2, Colonization and Settlement, 1585–1763) the previously included reference to the interaction of various groups, the "early arrival of Europeans and Africans in the Americas, and how these people interacted with Native Americans" (NCHS, 1994, p. 35). In the revised 1996 (NCHS, 1996) "basic" edition, the standards do not specifically mention Native Americans until Era 4, Expansion and Reform, 1801–1861. Generally, the experiences of other-than-European groups are grafted onto a conventional, chronological U.S. political chronicle.

In the social studies curriculum policies adopted in New York and California over the past decade, and in the 1996 revised national U.S. history standards, claims of national unity overwhelm acknowledgment of diversity and western cultural heritage is emphasized. The view that the nation was built by, and derives its strength from, diverse individuals and groups is minimized as if diversity and unity were mutually exclusive. Despite repeated reference to "the nation's commonalities," "common community," "shared community," "national unity," "common culture," and "ways people are unified by many values, practices and traditions," few specifics are provided beyond the rarely disputed democratic political ideals toward which the nation was founded. Nor do these policy documents explain how supposed commonality translates into unity.

All the curriculum policy documents refer to the individual rights specified in the U.S. Constitution and Bill of Rights (e.g., due process, equality before the law) and the core civic ideals set forth in these and other venerated documents such as the Declaration of Independence and Lincoln's Gettysburg Address. These individual rights and civic ideals, such as human dignity, liberty, and justice, constitute the so-called American Creed. How they unite us as a nation—for example, by serving as the rules of the game by which U.S. citizens and residents at least tacitly agree to play—is not spelled out. Beyond these short lists, one is left to wonder about the claimed commonality. New York's learning standards, for example, do not specify "the ways people are united by many values, practices and traditions" (NYSED, 1996, p. 2) beyond "basic civil values" including honesty, self-discipline, and "respect for self, others and property" (1996, p. 24). The California framework adds civic values such as "sportsmanship, fair play, sharing, and taking turns" and respecting "the rights of the minority" (History-Social Science Framework, 1988, p. 6). Property rights are more prominent in the New York than the California curriculum policy. Finally, all the policy documents portray the U.S. as having had problems in the past (e.g., slavery) but working to resolve them and come closer to realizing democratic ideals. (This theme also was evident in the western New York classrooms to be described in the next section.)

Multicultural national identities are muted in at least two ways in these curriculum policies. While the documents can be seen as allowing for or encompassing multiple perspectives and group experiences, specific examples are very conventional and rarely explicitly multicultural. Language such as New York's "significant reform movements" illustrates a major way in which racial/ethnic/cultural diversity can be diluted and diminished. Defenders of the language can and do point to it as enabling consideration of diversity (e.g., the civil rights movement, immigration reform since 1965). Skeptics point out that "significant reform movements" can be investigated without ever mentioning racial/ethnic/cultural diversity—by, for example, investigating the environmental movement. Second, without specification, educators who might be amenable to teaching about multicultural America but lack the requisite knowledge receive no guidance. By default if not explicitly, these curriculum policies also suggest that individual identities are monocultural (e.g., black or white or Asian), and each cultural group is treated as homogeneous.

Curriculum policymaking, including syllabus revision or creating a framework and standards, is always a matter of knowledge control—of trying to control the knowledge to be made available to students in classrooms across the district, state, or nation. Controlling curriculum knowledge means selecting some knowledge to be included and other knowledge to be kept out. One way to keep knowledge out is to ignore it. Omission is especially effective with newer knowledge that probably is not familiar to experienced teachers or other adults who completed their formal education some time ago. Another way to keep knowledge out is to include so much other knowledge that there is little or no room for anything else. Both of these tactics have been employed in New York to discourage meaningful attention to racial/ethnic/cultural diversity in social studies curriculum practice.

While New York seemed progressive on multicultural curriculum policy matters compared to California and the national standards project just a few years ago, prior to the 1994 mid-term congressional elections that brought Newt Gingrich et al. to national prominence, it now can be seen as trailing behind (Cornbleth, 1996b). Overall, both state and national curriculum policymakers have been downplaying the racial/ethnic/cultural diversity that has characterized the U.S. since its beginnings. How long or how well these containment efforts will hold remains to be seen. Curriculum policy is continually made, remade, and unmade both in official chambers and school classrooms.

In sum, this overview of U.S. curriculum politics and recent national and state-level curriculum policymaking illustrates how the policies reflect the broader politics, specifically the resurgence of conservative, nation-building efforts under the banner of common culture. Those politics and policies, however, do not map directly onto classroom curriculum practice. Instead they are transformed, ignored, or actively undermined.

Uncommon Curriculum Practices

In California

Returning to several Bay Area school districts and classrooms a few years after the 1990 California social studies textbook adoption controversy, Waugh (Cornbleth and Waugh, 1995, ch. 6) found that some teachers and administrators had been influenced by the policy debate to move beyond the modest multiculturalism of the state curriculum framework policy and approved texts. While these examples are not representative of the entire state, they provide evidence of the impact of political and policymaking processes and the surrounding discourse—as well as the influence of the policies made. They also well illustrate the (re)making of curriculum policy in school districts, schools, and classrooms (also, see Kon, 1995).

The official state policies and the political/discourse processes leading to them stirred educators and public awareness to move some local social studies curriculum policies and practices beyond a modest multiculturalism that simply adds a few heroes and contributions "of color" to the traditional story—or provides a black or women's history month. The textbook adoption controversy sensitized administrators and teachers in some school districts to the existence of strong concerns and perspectives outside their own experiences. In these cases, school people and community activists came to work together to move beyond reliance on the state-adopted textbooks and to steer the curriculum in more multicultural directions. Although only a few districts rejected the state-approved texts and fewer still created an alternative, literature-based social studies program, as did Hayward in the San Francisco Bay Area, a number of districts, including San Francisco, incorporated "supplemental" materials and "alternative" teaching units.

For example, in several predominantly white school districts south of San Francisco, administrators acknowledged problems with the textbooks raised by African Americans and organizations such as the Jewish Community Relations Council, the Council on Islamic Education, and the Association of Chinese Teachers. One administrator noted that when educators are brought up with the stereotypes, someone else has to point them out in the textbooks; otherwise they go unnoticed. Another administrator, admitting that he didn't see the stereotypes of Africans and doubted that many other whites would notice, said that the problems with the texts could be addressed through the use of supplemental teaching materials.

Palo Alto, home of Stanford University, had a history of responding to community curriculum concerns, including those of Japanese Americans who in the 1970s had challenged successfully the textbooks' silence on their devastating internment camp experience during World War II. According to the school district's curriculum director, "partly because of the [state] controversies, people were very aware of what was going on" (Cornbleth and Waugh, 1995, p. 168). Seminars and workshops were conducted to educate district staff who, the curriculum director said, hadn't noticed the problem areas until others pointed them out. "It's good that people look at these things, because some of that kind of stuff, depending on what your perspective is, you might look right over it" (p. 169).

Meanwhile, in San Francisco and elsewhere, teachers were using trade books and other materials to respond to the multiculturalism of the students in their classrooms and the world around them. A Chinese-American teacher, for example, used trade books that portray a diversity of families. An African American fifth grade teacher at another San Francisco school uses the new textbooks sparingly and employs a range of multicultural materials and activities. At the beginning of the school year, she focuses on the diversity of the students in her classroom, about half of whom are new immigrants.

> That's always the jumping off point for the first month of school—who makes up the United States, who makes up San Francisco, who makes up our classroom. And I try to instill in the children that everybody has something to offer and every culture has contributed something to the United States. So we start there and go on, dealing with acceptance and differences. (Cornbleth and Waugh, 1995, p. 166)

In summarizing events in California three years after the textbook adoption controversy, Waugh observed that veteran teachers, although varying in enthusiasm,

> often joined their younger colleagues in recognizing they had to provide a different kind of nurturing and learning context for their students. Their ideas were formed not only by their own backgrounds and education, and education reform movements, but by the reality of California's rapidly changing demographics—and the issues those changes engendered in the communities, the media, and their own personal lives and careers. (Cornbleth and Waugh, 1995, p. 165)

These brief descriptions also illustrate some of the range of contextual influences on curriculum practice, that curriculum knowledge is multiply controlled (e.g., Cornbleth, 1995b). U.S. teachers— shaped by their intertwined biographical, historical, and social-structural contexts—retain substantial curriculum discretion. Neither the political-policy discourse nor official policies should be mistaken for the lived worlds of teachers, students, and curriculum practice.

In New York

Systematic observations of elementary, middle, and high school U.S. history classes in urban and suburban schools in western New York, 1994–96, provide both agreement with and departure from the curriculum policy documents described above (Cornbleth, 1998). A major purpose of the research project was to identify the images of America actually conveyed to students in curriculum practice. While most of the teachers we observed and interviewed seemed unaware of, and largely unconcerned about, state policy specifics, they were aware generally of the America debate and its local manifestations (e.g., controversy about religious observances and teaching about world religions).[5]

No single America, or predominant image of America, was apparent in these classes. Instead, multiple and often mixed messages were observed within and across classes, and the messages frequently were brief snippets or fragments, like soundbites. Despite adherence to chronological historical sequence, there was no obvious narrative thread providing a coherent story of America. Nor was there evidence of multiple, interwoven threads or stories. At most, students were offered partial images or vignettes.

That the images of America conveyed in these classrooms were both multiple and partial is key to understanding contemporary curriculum practice. Students were offered numerous glimpses of some aspect of America but few more comprehensive images or bigger pictures; nor were students encouraged or assisted to create their own. Examples of comprehensive images, images with a capital "I," include Euro-immigrant America (i.e., we are all immigrants with experiences much like those of European immigrants, coming together to create and contribute to America), and both secular and religious versions of America as exemplar of onward and upward progress (e.g., the great democratic experiment, the American Dream, the City on the Hill). While some of these interpretations were evident during our classroom observations, they were not employed as broad conceptual frameworks.

The multiple and often mixed messages about America observed in these classrooms on the one hand, and their fragmentation or compartmentalization on the other, appear to be mutually constitutive. Acknowledging different points of view—incorporating multiple perspectives—necessarily interrupts a single story line. Without a means of bringing together these different perspectives or strands into, for example, a reciprocal or braided history (Cornbleth and Waugh, 1995; Cornbleth, 1996a, 1997b), the result is an MTV-like montage. With such fragmentation, contradictions among multiple messages may not be noticed or may be allowed to coexist.

The seeming disjointedness may be indicative of potentially

significant disruption of how most Americans have viewed the nation's history and likely future. To disrupt is to disturb or interrupt the previously established or generally accepted, orderly course of action—in this case, telling the history of the United States of America. By means of acknowledging different points of view or multiple perspectives, but especially by means of critique, the American history classes we observed engaged in disruption. It seems unlikely that national history standards or curriculum policy can either remedy disconnectedness or foster unity unless they are further revised to explicitly link, connect, and interrelate.

Both teachers and students in the classrooms we observed voiced critique of past and present actions and circumstances. Dissent, however, typically was neither sustained nor incorporated in ways that would substantially alter the image(s) of America conveyed. It was similar in this regard to individual instances of momentary resistance, in or out of school, that have little or no social or institutional impact. The data do not confirm the loudly-voiced fears of ideological critics who are certain that schooling in general, and social studies-history in particular, are either uncritically celebrating a flawed America or dismantling a magnificent one.

America comes into focus in these classrooms in moments of critique, celebration, and crisis. Most of the time, however, things just happen with little or no sense of causation or connection (e.g., exploration of the "New World," the War of 1812, government structure). Closest to an overarching theme was the recurring image of America as the best country in the world despite past problems, current difficulties, or one or another critique. In response to a 5th grader's story about how sometimes the government "rips you off," Donna defended the U.S. government, saying:

> So, what system is perfect? Do you know anything that is, besides me? [student laughter] It's a government for the people and by the people. In some countries people are told what job they can have, where they can live . . . (6/8/95, p. 3)

All three 11th grade teachers, on more than one occasion, and one 8th grade teacher conveyed explicit images of America as changing and making progress, as solving problems or righting past wrongs. Rob, for instance, conveyed an image of early 20th century America (with a focus on the 1920s) where there was "social intolerance." Though some problems remain, he informed his students, things are getting better. Examples of social intolerance mentioned in class, in a brisk review prior to the next day's exam, included denying women the suffrage and other rights, nativist attitudes against immigration, and Ku Klux Klan activities. Similarly, Stan conveyed an image of early 20th century urban problems being resolved by Progressive Era reforms: "political reform . . . improved democracy, less corruption" (2/23/95, p. 2, from transparency).

Conflict was evident in the discussion in Peter's 11th grade class about righting past wrongs by means of ongoing court cases regarding Native American land claims (some of which are in the local area; the class topic was the takeover of Plains Indians' land by "white men" in the late 19th century). Students were not agreed whether people should have to forfeit property now because past treaties were broken. One suggested that what happened in the past (100 years ago) should not be an issue now. When Peter suggested a parallel with African American experience, another African American female indicated that she was not ready to forget that past.

A second theme to be presented briefly here is "multiple America?"—the image of America characterized by multiple perspectives and divergent views—a multifaceted America more like a prism than a pane of glass. This image was evident in Bryce's and Rob's classes with respect to foreign policy (the Spanish-American and Vietnam wars) and more broadly in Lindsey's and Peter's classes in which students were the source of images of America more often than in other classes.

In both Rob's and Donna's classes, students interrupted the teacher's presentations with alternative views. For example, Donna not only side-stepped the government "rips you off" story but also a number of student questions including "Why is Christopher Columbus so famous when the Indians were the first ones here?" Donna seemed taken aback. "Well," she responded, "in studying history it has been chosen as an important event" (2/28/95, p. 3).

In Lindsey's classes dealing with late 19th century foreign policy, a number of critical images of America were student-generated, including America as self-preoccupied or selfish and America as not always right or good. Interestingly, clearly challenging and unappreciated student comments (government rips you off story, question about why Columbus is so famous) came in Donna's fifth grade class, interrupting her storybook version of a good, Euro-America.

In both Lindsey's and Peter's classes, multiple perspectives including student views seemed the norm. For example, students in

Peter's class not only recognized the different perspectives of Native Americans and westward-moving European American settlers, but disagreed among themselves regarding current Native American land claims. Native American perspectives received relatively less attention here as did the perspectives of late nineteenth century Cubans, Puerto Ricans, and Filipinos in Lindsey's class. Overall, the message conveyed in these classes was of an America where people (at least some people) have had the freedom or space both to dissent and to be wrong. Loyalty to America (as suggested, for example, by Lindsey and most of her students standing and reciting the Pledge of Allegiance along with the principal via the public address system) does not preclude critique. Such messages also appear to reflect the overarching image of imperfect but best, America as #1 despite past problems, current difficulties, and continuing dissent.

How might the various images of America conveyed in these western New York classes be understood? The absence of a single predominant image of America can be seen as reflecting the realities of U.S. history and contemporary society. The multiple perspectives and divergent views we observed seemed to reflect both the teachers' and students' understanding of some of America's complexity, past and present, and teachers' expressed interest in promoting critical thinking or thinking for oneself.

Unless one ventures into mythic realms, there simply is no single historical account. America as emblematic of democracy and progress is one such mythic narrative, largely oblivious to the counter experiences of those precluded from sharing the bounty (e.g., Appleby, 1992; Kessler-Harris, 1992). If school versions of U.S. history ever were stories of uninterrupted onward and upward progress toward realization of a Christian God's promise or a secular American Dream, they clearly are not so now. There was no direct reference to either, nor did we discern any subtler references in the classes observed. Hope for a better future seems to have been downsized.

It is wishful thinking, or simply mistaken, to assume that in some time past, school versions of U.S. history were coherent or connected. Supporting evidence simply does not exist. School history has long been caricatured as "one damn thing after another." This descriptor further suggests that chronology does not guarantee coherence. And text analyses repeatedly have pointed to the disjointedness of history and social studies textbooks (e.g., Beck and McKeown, 1991). Earlier school versions of America and of U.S. history may have been more internally consistent, however, with the repetition of themes such as progress and freedom. But repetition is not synonymous with either connection or meaningfulness.

Another interpretation of the images of America conveyed in these classes emphasizes the changes occurring in the U.S., including the historical and related social science scholarship that is enabling and providing impetus to efforts to construct a more comprehensive or multifaceted—or even reciprocal—U.S. history. With this interpretation, the U.S. is seen in increasing racial/ethnic/cultural complexity, the growth in understanding is uneven, and the messages conveyed are mixed. Partial and parallel if not contradictory images are offered. Teacher practice, like contemporary culture, is in flux, undergoing change.

For example, two middle school teachers who recognized problems with what might be called the received view of U.S. history, and who appeared to be trying to modify the images they offered their students to be more inclusive of different peoples and points of view, have not yet elaborated and refined them. In the concluding interview, Don reflected that:

> I think that probably, over time, I imagine that I would start trying to [pause] work that [multiple perspectives] into the curriculum in a little bit more regular way. Rather than, I mean, it's kind of haphazard, probably, the way it comes up now. But I don't know if that's bad or not, but, just making sure that it, that they do get pieces of it. (5/31/95, p. 7)

To an outside observer, the message is choppy or uneven—though perhaps in its own way an appropriate representation of U.S. history and an uncertain 1990s America recreating itself in a post-cold war world of global economic competition, increasing domestic diversity, and rampant technology.

Both of these interpretations point to disruption of the conventional story of America noted earlier. Merely tinkering with history curricula—by adding a few heroes and contributions from women and people of color to the existing narrative—embellishes it without changing its messages. In contrast, rewriting history so as to restore the experiences and perspectives of previously ignored (or barely mentioned) groups challenges not only the conventional wisdom but also the privileged positions of those individuals and groups who have benefited from dominant ideologies and prevailing distributions of power. Such rewriting, however, is of little interest to most policymakers and education bureaucrats.

Despite the warnings of self-appointed guardians of traditional U.S. history, such as Lynne Cheney, and recently enacted conservative curriculum policies in states such as California and New York, our classroom observations and teacher interviews suggest that many teachers and students no longer accept and convey images of an unsullied, progressive America. The conventional story has been disrupted, and there is no equivalent successor in sight.

Concluding Commentary

These classroom excerpts from California and New York reveal closer connections between curriculum politics and policy at the state and national levels than between policy and local curriculum practice. They suggest that the cultural containment policies of the past dozen years in the U.S. may be no more successful than its experience with prohibition. It may no longer be possible, let alone desirable, to press all U.S. citizens and residents into the same mold. We just won't fit or stay put. And modifying the mold probably won't make much difference. The U.S. simply has outgrown the melting pot, the salad bowl, the mosaic, and similar metaphors that assume, imply, or proclaim a single story—or set of standards or curriculum.

Changes in social studies-history curriculum practice are emerging out of tensions among past histories, present circumstances, and foreseeable national futures. Efforts to stave off curriculum and/or social change by imposing a common culture hegemony are not only undemocratic and unpleasant for those imposed-upon but also unlikely to succeed. At least since the turn of the 20th century, the scope of the history taught in U.S. public schools has expanded from Europe and North America to encompass much of the world geographically, historically, and culturally. And U.S. history has been broadened to include, sometimes only marginally, more of the peoples and cultures who make up the United States (Cornbleth, 1997b). These changes have seemed slow to many, they have been uneven within and among schools and regions, and they have been contested. This pattern is likely to continue, to provide a kind of continuity akin to the "divergent unities" mentioned earlier that Higham (1974) identified as keeping the

U.S. "hanging together." In the U.S., on both societal and school levels, recommitment to national principles and ideals may serve to more constructively unify diverse peoples than would attempted cultural coercion via national standards or curriculum. Government by consent of the governed, due process and equality before the law, minority rights and majority rule, and first amendment freedoms are among the most obvious examples. Like capitalism, representative democracy is a powerful unifier.

A further consideration is that evidence from my own and others' research (e.g., Barton and Levstik, 1998; Epstein, 1997; Seixas, 1993, 1997) indicates clearly that students do not simply absorb or adopt messages about America conveyed by schooling and other sources such as the mass media, family, friends, and personal experience. Consequently, even a national history curriculum taught in a standardized manner, however unlikely, would not be similarly received by students who come to school from different backgrounds and life experiences. When curriculum knowledge contradicts students' prior knowledge and experience, it is likely that schooling loses credibility for those students (e.g., McNeil, 1981). Curricular efforts at cultural containment may have just the opposite effects.

Whatever the specific outcomes of cultural containment policies and practices, it is clear that messages sent via curriculum policy and practice are not necessarily received as intended by students and other audiences. They are mediated or interpreted by recipients—if they are in fact received! Mediation is a function not only of attention, capacity, and effort but also of what recipients bring to the situation including their experiences, perspectives, and pre-existing knowledge. So, for example, while some teachers continue to convey, and students to accept, the conventional Columbus story, other teachers and students do not. In questioning the conventional version of events, the previously noted fifth grader in Donna's class was bringing outside knowledge into school and actively and publicly resisting the received story. Eleventh graders in McNeil's (1981) study, in contrast, resisted their teachers' versions of U.S. history passively and privately.

In addition to student mediation, curriculum policies are mediated by their surrounding discourses and sites of implementation as the glimpses of California and New York school districts and classrooms indicate. The face-to-face immediacy of life in schools, often different from that envisioned by policymakers, (re-)shapes the distant policies in ways that make sense to local individuals and groups. Once again, both curriculum policies and practices are not only enacted but also unmade and re-enacted.

Instead of national standards and curriculum, imagine efforts to create and gain support for model U.S. history curricula or curriculum samples that encompass us all and focus on connections instead of commonalties. Without neglecting those individuals and events that figure so prominently in most current school history, these model curricula would foreground social and political processes (e.g., expansion of civil rights protections, urbanization, globalization) so as to connect individuals and groups with longer term movements and developments in the nation's history and to demonstrate human agency. Such curricula would interweave our diverse voices instead of allowing one to outshout or silence others.

These hypothetical model curricula would neither oversimplify nor reify race/ethnicity/culture or the social identities of individuals, groups, and nations. More sophisticated (i.e., complex and dynamic) conceptions are needed in curriculum policy and practice—not merely the ticking off of one or another category of person, place, or event. Two options that I have suggested elsewhere and begun to develop are reciprocal history (Cornbleth and Waugh, 1995) and braided history (e.g., Cornbleth, 1997b). Reciprocal history examines the interactions and mutual influences among various individuals and groups, for example, slaveholders as well as enslaved Africans. Imagine a figure eight—or a spiraling figure eight—and moving back and forth along its path in the course of historical studies of questions such as: What is "American" about the centuries-long enslavement of African-Americans or contemporary U.S. popular culture? Examining various aspects of these or similar questions well illustrates the participation (not merely the "contributions") of and the borrowing-sharing-merging (not merely the similarities and differences) among several racial/ethnic/cultural groups. In this way too, the actions and perspectives of the full range of participants are considered, not merely those of putative heroes and leaders.

If a reciprocal historical lens seems daunting, consider a braided history that acknowledges points of contact and connection among various groups and related events such as continuing nativism and anti-immigrant legislation. The strands of seemingly different experiences and stories are both separate and overlapping or intertwining at various points like braids of hair, bread, or rope. Asking "What is the American experience with . . . ?" or "Who are we? individually, collectively, and in relation to one another?" shifts the emphasis from origins (be they African, European, Asian, or other) to interactions; it also tends toward inclusion and integration rather than exclusion and hierarchy. The strands comprising the braid could be the experiences, cultures, and perspectives of different individuals and groups of people—or political and social movements—or local as well as national and global issues—or women and young people as well as adult men—to cite just a few possibilities.

To take just one specific example, two students in my graduate curriculum course during the spring 1998 semester redesigned a U.S. history unit on the 1950s for urban eighth graders in order to encourage students to braid experiences and perspectives of different groups. The final assignment for the unit, which was taught in a school with a diverse student population (primarily Hispanic, African American, and Irish-American), asked students to choose three individuals from a list of 20 who were prominent in the 1950s and create a dialogue among them on one of seven issues considered during their study. Students were expected to "express genuine views from the individuals chosen with supporting reasons" and present the issue "in a straightforward comprehensive manner" (Gonzales and Baumgartner, 1998). Issues involved the new consumer society, new women's roles, African and Hispanic American loss of jobs to white servicemen, *Brown vs. Topeka Board of Education*, emergence of rock and roll, McCarthyism, and new Hispanic immigration. Prominent individuals included Joan Baez, Roberto Clemente, Dwight Eisenhower, a Ku Klux Klan member, Little Richard, Joseph McCarthy, Rita Moreno, Elvis Presley, and Justice Earl Warren.

Both reciprocal and braided history curricula model what episodic add-ons or asides about, say, female heroes or contributions, cannot do. They modify the received historical narrative rather than embellish it. They reject a weak form of parallelism (segregation?) that maintains traditional, elite, and individualist views. Both reciprocal and braided curricula also are more likely to connect with students' lives in ways that support their own social identities as well as the nation's. I would like to see a range of curricular responses to how-to-do-it questions, as long as the focus remains on interconnections and change—in people's experiences, knowledge, and interpretations.

Other nations are facing similar dilemmas regarding their histories and images, and the national history to be taught in their public schools. The parallels suggest the seriousness of the issues and the possibilities of learning from one another across our various, often self-created, boundaries. They also suggest that diversity and multifaceted identity are transnational, 21st century phenomena, perhaps better understood on a global stage in addition to or instead of on national ones (e.g., Kalantzis and Cope, 1992). At the least, consider the ramifications of no longer conceptualizing multiculturalism only nationally, within U.S. or other national boundaries.

Throughout this examination of national standards and curriculum as efforts toward cultural containment in the U.S., I have noted cross-currents and described the resulting tensions within and among curriculum politics, policy, and practice. These cross-currents are endemic in the U.S. as conditions, interests, and political coalitions change. Curriculum *is* continually contested, and both curriculum policies and practices are not only made, but unmade and remade by numerous official and unofficial education policymakers and practitioners. As Maxine Greene (1993) has observed, "The heteroglossic conversation moves on, never reaching a final conclusion, always incomplete, but richer and more densely woven, even as it moves through time" (p. 213).

Notes

Earlier versions of this paper were presented in Moscow at "The Cultural Historical Approach: Progress in Human Sciences and Education," an international conference in honor of the 100th anniversary of Vygotsky's birth, October 1996, and in Manzanillo, Cuba at the "IV Seminario Cientifico Sobre la Calidad de las Education: Intercambio de Experiencias de Profesionales Cubanos y Norteamericanos," January 1997. This revision has benefited from the helpful comments of participants in those meetings.

1. I use "America" rather than the United States of America because this is the more common usage in the context of nationalism and national identity, e.g., the American nation. Unfortunately, some conservative participants in "the America debate" (Cornbleth and Waugh, 1995), about what it means to be an American in the 1990s and what vision of the nation is to be passed on to future generations, have tried to cast their opponents as "un-American."

2. National identities, too, are social in the sense of being socially constructed and reconstructed, and of existing in relation to the identities of "other" nations.

3. This is my interpretation of a position suggested by Seth Chaiklin of Aarhus University, Denmark at the Moscow conference where an earlier version of this paper was presented.

4. Not specifically mentioning or naming individuals or groups is one way of muting multiculturalism. Typically, we found these documents to name European groups and male individuals while referring to "others" only by a general group reference, e.g., "The role of free blacks in the battles of the American Revolution should be considered" (History-Social Science Framework, 1988, p. 53). I am indebted to graduate assistant Angela Stevenson for careful analysis of the New York, California, and national curriculum framework and standards documents.

5. While teacher gender and grade level were confounded (most of the women taught in the lower grades), they did seem to matter with respect to the images of America conveyed. With the exception of Lindsey, the African American 11th grade teacher, the female teachers offered more conventional images of a simple, perhaps even storybook, Euro-immigrant America. The male teachers were among the most critical and the most conventional. America was portrayed as more diverse, and a wider range of views was apparent in 11th than in 7th-8th grade classes, and in 8th compared to 5th grade classes. There were no clear differences with respect to the images of America conveyed between urban and suburban schools and classes or between more and less experienced teachers.

References

Almond, G.A., and Verba, S. (1963). *The civic culture*. Princeton: Princeton University Press.

Anderson, B. (1991). *Imagined communities*, 2nd ed. London and New York: Verso.

Appleby, J. (1992). Recovering America's historic diversity: Beyond exceptionalism. *Journal of American History*, 79(2), 419–431.

Archer, M.S. (1984). *Social origins of educational systems*. London: Sage.

Baldwin, J. (1985). *The price of the ticket: Collected nonfiction 1948–1985*. New York: St. Martin's/Marek.

Barthes, R. (1957/1972). *Mythologies*. New York: Hill and Wang.

Barton, K.C., and Levstik, L.S. (1998). It wasn't a good part of history: National identity and ambiguity in students' explanations of historical significance. *Teachers College Record*, 99(3), 478–513.

Beck, I.L., and McKeown, M.B. (1991). Substantive and methodological considerations for productive textbook analysis. In J.P. Shaver (ed.), *Handbook of research on social studies teaching and learning*. New York: Macmillan.

Boli, J., Ramirez, F.O., and Meyer, J.W. (1985). Explaining the origins and expansion of mass education. *Comparative Education Review*, *47*(1), 145–170.

Collins, R. (1977). Some comparative principles of educational stratification. *Harvard Educational Review*, *47*(1), 1–27.

Cornbleth, C. (1990). *Curriculum in context*. London: Falmer Press.

Cornbleth, C. (1995b). Curriculum knowledge: Controlling the "great speckled bird." *Educational Review*, *47*(2), 157–164.

Cornbleth, C. (1996a). Multicultural education and the politics of constructing the New York State social studies curriculum. Keynote address presented at the SUNY College at Buffalo conference, National standards and New York State social studies frameworks, April 27, 1996, Buffalo.

Cornbleth, C. (1996b). Discouraging diversity: Making education policy New York-style. *Social Science Record*, *33*(2), 7–14.

Cornbleth, C. (1997a). On the wings of dreams (response to review of *The great speckled bird*). *Curriculum Inquiry*, *27*(1), 113–120.

Cornbleth, C. (1997b). Birds of a feather: People(s), culture(s), and school history. *Theory and Research in Social Education*, *25*(3), 357–362.

Cornbleth, C. (1998). An America curriculum? *Teachers College Record*, *99*(4), 622–646.

Cornbleth, C., and Waugh, D. (1995). *The great speckled bird: Multicultural politics and education policymaking*. Mahwah, NJ: Erlbaum. Previously published by St. Martin's Press.

Eliade, M. (1963). *Myth and reality*. NY: Harper and Row.

Epstein, T. (1997). Sociocultural approaches to young people's historical understanding. *Social Education*, *61*(1), 28–31.

Fuchs, L.H. (1990). *The American kaleidoscope: Race, ethnicity, and the civic culture*. Hanover, NH: Wesleyan University Press.

Gonzales, L., and Baumgartner, T. (1998). *The 1950s· Happy days?* Unpublished final project for the Social Studies Curriculum Seminar, University at Buffalo, Graduate School of Education.

Greene, M. (1993). The passions of pluralism: Multiculturalism and the expanding community. *Educational Researcher*, *22*(1), 13–18.

Higham, J. (1974). Hanging together: Divergent unities in American history. *Journal of American History*, *61*(1), 5–28.

History-Social Science Curriculum Framework and Criteria Committee. (1988). *History-social science framework*. Sacramento: California Department of Public Instruction.

Kalantzis, M., and Cope, W. (1992). Multiculturalism may prove to be the key issue of our epoch. *Chronicle of Higher Education* (4 November), p. B3.

Kessler-Harris, A. (1992). Multiculturalism can strengthen, not undermine, a common culture. *Chronicle of Higher Education* (21 October), p. B3, 7.

Kon, J.H. (1995). Teachers' curricular decision making in response to a new social studies textbook. *Theory and Research in Social Education, 23*(2), 121–146.

McCarthy, C. (1995). The problem with origins: Race and the contrapuntal nature of the educational experience. In C.E. Sleeter and P.L. McLaren (Eds.), *Multicultural education, critical pedagogy, and the politics of difference*. Albany: State University of New York Press.

McNeil, L. (1981). Negotiating classroom knowledge: Beyond achievement and socialization. *Journal of Curriculum Studies, 13*(4), 313–328.

Mills, C.W. (1959). *The sociological imagination*. New York: Oxford University Press.

NCHS (National Center for History in the Schools). (1994). *National standards for United States history, Grades 5–12*. Los Angeles: University of California, Los Angeles, NCHS.

NCHS (National Center for History in the Schools). (1996). *National standards for history*, Basic Ed. Los Angeles: University of California, Los Angeles, NCHS.

NYSED (New York State Education Department). (1996). *Learning standards for social studies*, revised ed. Albany: NYSED.

Olneck, M.R. (1989). Americanization and the education of immigrants, 1900–1925: An analysis of symbolic action. *American Journal of Education, 97*, 398–423.

Olneck, M.R. (1990). The recurring dream: Symbolism and ideology in intercultural and multicultural education. *American Journal of Education, 98*, 147–174.

Seixas, P. (1993). Historical understanding among adolescents in a multicultural setting. *Curriculum Inquiry, 23*(3), 301–327.

Scixas, P. (1997). Mapping the terrain of historical significance. *Social Education, 61*(1), 22–27.

Toulmin, S.F. (1982). *The return to cosmology: Postmodern science and the theology of nature*. Berkeley: University of California Press.

Tyack, D. (1974). *One best system*. Cambridge, MA: Harvard University Press.

Tyack, D. (1995). Schooling and social diversity: Historical reflection. In W.D. Hawley and A.W. Jackson (eds.), *Toward a common destiny: Improving race and ethnic relations in America*. San Francisco: Jossey-Bass.

Tyack, D.B., and James, T. (1985). Moral majorities and the school curriculum: Historical perspectives on the legalization of virtue. *Teachers College Record, 86*(4), 513–535.

Waugh, D., and Hatfield, L.D. (1992). Rightist groups pushing school reforms. *San Francisco Examiner*, 28 May, A-18.

Williams, R. (1961). *The long revolution*. New York: Columbia University Press.

Contributors

Angela Calabrese-Barton is assistant professor, Center for Science Education, University of Texas at Austin. She is the author of *Feminist Science Education* (Teachers College Press, 1998) and "Liberatory Science Education: Weaving Connections between Feminist Theory and Science Education" in *Curriculum Inquiry*.
(acalabresebarton@mail.utexas.edu)

Catherine Cornbleth is professor, Graduate School of Education, University at Buffalo. Co-author of *The Great Speckled Bird: Multicultural Politics and Education Policymaking* (Erlbaum, 1995, 1999), she continues to work in the areas of curriculum politics-policy-practice and the social identities of young people and nation states.
(ccorn@acsu.buffalo.edu)

Nadine Dolby was Postdoctoral Research Affiliate, Institute of Communications Research, University of Illinois and is now at the Center for Research in International Education, Monash University, Melbourne as a Lecturer. She has published in *Journal of Curriculum Theorizing, Educational Researcher,* and the *International Journal of Inclusive Education.*
(nadine.dolby@education.monash.edu.au)

Vivian Forssman created *Knowledge Architecture, Inc.* in 1994 to build models of project-based learning, helping young adults develop workplace-ready skills in information technologies

(IT). Her career has taken her from Vancouver to the Yukon to the Philippines, doing IT projects including strategic planning, software development, and network development.
(vivian@knowarch.com)

Diana Lawrence-Brown is now on the faculty of St. Bonaventure University, following more than a decade as an educator in both general and special education. Her research interests include the accommodation of diversity in general education classrooms, teacher learning, and how power is exercised in schools.
(bywater@madbbs.com)

Suzanne Miller is associate professor of English education, Graduate School of Education, University at Buffalo where she also is co-director of the Collaborative Research Network. Her recent ethnographic work has traced how students develop pluralistic understandings in discussions which emphasize thinking critically about perspectives.
(smiller@acsu.buffalo.edu)

Margery D. Osborne is assistant professor, Department of Curriculum and Instruction, University of Illinois at Urbana-Champaign. She is author of *Constructing and Framing Knowledge in the Elementary School Classroom: Teachers, Students and Science* (Peter Lang, 1999).
(m-osbor@uiuc.edu)

Jason Tan is assistant professor, Division of Policy and Management Studies, National Institute of Education, Singapore. Co-editor of *Education in Singapore* (Prentice Hall, Singapore), he has published on issues of school privatization and the educational achievement of the Malay ethnic minority in Singapore.
(etjtan@nie.edu.sg)

Gina DeBlase Trzyna was a doctoral student in English education, Graduate School of Education, University at Buffalo and is now an assistant professor in the College of Education at Wayne State University, Detroit. Her research interests include gender and literacy, multicultural literature, and critical pedagogy.
(gdeblas@coe.wayne.edu)

Gaby Weiner is professor of education, Institute of Teacher Education, Umea University, Sweden, having recently moved from a similar post at South Bank University, London. Involved with social justice issues since the 1970s, her publications focus on issues of feminism, gender, and equal opportunities.

(gaby.weiner@educ.umu.se)

John Willinsky is Pacific Press professor of literacy and technology, University of British Columbia, Vancouver. Most recently, he is author of *Learning to Divide the World: Education at Empire's End* (University of Minnesota Press, 1998) and *Technologies of Knowledge: A Proposal for the Social Sciences* (Beacon, 1999).

(john.willinsky@ubc.ca)

Index